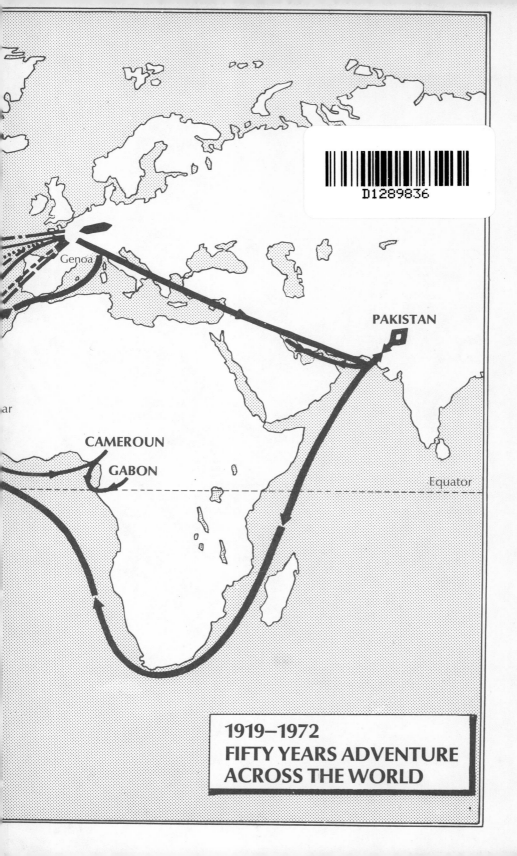

Genoa

PAKISTAN

CAMEROUN

GABON

Equator

**1919–1972
FIFTY YEARS ADVENTURE
ACROSS THE WORLD**

DON FERNANDO

DON FERNANDO

The Story of Fernand Fournier-Aubry

recorded by Andre Voisin

and translated from the French by
Xan Fielding

G. P. PUTNAM'S SONS, *New York*

Third Impression

FIRST AMERICAN EDITION 1974

Copyright © 1972 by Editions Robert Laffont

Translation copyright © 1974 by Talmy Franklin Ltd.,
London SW1

SBN: 399–11206–5
Library of Congress Catalog Card Number: 73–78590

PRINTED IN THE UNITED STATES OF AMERICA

LIST OF ILLUSTRATIONS

Between pages 120 and 121

v

At Satipo, my headquarters built of solid mahogany, with my horse and my Harley-Davidson on which I crossed the Andes to put paid to 'the Tyrant' who was terrorizing the neighbourhood.

Napoleon, my valiant and loyal henchman in the jungle.

Kinchokre, my 'brother', a pure Campa Indian, chief and witch-doctor – nobility personified.

Standing in front of me, Pangoate, my wife according to the law of the Campa Indians. She bore me two children. All three of them were shot dead, victims of 'civilization'.

'Horse', my horse at Satipo. I rode him without spurs. I taught him to salute by raising his hoof and wagging his tail.

1943: I become a 'vitamin fisherman' and my catch saves thousands of human lives.

Ecuador, 1943. My first base for my shark-fishing expeditions in the Pacific. I provide tons of shark livers which save the lives of thousands of wounded and sick.

My first boat, the *Pelicano*, and my first catch: shark livers rich in Vitamin A, bonitos yielding Vitamin D2.

Myself with Victoriano Suarez, an Indian from Ecuador, my henchman on the high seas.

My crew. They were unpaid but, apart from the sharks, everything we caught was theirs. This suited them better than trade union rules and regulations.

A shark's jaw: twelve rows of razor-sharp teeth.

No launch on the *Pelicano*, only a balsa raft from which to spot the sharks.

A shark's liver, loaded with vitamins, a quarter of the total weight of the beast.

My first refrigerator ship, the *Cecilia*. Things are looking up!

Myself during the war, when I was known to all and sundry as 'Captain Shark'.

Ayde: her image was engraved on my mind during my shark-fishing expeditions.

Ayde: before the end of my shark-fishing days. Parting from her almost broke my heart.

Tierra del Fuego, the tip of South America, not far from the Straits of Magellan which my father knew.

In the Guaytecas Archipelago, on my initial reconnaissance of the area.

At Chiloe. Carmen in the centre. Working on a fishing-boat, she disappeared at sea one night in a storm.

My four *sufridos*, cheerful rascals in spite of the harsh living conditions in the worst climate in the world.

Our 'castle' in the Guaytecas, built with the only materials available.

In the harshest climate in the world I break my arm and leg.

The longboat turns turtle, I break my arm and leg. No doctor. Home-made splints of planks and cords. But never say die!

On the opium and gold route in the north of Afghanistan. A forbidden zone controlled by the big contraband tycoons. The motor road ends here. No more jeeps, only camels.

At Kabul. To film this *buzkachi* of Uzbeks (the best horsemen in the world) I had to kneel down with my camera in the path of fifty horses at full gallop. This gesture served as an open sesame enabling me to penetrate into Forbidden Asia in 1955.

With my guide and 'brother', Cheul the Terrible. Thanks to him I was able to advance, lap by lap, along the track leading to the secret gateway of China. Using jewels as money, I buy my white horse and my camel. On the secret track there is no more day or night, time ceases to exist.

Azyade. Love, so pure and powerful that it transcends everything, even death.

Our first caravan. The tents are of raw camel hide. The wind blowing over these steppes, the *bouran*, drives the swallows towards the north. By day the reflection is blinding, at night it's icy cold.

Tachki, my friend and bodyguard, on guard at my door after Azyade's death. He shared my grief and my indifference to being still alive.

These walnut-trees in Upper Kashmir saved me. I insisted on uprooting them and rolling them up hill and down dale, without equipment, by manpower alone, as far as a Decauville railway.

1972: At the age of 71 I plan more adventure ...

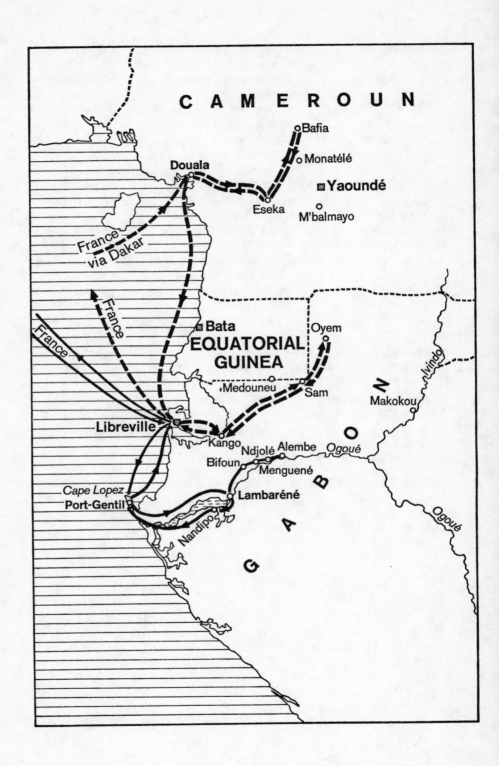

EQUATORIAL AFRICA

1919-1929

1

There's no resisting the wind of adventure. When it blows I feel it and I obey. As far as possible I try not to think and simply follow my instincts.

Why have I chosen today, for instance, to record the long week-end which is my life? For ages I refused. But now it appeals to me, I feel the urge, because subconsciously I know that the time has come.

If I get it off my chest I hope it will serve as an example and encourage others, the boys and youths who read it, to dream as I once dreamt and to set off in their turn in quest of adventure. I also hope they will get some fun out of it, as I do here and there.

At the start I had no idea where adventure was going to lead me. Even today I'm not quite sure. But I keep going. That's the lovely part about it.

In a few months I shall be off again. But this time, before I leave, I want to unburden myself of everything: my joys and woes, my struggles and secrets. I want to give them all away – or rather give them back: for they are not really mine to give. Life bestowed them on me day after day, even though I occasionally lent a hand myself. Life lavished everything upon me: love, travel, mishaps, sickness, encounters, hazards – even my name.

I've had all sorts of names. And I've lost my own. In the basin of the Amazon I'm known as Don Fernando, because one day the skipper of an old steam tub spontaneously called me by that name. The half-caste rubber tappers, my friends the *seringueiros*, adopted it and spread it all the way along the river.

And so I've become Don Fernando. Even so, at the age of seventy-one, after over half a century of adventures, I still don't know who I am. Thousands of memories jostle in my head, but I still have a job to identify myself. Maybe it's easier to identify others.

I've made a lot of money in my time. How much? If we bothered to count we shouldn't be what we are: men of adventure. Money

2

– what's left of it – is a good thing, if only for setting off and getting going again. Then one also has to cater for setbacks and delays, friends in need – and fun.

I learnt about life from men's faces, the faces of bandits and pioneers. I travelled across Africa, South America and Asia, with a passion for observing, prospecting, devising, understanding, helping, and always by the sweat of my brow. I survived because I loved it. I loved it all: misfortune, hunger, hardship, danger, courage, fear, death. Life offers its beauty only to those who grasp it in both hands.

When you press on to the point of exhaustion, to the verge of death, the jungle truly becomes the jungle, the sea the sea, the desert the desert. At last you see them as they really are. And the same applies to yourself. Laid low by malaria, I switched to shark-fishing in the Pacific since the jungle was declared out of bounds to me by the doctors. I got to know Asia and the five forbidden frontiers of North Afghanistan through saving a friend from death. Yes, you have to get down to fundamentals – it's only when you've reached the end of your tether and are on your last legs that you have a chance of discovering who you are.

One day, in the depths of the jungle, I had the good fortune to meet a tribe of Indians protected by their witch-doctor chief. Everything about these simple men was a revelation to me: their beauty, the natural harmony of their gestures, their nobility, their eyes devoid of hypocrisy or deceit. With them, time no longer existed; nor did my white carapace; I revelled in the sensation of being nothing beneath this immense vegetation. I wanted, like them, to steep myself in its aromatic scent and sap. I should have liked to be an Indian.

My desire must have been so genuine, my attitude so free from affectation, that after observing me for a few weeks the witch-doctor introduced me to Pangoate, who became my wife according to the law of the tribe. We had two beautiful children. The boy used to go fishing with small harpoons; the girl handled the pirogue. They led a happy life, almost stark naked. Their skin, like that of all Indians, was soft and odourless. They lived in the midst of greenery, under the vast ceiling of the virgin jungle. They used to go bathing five times a day, in a river saturated with mineral salts and rich humus seeping from the undergrowth.

Twice over I lost this wife of mine and our two children. The first time was when, almost dying of fever, and on orders of the witch-doctor chief himself, I had to leave the tribe and the forest under pain of expiring there and then. The second time, years later, was when I heard they had been killed, shot dead during an abominable expedition described as 'punitive' in order to conceal the real motives of cruelty and cupidity.

When I managed to get back, after long journeys in Tierra del Fuego and Asia, I had only one thing in mind: to wreak revenge. But on whom? Some dirty little rat? But which? Striking out at random was no remedy and wouldn't restore life. In the end I said to my friends: 'We're not policemen or public prosecutors. Anyway it's now too late. The priests accompanying the conquistadors should have flung themselves in front of their swords and muskets as soon as they landed on these shores. Then the massacre might never have occurred, still less continued. Let's think of something more practical and positive than revenge.'

I tried to work out the chances. The truth is that contact with us Whites kills the Indians off in any case: they are too pure, they are not immunized against our microbes. It's impossible to coop them up in reserves, to restrict them to our wretched little laws. And so? So: 'Indians, withdraw to your forests, far from the cynical exploiters of the soil and the subsoil. Depart from these lands, where the traders, the ruthless, avaricious foreign merchants, are death to you.' And the Indians withdrew.

They have continued to withdraw, to the regions where there is no more water. No more water, no more rivers, no more bracing dips five times a day, no more fish. Lack of water is tantamount to a death sentence. And the tragedy is that it can't be reversed, that our very compassion compels us to say: 'Let's show our respect for these people by letting them die alone – above all without us. Since we can do nothing about it, let's stand aside and in silence pay tribute to beauty as it dies. Let us acquiesce, and above all no hypocritical lamentation. No. Nothing but respect.'

If I mention this tragedy it's because I was affected by it personally, body and soul. And also because it's only one example of similar tragedies occurring all the time all over the world. Elsewhere I witnessed with my own eyes the extermination of the Mongols.

But nothing ever dies completely, I'm certain of this now. Even those murdered Indians have bequeathed us their blood. It flows in the veins of all the little half-castes inhabiting the banks and forests of

4

the Amazon. The thousands of *seringueiros*, who tap the rubber trees, have also inherited it. Just because they are nowadays destitute, vulnerable, exploited and starving, must these half-castes be left to atone for the crimes of the white half of their parentage?

At the sight of them struggling for survival, without complaint, in their own heroic way, I realized they still revealed the purity and innocence of their Indian ancestors; and I swore that my revenge would consist of helping them, and others like them, to survive.

Besides, it's here that I belong. Imperceptibly the jungle and tropical forest, the tributaries of the great River Amazon, have become my real home. How did this come about? It just did, that's all, without any effort on my part. I'm not an ethnologist or explorer. I have no staff, no private income, no fixed salary, no showy or elaborate equipment. I am what I have been all my life: a pioneer, at my risk and peril.

I have learnt that adventure is always where other people fail to see it. All I can hope is that my own experience will show the long-haired youths of today, their fathers, even their grandfathers, whoever is bored and fed up and at a loose end, that everything is still possible.

For my part, on this point, I have always had the soul of a child. That's the first step.

2

I was born on 23 November 1901, at Saint-Maur-des-Fossés, the youngest of a family of six. My father was a quiet man and never raised his voice, even to give orders. My mother and my sisters were well-favoured, elegant and distinguished. Their unobtrusive perfume, the rustle of their skirts, their gentle voices, contributed to the pleasant atmosphere at home.

One day we moved and went to live at Nantes. Our apartment in the Rue Grasset is a clear image. I think in images. They are engraved on my mind. I can still see the balcony, the Rue Crébillon, the Place du Calvaire, but especially the balcony. It is connected in my mind with the Nantes Carnival.

This was a fantastic celebration in which the whole town took part. The jollifications lasted nearly a week. There was Shrove Tuesday. An endless pageant unfurled at our feet: decorated floats, brass bands, masked groups parading arm in arm. We would throw streamers over the procession of men and women in motley, with phosphorescent eyes. Right at the end came a float decorated with flowers, bearing the fattened ox with its horns painted gold.

It was not long before we moved again, this time to Le Vésinet, just outside Paris, where my father had found us a big bourgeois villa with a large garden. There were trees everywhere and – lovely surprise – a little pond fringed with rough-hewn stones. This became the focal point of our games. My father kept it stocked with carp which he caught in Ibis Lake, and my brothers constructed a couple of boats out of the wooden tubs in the laundry. Our two housemaids from Noirmoutier occasionally found themselves adrift in these makeshift vessels.

Supper was at half past seven in the evening. We would gather round the big table in the kitchen. There were noisy altercations, squabbles over who was to sit in which place, then peace was restored with the entry of our parents. In winter there was always a log fire, which my father and mother both loved. When the meal was over they would sit there together conversing quietly, like lovers.

The signal for our bed-time was given by old Marie coming in with the 'Pigeon' lamp. This was made of brass and bore the challenging inscription: *A thousand francs to anyone who can make it explode*. It was left burning all night in the room I shared with my elder brother, because we both suffered from nightmares and I used to walk in my sleep.

My eldest brother, too, was a somnambulist. One of the maids gave notice because he kept coming into her room in his night-shirt. Had she taken him for a satyr? Was he one? I never knew.

For a long time my mother and sisters used to give me lessons at home. I was made to trace pot-hooks, then letters with down-strokes and upstrokes. I tried to be clever and attempted to write, like my brothers, in round-hand. But learning meant little to me. I have a clearer memory of our dogs and guinea-pigs than of the primary school I eventually attended.

What I liked most was my father's stories; he used to come up to our room sometimes, sit down on one of the beds and describe the adventures he had had in his youth. He had a great gift for story-telling, never being too long-winded and leaving enough to our imagination without ever confusing us. He told us about grand-pa, a worthy blacksmith from the Var, who eventually became a jeweller in Paris. His forebears didn't even have the means to be bakers; they merely hired the ovens and kneaded the dough. Thus we were able to appreciate what sacrifices each generation must have made for grandfather to end up as a Paris jeweller. And this wasn't all, he had also allowed his son to court adventure and negotiate the Straits of Magellan in a three-master. And it was as though we were there ourselves, in the Straits of Magellan, in Chile, in the Cordilleras. We knew that in Santiago the hogs were black and people pissed in the streets and squares without the slightest embarrassment. We would follow our father on his expedition through the Andes in search of iron. We would sail with him down the Amazon. It was like being at the theatre, with him the hero of the play. He described how he arrived, dizzy with malaria, at Belem do Para . . . and my fancy would take flight. That's how it all began perhaps. For me, who was one day to follow in his footsteps, the virus probably dates back to those stories of his.

Other evenings were devoted to dominoes, lotto and above all network. Old Marie taught us this craft. We each had our bobbin, cotton and wooden frame and within a few weeks we all knew how to weave. Then we learnt to embroider. The design allotted to me was a kneeling figure, a sort of Greek dancer. In the end we were able to present my mother with a superb bed-cover composed of these assembled pieces. It must have been a quaint sight: all of us at work in front of the huge fireplace, while our parents conversed together. Such was our family life.

We had no radio or television, but my father provided ample opportunity for us to use our eyes in other ways. Through him we discovered the joys of the theatre and the charms of the country-side. The Wild West show at Luna Park was sheer delight: there were Redskins and then Buffalo Bill would enter, toss a piece of coal into the air and blow it to smithereens with a shot from his pistol.

The Chatelet was even more fascinating. We used to go to matinée performances, *Helen of Troy*, *The Thief of Baghdad*, *The Great Mogul* – what images, what dreams they evoked! I would come back to Le Vésinet longing to recapture them, to live for weeks and months in that world of marvels which has ever since seemed real to me.

Everyday life was also full of surprises and no less exciting. These were the early days of aviation, when Blériot and other pilots used to take off from Le Pecq. Yet my father, who was so adventurous, thought them crazy. But then most people did. I was baffled. To me, aviation was magnificent. One day a balloon actually got caught on the roof of a house near the Chatou Bridge. A chorus of solemn gentlemen swarmed round it, showing contemptuous amusement or crying shame. I have always remembered their ironic expressions. Those who protest nowadays, when men land on the Moon, that it would be more useful to buy farm equipment, have the same look in their eyes.

Meanwhile there was school, which was not such fun. A coach-man in a four-wheeler fetched us from home every morning. Car-men pulled the four-wheeler and we picked up three or four of our class-mates on the way. They were mostly boys: Swiss, English, one Scotsman. God knows what we were meant to learn at school. I received no benefit from the teachers, who were no doubt worthy, but crammed our heads with such out-of-date stuff that none of it applied to us. I wasn't going to model myself on Roland, still less

8

on the young Napoleon. I couldn't make head or tail of the principles they wanted to inculcate in me. The only thing I liked about school was playing truant. I was neither proud nor ashamed of being one from bottom in my class.

Our desks were fitted with padlocks. This was allowed and amused us, bestowing an aura of secrecy on our meagre personal belongings. The Scottish boy kept a bottle of whisky in his; no doubt filched from his parents. It was fitted with a rubber tube, like an enema, and from time to time he let us take a swig.

On Sundays, like the rest of the local gentry, we went to church *en famille*. My grandmother, though very old, insisted on coming with us, wearing a jerkin and leaning for support on one of the maids. She looked rather grim, but wasn't particularly unpleasant as far as I was concerned. To me, Mass was a thing of beauty. There was poetry in it, in the church building, in the details of the service, the smell of the incense. The atmosphere was faintly awe-inspiring. For a long time I was a choir-boy. I found the priest very old and kind, and his light communion wine excellent.

One day my father appeared at the wheel of a motor-car. It was a De Dion Bouton, with handsome seats facing each other. He took us out for a spin, driving at fifteen miles an hour. People stared at him as though he was out of his mind: 'He's going too fast! Is he allowed to drive as fast as that? ...' There's no limit to the nonsense people talk!

A few months later I had a bicycle. Not that it happened often, but, without our having to ask, things materialized. Were our wishes, our desires, our prayers anticipated? Hardly. My father was earning a good living at Peugeot's. He loved his brood but didn't pamper us or bother unduly if any of us cut himself, caught his finger in a door or got a nail embedded in the sole of his foot. 'Go and put it under the cold tap and stop making such a fuss; it won't kill you' – that was his method.

Scene: the school playground. Time: the morning break. I was twelve years old. The game we were playing consisted of turning a somersault and landing on a pile of sand. I made a bosh shot. It happens even to champions and professional acrobats. I landed on my back, on the concrete. I went white in the face, a sorry sight. The four-wheeler was summoned, then the ambulance, then the doctor. Apparently I had broken something.

Why did I land on my back and miss the pile of sand? Destiny?

No doubt. As a result, I had two years away from school. There was no miracle cure. 'He must stay at home and rest. It won't prevent him from walking, eating and reading.'

So there I was, confined and coddled. Every morning I woke and listened to the house coming to life; the maids brought me breakfast in bed; my sisters practised the piano. It all seemed unreal. After a few days I started going for walks in the forests of Bougival or Saint-Cucufa, taking the dogs with me. Sometimes, since my parents didn't mind, I took a picnic lunch and didn't come back till the evening. On my return I would find my mother more beautiful than ever, my sisters even more elegant. I felt I was on the mend and enjoyed my freedom.

One evening I diffidently told my father that school didn't interest me, I couldn't help it, but I didn't want to go back. He understood at once: 'All right, my lad, all right. If you don't like it, you needn't go. But you must have some sort of education. Get down to some serious reading, go on with your maths and geography.' I did so. I solved equations, pored over the atlas, lapped up Jules Verne, Gustave Aimard, Leonardo da Vinci, Confucius and *The Odyssey*.

I was a denizen of the jungle, of the virgin forest, surrounded by Negroes and cannibals. I roamed the woods like Fenimore Cooper; my daily walks assumed another aspect. I followed my instinct like Ulysses. His adventures enthralled me. What intelligence! Curling up under the belly of a sheep and making the Cyclops himself push the rock away from the entrance of the cave! Here was someone I could understand.

I now realized how lucky I was to have injured my back – a destiny my school-mates couldn't understand, since they were restricted to a prescribed curriculum. I was vaguely aware of the difference between us. At the age of thirteen or almost I was still rather small and not particularly strong. Appearing stripped to the waist or stark naked in front of other boys, for games or swimming, didn't appeal to me at all. I was shy of being considered a weakling; and so I tended to keep to myself. My father said to me: 'Stand in front of the mirror, put up your fists and fight your reflection.' I did so, every morning, and didn't feel silly at all. In fact I gradually felt stronger. I had no wish for friends of my own age. I meditated, I pondered, I took counsel with myself. Lightly clothed, winter and summer alike, I soon recovered from my injury and was more or less completely immune to colds and influenza.

One evening my father came home in a state of dejection. My uncle, his brother, had died. It was only later that I learnt how – while making love to two ladies simultaneously. He must have been seventy years old. It was a better way to die, after all, than giving up the ghost in a hospital or getting killed in a war.

War did break out eventually and, much to my parents' sorrow, my eldest brother went off to fight. He never returned. For safety's sake, my father moved his brood to Normandy and we didn't come back to Le Vésinet until after Big Bertha had stopped lobbing over her shells.

I still read voraciously. I was hale and hearty, and as keen as ever on flowers and wild life. One day, on the estate of one of my father's friends, I met a fellow who was acting as game-keeper. Seeing I was alone, he befriended me. Thus I learnt he was really a poacher. Instead of guarding the estate, he used to set snares which he constructed himself with guitar strings, boot-laces and bird-lime. With his whiskers and corduroy trousers, he was a character straight out of a novel. I didn't approve or disapprove of his poaching. We used to snare rabbits or pigeons. Sometimes I even took my trophies back home. 'A fellow I met gave them to me,' I would explain, and nothing more was said. One day a shrew of a woman came and told my father we were eating stolen rabbit. He promptly showed her the door. He had no need of a third party to bring up his children.

Things happen without rhyme or reason. In the villa there was a trap-door for lowering barrels of wine into the cellar. This gave me an idea and I said to my father: 'I'd like to do some woodwork down there.'

'What do you need?'

'Well, a work-bench. Also a saw-horse and some tools.'

He bought them for me and I set them up in my cellar-workshop. Then I hopped on to my bike and went round to the local wood merchant. I didn't know the difference between oak and beech. All I could see was a lot of logs and blocks, and some smaller pieces which I brought back. The first thing I carved was a duck. Then I saw some stove-pipes lying around. I hammered them flat, sawed them into strips and ended up with a duck-shaped ash-tray.

I also made some furniture, especially a big arm-chair on which I toiled for months. The seat was absolutely flat and not very comfortable. The back was adorned with palmettes, on which I carved a dog and a fox. I waxed it all over with the maids' furniture polish and stood it by the fireplace. I hate to think what it looked like.

As I grew older, I began looking round for a job. I was deeply in love at the time with a girl of my own age. She went off one day, far overseas, with her parents. I felt bereft. Then I joined forces with a friend of mine called Jean, a tall, handsome, well-educated, blue-eyed Jewish boy. We were inseparable and got taken on together by a firm of furniture-removers. We both drank quite a lot, but never got tipsy. We knew when to stop, instinctively. It requires no effort. We merely refused the little nips at the bar in which our colleagues indulged. We were employed regularly until, one day, we got a piano jammed in a staircase. We couldn't move it up or down and just stood there roaring with laughter. In the end we gave up and left it where it was.

So we turned to coal-heaving. Once again we had great fun and were always in fits of laughter at our Negro-minstrel faces. We used to fetch the coal from the goods station where it was dumped in bulk, put it into 50-kilo sacks, and deliver it. Every evening, when I got home, I had to scrub myself all over to make myself reasonably presentable.

After several months of this I began to feel restless, I longed to get away — no matter where or how. I couldn't account for this sensation, it happened spontaneously. Maybe it had been at the back of my mind for some time; perhaps I had mentioned it to Jean. All I know is, I was in need of adventure, and adventure meant leaving home and striking out on one's own.

One evening I said to my father:

'You know, I'm not interested in anything here, I haven't got my school certificate. I want to get away, I must get away ...'

He said nothing, but looked at me and gave a little nod. Next day he took me aside and said with deliberation:

'If you leave here, you'll leave like a gentleman. Go to the Chargeurs Réunis in the Boulevard Malesherbes: I'll pay your fare. Get a first-class ticket to Douala. That's in the Cameroons. Good luck, my boy.'

I was deeply moved and thanked him.

My friend Jean wanted to come with me, but his father objected: 'You're only eighteen. If you try to run away I'll have you locked up in a reformatory.' I solved the problem by exchanging my first-class ticket to Douala for two third-class tickets to Dakar.

On my last evening, my dear father came up to my room with

two presents: an old-fashioned revolver, which I have since lost, and his muzzle-loading gun dating back to the time of Napoleon III, which I still have after fifty years of adventure.

Next morning Jean and I climbed into the train to Bordeaux. From the window of our compartment we had a last look at the Gare d'Austerlitz. On the platform, in a frock-coat, alone, stood my father. His face was set and grave. He looked slightly older than usual. There were tears in his eyes, but he was smiling. He seemed happy to have allowed me to do what I hankered after. It's splendid to enable someone to do what he wants. When you can't do it yourself, then at least help others – that's what his smile seemed to say. The train gave a sudden jolt. Clanking and puffing, it pulled out of the station.

3

At Bordeaux we felt we were really on our way. Elegantly dressed (suits from Nicole in the Rue Tronchet, with superb shirts to match) we looked perfect little gentlemen; this reassured the parents and attracted the girls. Jean, as I said before, was extremely handsome and where the girls were concerned I always came off second-best. The loveliest were for him; I got the left-overs. To celebrate our departure we went and had a drink in a café opposite the big theatre, then spent the last night in a little hotel which my father had recommended.

Next morning, dapper as ever, though still perhaps somewhat too genteel, we were at the foot of the gangway, each with his little case in his hand. The ship looked splendid to us. Yet she was only an old freighter, converted to take passengers, that was ending her days on the Africa line.

At the top of the gangway stood an impressive figure in white gloves, with a suitcase open in front of him. His patter was convincing: 'Gentlemen, Africa is deadly. All the old hands will tell you. Be prudent. Malaria, mosquitoes, the dread anopheles. A simple precaution: this miracle cure, this little packet. Directions for use are inside. Exclusive. Efficacious. Only five francs. A word of warning: for scientific and climatic reasons, to be opened only in the tropics. Five francs!' Five francs at that time was a lot of money, but everyone forked out. We thought we had better follow suit and bought one packet between us. Out at sea, we had a good laugh. I opened the famous miracle cure. It contained two little squares of wood, with a notice sandwiched between them: *Hold one square in your right hand, the other in your left. Take aim and squash the mosquito between them.*

At Dakar we disembarked, gullible, innocent and overawed as ever. We found a hotel, hired a car and set off to explore the town. It was like being at the theatre again. Beautiful plants everywhere, brightly coloured lizards in the gardens, black-skinned women. Our chauffeur drove barefoot, accelerating with his big toe. I waved at a merry group of Negresses and one of them replied, like a cheeky brat sticking his tongue out, by lifting her loincloth and revealing a superb pair of black buttocks. Laughter all round. Our chauffeur went on guffawing as though he would never stop.

Next day I got bitten in the ankle by the hotel monkey but this didn't prevent us from pursuing our exploration: the coast, Gorée, Slave Island with its prisons and little harbour. Our money melted away. To make matters worse, Jean suggested going to a brothel. Well, why not? The idea didn't appeal to me, but one has to improve one's mind. At the brothel there were two sisters, one of whom was called Fernande. No sooner had we sat down than a crowd of French sailors burst in. A drunken orgy ensued. In the heated atmosphere Jean must have said something which Fernande took amiss. Anyway I saw his smart jacket gripped at the hem and ripped in two by the madame of the house, to the applause of the sailors. He was understandably annoyed and gave Fernande a slap in the face; the squabble developed into a free-for-all. Somehow I managed to get him out and we made our way back to the main square, where the sailors took it into their heads to uproot a lamp-post with the intention of bashing us over the head. A police car drove up, full of black and white cops – no more sailors! There we stood, all by ourselves, a couple of mugs in front of the broken lamp-post.

Next day I persuaded Jean to tot up our accounts. Our funds were dangerously low. We had to get a job. There was a gang of Negroes digging drains in the Place Proet. We made enquiries and were consequently engaged by the Public Works Department. We set to work with spade and pick and shovel. In those days white men labouring side by side with blacks had never been seen before. We didn't care, we had to eat and we didn't want to beg; but we were very conspicuous. At this time of year the heat was unbearable and we probably wouldn't have lasted long. In fact we had worked for only three days when, one fine morning, up comes this rather shabby character in a sailor's cap, a real Portuguese by the looks of him, with one ear pierced by a gold ring. Not a bad fellow, on the whole. He must have noticed us straight away: two little green-horns, strong, innocent and hard-working. He gets down to brass tacks: 'I'm a sea-captain, would you like to work for me?' We had no idea what he had in mind, but we followed him aboard his ship.

'Where are you heading for?' he asked.

'Cameroons.'

'Fine. I'll take you there free of charge. All I ask in exchange is a small favour. I'll drop you offshore in the dinghy. A pirogue will come out. My men will load two or three cases on to it; you'll merely have to keep an eye on these cases. They're for a Chinaman at Soualaba to whom we deliver a little contraband. It's not very complicated. You just have to make sure the cases get to the Chinaman.'

It was a godsend. This sea-captain with his ear-ring stepped straight out of the pages of a book. Jean, however, was not so enthusiastic.

'I'm going to stay here,' he said. 'You go, though, and if it works out I'll join you.'

I remained on board and watched him as he walked away from the wharf, looking back every few steps. I was bound for Cameroons, and alone for the first time.

A couple of weeks afterwards we were off Douala. I had an easy time. Whenever I tried to make myself useful I was reminded that I was a passenger. I appreciated the peace, the harmony, and day-dreamed for hours on end. I watched the dolphins at play. I was myself engaged in a game, and beginning to learn the rules. These consisted in not knowing and not wishing to know the future, living intensely in the present, revelling in every new sight, sound and smell. I recalled the exotic gardens at Dakar, the flowers in full bloom, the bougainvillaea, the markets, the dried fish. It was a far cry from the park at Le Vésinet with its geraniums, dahlias and camellias that my father used to fetch from Nantes every year for my mother to be surrounded by flowers. This cosy picture was receding, eclipsed by the enthralling image of Black Africa.

As we sailed across the Bight of Benin, I heard certain place-names mentioned that were music to my ears: Lomé, Cotonou, Lagos. At last we approached Douala, after sailing past the big island of Fernando Po. The coast appeared, with Mount Cameroon towering in the background. The time had come to launch the dinghy and ship the cases. I shook hands with the Portuguese captain, thanked him for my passage, then climbed overboard.

In the bay a pirogue drew alongside. The cases were transferred. The Chinaman was waiting further off.

'Here's your contraband,' I said.

He scarcely listened and guided me to another pirogue, explaining:

'You can't sleep here. I'm going to show you your hut. It's not very near, but come along.'

We set off across the estuary, past countless islands planted with mangroves. The sky lowered, the sea rose, the storm broke. The giant silhouettes of the mangroves, the backs of the Negroes wielding their paddles sprang into view at every flash of lightning only to be swallowed up again by the dark. The smell of the water grew more pungent; we approached a group of huts. Voices, shouts, bursts of laughter could be heard. I noticed a few Negroes and half-castes. The Chinaman showed me into my quarters, a hovel made of branches, then shook hands and set off again.

It was only next day, when I read the paper, that I understood. The Chinaman had been found with his head cut off, and the cases were stolen. A sordid incident between gold smugglers. Gold in 'my' cases? I was flabbergasted. The old boy had saved my life by guiding me to this distant hut. Without knowing me, he had insisted personally on keeping me out of harm's way. I folded up the paper and went off to the Hotel de la Poste in search of a job.

The lobby was full of Whites, labourers, foresters – strangers. I made enquiries and was introduced to a man who dealt in mangrove-trees at Soualaba. 'I make railway sleepers,' he told me. 'The Negroes work with axes and adzes. They fell the trees and square the timber. You don't look like a labourer, but you can be an overseer. I'll settle your hotel bill. To begin with, your monthly salary will be a pair of trousers, a shirt, three pairs of espadrilles. You'll eat with the Negroes. Agreed?'

'Why not?'

So there I was, in the *poto-poto* – the region of swamps, marshes and torrential rain – with my first employer. Big hefty Negroes squared the mangrove-trees for twelve hours a day, by hand. The malarial mosquitoes, the troops of monkeys, the sound of falling timber were all new to me; so were the various scents exhaled by the heat and humidity.

At first all went well. I worked hard, fed like a rustic on bananas and manioc, slept on the ground among my men. After a few days my boss lent me his double-barrelled shot-gun to supplement the rations and give the Negroes a treat. But I saw this was really for the sake of economy. I also noticed he always carried a home-made rhinoceros-hide whip. I began to find him less amusing.

For me, my Negro foresters were friends. They were hard-working and cheerful. Why strike and curse them? Having nothing to do but supervise, I made myself responsible for lighting the fire and cooking the rice in the huge cauldron. I also went fishing in the estuary and grilled my catch. The only thing at which I drew the line was shooting monkeys for the pot. On Sundays the Negroes slaughtered them wholesale. I disapproved, but they replied with a grin: 'We eat *anything*, boss!' Apart from this, we saw eye to eye and they regarded me with affection. In the evenings I would listen to their palavers, story-telling and singing. The rush torches gleamed red in the dark; the wood smelt of incense; the beaten earth floor of the huts, the soil of the logging-camp exuded a sweet, heady scent. Darkness made equals of us all and I felt I was at one with them.

One evening I entered my hut and found a black figure clad in a loincloth sitting on my bed. A young Negress. I turned round and saw one of the heftiest lumber-jacks and his son smiling at me through the door. They came in, lifted the girl up and stood her in front of me. Then I understood and was thunderstruck. They burst out laughing and Soualaba – I called her by this name straight away – drew closer. I put my arms round her and kissed her on the forehead. The hilarity increased. What was I supposed to do? What was the custom? I felt helpless.

Her brother then took me by the arm and said: 'This is your wedding-day, Fernand. Come along.' He led the way down a freshly made track in the forest, at the end of which stood a pretty little hut of bamboo and palm leaves. 'This is your new home,' he exclaimed. 'Soualaba built it herself. Look at her hands.' I noticed they were cut and grazed. There was a trickle of blood on her right arm, but her smile was dazzling. She leant forward, grasped my shoulders and applied her thick lips to my bare chest.

'Off you go now!' she cried. 'Off you go, both of you!'

Her father and brother obeyed, almost meekly. This was my first real Cameroon night. Soualaba was my first black wife. I was overwhelmed by the beauty of her gleaming black body lying naked beside me. What a gift from heaven! I accepted it thankfully.

In the morning I followed her down to the estuary. We bathed together and I couldn't keep my eyes off her as she rubbed herself all over with a herb she had picked in the forest, which made her body smell like a beautiful plant.

18

Everything was going well. The Negroes were making a good job of squaring the timber, at least I thought so. I never treated them harshly and refused to carry a whip, which seemed to irritate my boss. Then, a few days after my 'wedding', the incident occurred. I was with Soualaba fifty yards or so away from the camp. She had just used my hatchet to cut down some branches for our fire and I was admiring her strength and agility as she launched the pirogue I had given her to go fishing, when suddenly ...

I heard a sharp thwack, a hoarse cry. I rushed back to find my boss using his whip on one of the lumber-jacks, an absolute giant of a man but terrorized into acquiescence. That's how it was in those days: in front of a white, a black lowered his head. My reaction was instantaneous. I saw that white face and my arm shot out, of its own accord, and delivered two resounding slaps. A deathly silence ensued. All the Negroes waited, in consternation.

My boss sat down on a tree-trunk, with his feet in the mud. He held his head in both hands and burst into tears. He didn't fight back, he wept. He wept so bitterly that I held his hand, almost like a friend. He mumbled incoherently, as though at the end of his tether. Drink, the climate, the food had reduced him to a wreck. He wasn't a bad fellow. There was a better side to his nature, for he produced a wad of banknotes from his pocket and said: 'Take this. You're fond of these people; go and work with them in another camp. I'm finished.'

He went off, alone, in his own pirogue, in the direction of the town. As soon as he was out of sight, he must have paddled out to sea. Next morning his body was found floating in the estuary; he had committed suicide.

4

So there I was, without an employer, but with a gang of blacks who led me to a nearby village. Soualaba and I were allotted another hut and there we remained for several weeks with never a thought of work. I spent my time carving wood and hunting with my father's gun. I was pampered, cossetted, immortalized in a long plaintive ballad punctuated by laughter, on account of my defence of the ill-used Negro.

As my blacks had noticed on the very first day, I never wore a solar topee. Any white who didn't wear a topee in the equatorial zones was looked upon as a madman. All I had was a broad-brimmed felt hat which I had bought at Léon's on my father's advice. 'Don't ever wear a topee,' he had told me, 'it's a lot of rot. It's like having a dish-cover over your head, it makes you go weak in the noodle. Wear a hat.' None of my blacks wore a topee and I was happy to live like them, observing the plants, the trees, the birds, the monkeys, the cruel fairyland of the tropics. There was everything here to gratify my heart's desire.

One morning, however, I felt an urge to go to Douala. The money had been paid out and something had to be done to replenish the coffers. The Hotel de la Poste was still the meeting-place of the foresters, adventurers, officials and merchants. I was given a tip about a job up north, in Esséka, and decided to take Soualaba there with me. Meanwhile I booked a room for us both and went back to the village to fetch her.

The first thing we did was go shopping. She bought herself a bright red loincloth and I bought her some jewels. She looked absolutely dazzling, but was still barefoot. Nothing suitable could be found for her in the shoe-shop: the small sizes for European ladies made her laugh and were obviously out of the question. I left her and went off to buy myself a pair of trousers and a couple of cotton shirts. When I got back, she was triumphantly wearing a pair of men's patent-leather pumps.

Spick and span in our new clothes, we went round to the hotel. Seeing me arrive with a black woman, the porter protested sharply: 'This isn't a brothel, Monsieur.' Soualaba, who had no idea what a brothel was, smiled innocently. 'This lady is my wife,' I retorted. 'She's travelling with me. We're leaving in two days' time.' Astonished, but delighted that a white should have chosen a Negress as his wife, the man gave a respectful bow. I took Soualaba by the arm and led her up the stairs. Peering over my shoulder, I was pleased to see the dismay on the faces of the dirty-minded little colonial officials who were only too inclined to regard all black women as whores.

The Esséka train was wonderfully old-fashioned, with carriages like those in a Wild West film or Buffalo Bill illustration. As we chugged along, Soualaba preened herself in her loincloth and I gazed in admiration at her bare breasts. And such was the pure-mindedness of our black fellow passengers that no one even noticed.

Esséka was a sort of outpost, a bush trading-station, where some sales and barter companies maintained a few agents. I reported to the office I had been told of in Douala. The Frenchman in charge, a former captain who had risen from the ranks, signed me on without a word. This was a new apprenticeship for me: trading in palm kernels, areca, coconuts and every kind of oil-seed used in the manufacture of soap. The raw material was produced by the Bafias and other local tribes, who had the curious custom of wearing a small leaf on the end of the penis as a protection against the flies. Thus files of stark naked porters could be seen entering the village, each with a little green plume on the afore-mentioned part of his anatomy, and a 50-kilo sack on his head. My job was to deal with them in pidgin-French and generally make myself useful.

I soon realized that the manager monkeyed with the scales, diddling the blacks and his own firm. The set of weights he used enabled him to deduct a few kernels from every sack and thus build up a stock of his own. He also traded in goods which he himself filched. Every week he reported the theft of various items: 'With blacks it's inevitable, they're thieves by nature. These items will have to be written off as a loss. We keep a check, but as you can see for yourself ...' Meanwhile, all the goods he had pilfered were resold by him to the very people he accused. I was sadly disillusioned. But what I disliked most was his attitude to his own black girl; he

21

always introduced her in a shamefaced manner, as though she was a harmless idiot whom he kept out of pity or from habit.

One day he summoned me and pompously informed me that for fear of local gossip, and for the sake of the firm's good name, I should make it clear to the village that Soualaba was only my servant.

'Why not my cousin, while you're about it?' I retorted. 'She's my wife. I don't like hypocrisy. I'm handing in my resignation.'

And that was that. I rejoined Soualaba in our hut, a sort of out-house which I rented for next to nothing from a Frenchman by the name of Coudestreaux. A man of sterling quality, the son of a forester, he had been here for ten years and ran a grocery-cum-general store. He too had a black wife, built on the same scale as himself. She was well over six feet tall and must have weighed at least 200 lbs. Her name was Vérité.

This unique couple had befriended us right from the start. When I was busy at the trading-station, Soualaba used to spend her time chatting to Vérité and, when the day's work was over, all four of us would go down to the swamp. In bush country a swamp has a characteristic smell. The stagnant water exudes an odour of sludge and grass. Because of this, most of the whites objected to it and looked upon it as something unclean: a bog or even worse. Coudes-treaux taught me to take a different view: 'Of course they'll say it attracts mosquitoes, but what if it does? Look how pretty it is! And where else can one go for a nice cool bathe? So come on ...' And in he went, stark naked.

When I told him how I had resigned from my job, he offered me our hut rent-free and said: 'I'm arranging a deal with some fellows from Garoua. I'll see how I can fit you in. You're new here, you're young, it's right up your street.'

A few days later, in great form and with several drinks inside him, he introduced me to a dozen jovial blacks, one of whom spoke very good pidgin-French. 'It's all settled,' he said. 'Here's your guide if you want the job. There's nothing crooked about it, it's natural contraband. Down here there's a shortage of meat. Up north there's a surplus and no one benefits from it. So this is what I suggest: you go up to Garoua with these fellows; it's their part of the country. At that altitude you'll be in the vicinity of natural pasturelands teeming with oxen and buffalo. To the north there's Lake Chad, no good for smuggling; but to the west there's the British frontier of

Nigeria. The cattle aren't particular, they'll follow you across. You must bring me back a nice big herd on the hoof. I'll pay for it here in goods and give you the cash for the first instalment.'

'But my dear Coudestreaux,' I protested, 'I don't know a thing about cattle.'

'You don't need to. Your job is to look after the cash and supervise the convoy.'

The group of blacks awaited my decision. The French-speaking guide kept wiping his nose on his shirt-tail and motioning me to accept. I was tempted. I went off for a moment and came back hand in hand with Soualaba, so that all of them might see that we were man and wife and had decided to leave together.

Our little column set off next morning. It was a real honeymoon and lasted several months. We would halt for the night at least an hour before sunset, since darkness fell abruptly at six o'clock. Our escort would help us build a little shelter of branches roofed in with foliage. The focal point of the camp was our big five-litre cauldron. We had rice, salt, fat, sugar and coffee, and we supplemented these rations with game. I hardly ever used my gun; our Bafias still hunted with bows and arrows. I admired their dexterity all the more when I saw they caused no damage to the countryside, took only what was strictly necessary and never disturbed the harmony of the landscape even by the noise of a fire-arm.

The vegetation gradually changed. The forest became less dense. Other species of trees and plants began to appear, and other animals. The roof of our shelter was no longer made of foliage but of dried grass. We were skirting the Nigerian border. The Bafias dis-appeared with the letters Coudestreaux had given me. They returned two days later with four men who were to negotiate the sale. I handed over the money and we arranged another meeting-place. If all went well, we would start back ten days later with a fine herd of thirty zebu.

In those days the frontier was a mere symbol: no barriers, no guards, no Customs. Our rendezvous was near Mokolo. We there-fore made our way up there, without the slightest misgiving, but rather restless after waiting so long. We camped out as usual and in the morning the first batch of oxen arrived, driven by a Bafia beaming with pleasure at seeing us again. The 'English beef' was stupendous: huge hulks of flesh with widespread horns, absolute monsters. I had arranged for the remaining batches to join us at

24-hour intervals, after we had already started back, and this arrange-
ment worked perfectly. I felt very pleased with myself and looked
forward to making a triumphant entry into Esséka.

Alas, after ten days or so, in spite of the herdsmen's know-how
in choosing camp sites and water points, the oxen began to look out
of sorts. Then one of them keeled over and died. The death of an
ox isn't a great calamity but when it repeats itself every other day,
one can't help worrying The poor beasts were suffering from a
disease of the knee-joint and were dying one after another. They
would start limping, then – crash ! – keel over, and we would have
to finish them off. By the time we got back to Esséka, there were
only half a dozen of them left.

A few days afterwards I heard some shrieks coming from a hut
which served Coudestreaux as a store-room. I rushed inside and saw
a big Negro, stark naked, flat on his stomach, tied to a bench. I drew
closer and noticed a piece of wood protruding from his arse. It
looked like the shaft of an arrow. I plucked it out and released the
victim who rushed off, still shrieking, down to the swamp. Then
Coudestreaux appeared : 'What the hell are you doing ?'

'That's a fine thing to ask ! I heard a Negro shrieking, so I came
to see what was wrong. He had this piece of wood rammed up his
arse. I removed it, that's all. What's going on ?'

Coudestreaux looked rather odd, almost shame-faced :

'I did it, and I'll tell you why. There was no need for him to kick
up such a fuss. I let him off lightly in fact. I rammed it up with a
piece of cotton-wool dipped in red pepper. It doesn't hurt too much.
If it burns his arse, it'll teach him a lesson. Because there's one thing
I can't stand : having my tinned cassoulet stolen. My cassoulet is
sacred, and he knows it. I'm fond of the blacks, as you've seen for
yourself. But I won't have them filching my cassoulet ! That's all !'

I suppose I looked rather puzzled, for he went on to explain :

'You're a newcomer, Fernand; don't judge me too hastily. I was
a newcomer myself, ten years ago. I was as soft-hearted as you. But
no longer. I'm not a nasty character, maybe it's the effect of the sun,
but every so often something goes snap in my head. I won't have
anyone stealing my cassoulet. My advice to you is to push off before
you go crazy as well. Maybe I drink too heavily ... But, believe me,
no one loves the blacks as I do. Look at Vérité, she really is my wife.
Seven years ago I was as tough as they come, working on the Esséka–
Djole railway. The blacks there were dying like flies, treated like

slaves. But I stood up for them. One day, a fellow from the same village as that idiot who's now dipping his arse in the swamp had his legs reduced to pulp by a tip-truck. The white foreman refused to transport him on the decauville to get to the first-aid post. There was a hand-operated shuttle-train there which plied to and fro on the single line. The blood rushed to my head. I knocked the foreman down, picked up the injured Negro and put him on the shuttle. The whole gang watched me. I set off like a maniac, and kept going for dozens of miles until I reached a friend of mine who had some medical supplies. I saved the black's life. Don't judge me, Fernand. Go on, take some money and push off.'

By a happy coincidence a postcard from Jean arrived that week. It had been posted in Gabon. He had left Dakar, signed on as a lumber-jack in Cap Lopez, and suggested I join him there. I regarded this as a good omen. I already saw myself felling giant trees in the virgin forest, and I knew Soualaba was willing to come with me. But I had reckoned without her family. When I told them my plans, they looked grave and pensive. Then a lengthy palaver ensued. Finally her father said : 'Soualaba will not accompany you to Gabon. There are big tribes of Pahuin cannibals there. She will stay here with us.'

I knew his decision was irrevocable. I didn't know what to say. Soualaba herself broke the silence. 'I'm pregnant,' she announced, glowing with happiness.

'The child will be of our family,' her father went on. 'All of us appreciate the gift you are leaving with us. In your absence it will keep your memory alive. If the cannibals don't eat you, you'll find it grown on your return.'

Soualaba seemed only faintly sad. My own heart was infinitely heavy; I was still ruled by the code of civilized man. On the last evening she clung to me, as though wishing to imbue me with the strength and courage she derived from nature. She was fore-armed against tribulation of every sort and wanted to make me share her peace of mind.

On the departure quay we kissed each other on the forehead. Her big eyes opened wide. I smiled, but a tear trickled down my cheek. I let it trickle.

5

The *Tchad*, an old Indochina vessel, steamed out of harbour and headed south, past the Rio Muni enclave, towards Libreville and Cap Lopez. I had no idea what to expect. Gabon in 1920 was still relatively unknown territory. Jean was no doubt up country, in the depths of the forest. Apart from the money Coudestreaux had given me, my sole possessions were a drill jacket, two cotton shirts, a small tin trunk, my shot-gun, a few skins and an old blanket. Yet I felt rich and optimistic.

On landing, I followed my usual practice and enquired after a small hotel. I was recommended Uncle Lan's. I made my way there on foot, entered the lobby and looked around. To my surprise, the first person I saw was Jean, in a group of other whites who were clearly foresters. He introduced me to one of them, a huge fellow with a heavy moustache: 'Maxime, this is my friend Fernand. I can vouch for him.'

Maxime sized me up with a rather superior smile. 'If you want to join me,' he said, 'I'm up Lambaréné way. We're felling okoumé trees and floating them down by raft.'

'What would I have to do?'

'Learn the job. Health all right?'

'Yes.'

'Don't drink too much? Or smoke?'

'No.'

'Tummy trouble?'

'No.'

'Run after girls?'

'Not more than anyone else.'

'Not queer? No perversions?'

'No.'

'All right, then. I'll take you on.'

Business was booming at Port Gentil. The great timber rush had just started. The pioneer foresters had been producing okoumé for two or three years. Scattered in small groups throughout the interior with their Bapono labourers, they were permanently in need of additional staff for locating sites, staking claims and negotiating with the blacks or the buyers. The death rate was high along the banks of the Ogoué: mosquitoes, tsetse flies, alcohol, even poison decimated the white personnel. I was therefore made welcome in this paradise of tough guys. I listened to them talking shop and Jean, who had been there a month, put me wise:

'It's simply terrific. If you don't mind roughing it and taking risks, you can make a fortune. If you go far enough up stream, by the rapids, you can still buy a ton of timber for half a dozen tobacco leaves. That same ton sells down here at forty-five francs; one day it will be worth ten times more. From Maxime's you'll be able to come and see me; I'm working on the shores of a lake north of you.'

So there I was, in work again, this time as a forester. My new boss, Maxime Fouet, went on boozing steadily as he gave me my instructions.

'Tonight you get some sleep; tomorrow you leave for Nandipo with my men. I'm putting you in charge of the food supplies for the camps. Rice, coffee, sugar, cooking fat and salt have to be loaded on to the pirogues. We'll see about your job when you get there.'

'You're staying here?'

'No, but you don't think I'm going to wear out my arse sitting in a pirogue? I'm taking the *Alambé*. She's a nice little tub belonging to the Chargeurs Réunis. So I'll be in Nandipo long before you.'

We shook hands; his clasp was enough to crush one's fingers. I was very glad to have a boss with such a character and I thought he was doing me a great favour in letting me travel by pirogue up the Ogoué: a new experience for me.

In the morning I was up bright and early. The flotilla was waiting for me. We loaded up in high spirits and started off. What a treat! What a splendid holiday was this three-week voyage! The river meandered playfully, past sandbanks dotted with curlews which took wing uttering their plaintive cry. My boatmen belonged to the most handsome race I had ever seen: the Eschiras. Slim, muscular, in perfect physical condition. I gazed in admiration at the smooth rhythmic swing of their paddles. Their voices reverberated over the water. Like the flow of the river itself, they gave an impression of economy and sustained effort. One of them stood in the bows, beating out the time and chanting, punctuating his song with a jerk of the hips and a clank of metal anklets. He sang, now improvising on whatever he happened to see, now addressing himself to one of the crew who replied in kind. The words were translated into pidgin French for my benefit:

'The white soldiery ... the white soldiery ... a lousy lot ... a lousy lot.'

Every so often my attention was drawn to an isolated hut or a group of several, set back from the bank on a slight rise because of the danger of flooding: the residence of a white plantation manager, the chapel of a missionary. My eyes feasted on the landscape, the brilliant colours, the richness of the vegetation. A heady scent, more pungent even than in Cameroon, imperceptibly assailed my nostrils.

Further up stream, to my delight, I caught sight of hippopotami bathing, displaying their huge snouts and tiny ears. The way they snorted and slowly submerged, just like ships sinking! One of the Eschiras told me we would be seeing more and more of them the nearer we approached the River Niaie. They were not vicious, he explained, only playful; but one of their favourite games was to overturn a pirogue with a heave of their backs. From then on I kept a close watch.

A few hours later we stopped at Father Barroux's missionary, which was evidently a regular halting place for my Eschiras. We were given a warm welcome. Some Baponos and Fangs came down to meet our pirogues, and I was carried more or less bodily to the mission-house. Father Barroux was one of the greatest hippopotamus hunters on the Ogoué, and a number of severed hippopotamus heads lay rotting in the shallow water. They were over a yard long, and attached to iron stakes so that the little fish could pick them clean. The villagers now dragged one out of the water and my boatmen gave me to understand that they were going to feast on this putrefying flesh. Instinctively I tried to discourage them – it looked so dreadful – but they burst out laughing and replied: 'Smells bad, but tastes good!' What could I say? Once again I had reacted like a white.

Father Barroux was very popular and stood high even in the estimation of the witch-doctors. He would set off alone in his little pirogue and disappear into the interior for months at a time, preaching the gospel of mutual aid and goodwill. I was deeply moved by the genuine feeling with which he spoke about his primitive blacks. His was another form of adventure.

The morning we left, I had another shock: a dying black was brought into the mission-house. I hadn't worried about disease since my arrival in Africa, but even so the truth had to be faced: this man, according to Father Barroux, was suffering from sleeping sickness. There he lay, prostrate, dazed, stupefied. 'His eyes are already set,' said the priest. 'He's going to waste away even more, then lose the use of his limbs. There's no way of getting him to Port Gentil in time. Anyway those newcomers in the Institut Pasteur can't do much about it.

'Fernand, look after your health. The sleeping sickness fly is black, it flies sideways and very fast, and lands on your neck behind your ears. It flies off just as fast, in a series of zigzags. Watch out for them when you arrive: there are any amount on the shores of the lake.' Thanks to this warning perhaps, I never had sleeping sickness, nor did my blacks.

We started off again. The boatmen had eaten their fill and were hardly at all affected by the sight of the dying man. We halted at various other places along the river, either in black villages or backwaters inhabited by white settlers. At Achouka we stayed with a planter and his wife who grew bananas and coffee. They made this an occasion for a little celebration and I had the pleasure of tasting Pernod again. Next morning we resumed our journey. The Eschiras at once fell into their usual rhythm and the planter shouted after us: 'They're better than an outboard! No mechanic or spare parts needed! Your boss is so mean he prefers a banana motor!' That was what native man-power was called out there.

A few days before we were due to arrive, I thought I would like to have a go at paddling myself: I soon had to admit that I lacked the stamina, dexterity and strength of my Eschiras. They laughed heartily at my efforts, but not unkindly. We reached the Fouet concession in high spirits and on the best of terms. The holiday was over. Maxime was already on the spot; there was no time to waste; my hut was ready and I had a new job to learn.

Maxime took me in hand for several weeks. He worked hard himself and expected his staff to do likewise. My training started with the maintenance and sharpening of the tools, for everything was still done by hand.

'Here are the grindstones, these ones are worked by foot, the others by hand. You see that Bapono over there? His name is Maila. I'm handing him over to you. You can keep him when I send you into the forest.'

'When will that be?'

'The forest is a reward. First of all, the tools. There are three ways of sharpening an axe ... Now pay attention.'

I was only too keen to learn.

'Watch me. I hold the axe by the head, not by the shaft. Now you try.'

I tried.

'You're forcing too much. Gently does it. Get the feel of the tool!'

When he considered I had mastered the art sufficiently, he went on to teach me the various species of trees. Whereas in France I was just able to recognize an oak, poplar, plane or pine, here everything was unfamiliar. But this didn't disturb him. 'All the foresters in Gabon are birds of passage, except for a few madmen like myself. You're sound in wind and limb, therefore you're a forester. Go ahead!'

I set off with Maila, who was familiar with the forest and knew every species of tree. We were prospecting for *okoumé*, because of its success in industry. The war had put paid to the use of massive wood; there wasn't enough of it for rebuilding; the timber yards had no more supplies of seasoned wood; the heyday of veneers was at hand. We made our way through the forest, blazing a trail with our machetes. Maila taught me how to recognize the best trunks: from the sap they exuded when nicked by a machete. I would dip my fingers in it, contemplate it, smell it; he would give a friendly chuckle. There was no point in studying the shape of the leaves. The tops of the trees touched and intertwined; the virgin forest formed such a dense covering, the light was so glaucous, that a tree could be evaluated only by its bark. I would also assess its circumference at ground level and mark it by notching the bark. Every morning we would go off in one direction and return by a different route, crossing little streams and swamps; and not once did Maila lose his way. Every evening, towards five o'clock, we would reappear at Maxime Fouet's camp.

The evenings were another story; I would discover another Maxime, the man known as 'the champion liar of the Ogoué'. Bragging and blustering in his anxiety to be cock of the roost, he

30

often showed himself up in the worst light. I would sit and listen; it was like being at the theatre. The day's work was over, so why not allow myself to be lulled by the sound of the boss blowing his own trumpet?

'Certainly I fought in the '14-'18 war!'

'You did? You were too young to be called up.'

'I volunteered. I was in the air force. A machine gunner, actually.'

Sceptical silence on the part of Henri Lehurteaux, the forester across the way, who was also a liar. So Maxime would pile it on: 'I used to fly in such-and-such a plane, so balls to you!' And he would make a dignified exit. Lehurteaux would put us wise: 'Balls to him. Such-and-such isn't the name of an aircraft, it's the name of an airbase!'

'What about you?' asked Miquette (a lumber-man who had just been given an official forestry concession of 6,000 acres, duly signed by the Governor of Port Gentil). 'Were you in the war?'

'I was a naval officer, before coming out to this lousy country.'

'Your health, Skipper!'

And Lehurteaux would tell us all about his ship. This was until the day Tanguy, who actually was a skipper (in command of the *Alambé*), revealed that Lehurteaux had been a deck-hand, nothing more.

Such were the evenings spent among liars. When Maxime was asked to play cards, he would assume his most imposing manner and haughtily refuse: 'I swore never to touch another card as long as I lived. I've lost such terrific sums at Monte Carlo. Please don't insist.' In point of fact he didn't know how to play any more than I did, but all of us pretended to believe his story about the casino. I sat and listened, but I also pondered on my encounter with the virgin forest. This time I was right on the spot: under the huge green vault which no wind can penetrate, where every tree stands upright until it dies, so firmly is it wedged between its fellows. I found it even more beautiful and life-like than in the books I had read. Against this background of teeming vegetation Soualaba's face would appear. I had a vague feeling that I had landed in a god-forsaken spot and would probably never see her again. I would pick up my hurricane-lamp, bid the company good night and go back to my hut.

It was after one month, or thereabouts, that a strange incident occurred. The sun had set and I was going back to my camp, when a witch-doctor of Bapono stock got Maila to lead me into a little clearing fenced in with wooden stakes. Maxime, who was fairly hard on his lumber-jacks, whether Bapono or Benjabi, had not been invited; nor was such an invitation usual in fact. I accepted it as an honour, but remained on my guard.

The feet of the giant trees were draped in lianas. A huge fire in the middle of the clearing flickered intermittently on a number of human figures. Several statues of animals were brought in, placed on the ground and daubed with vegetable dye. Some big wooden tom-toms started up and the drummers appeared; they looked like huge demons in the light of the torches. I was impressed by the gravity of their faces – they were all men and five or six of them were daubed with kaolin – but I couldn't understand what it was all about. The witch-doctor stood up, clad like a prince, like a king, more majestic than any monarch. His dress was made of feathers and pieces of mirror sewn together. The haunting music started again and went on for about an hour. I felt vaguely apprehensive but was unable to account for this feeling.

All of a sudden there was total silence. Two blacks, terrifying under their coating of kaolin, appeared from behind the wooden fence pushing a young Negress in front of them. She was stark naked, glistening with some oily unguent, and must have been about twenty years old. She allowed herself to be dragged to the centre of the clearing, serene, compliant, bemused. The witch-doctor spoke and a long palaver with the lumber-jacks ensued. I couldn't understand a word. Every now and then I gave Maila a questioning glance; he was following the conversation intently. I didn't bother him. In his own time he took me by the arm: 'That woman isn't a Bapono. She's a Pahuin. From up North, where they eat people.'

'What of it?'

'The pirogue in which she was travelling with her husband and children capsized here – it was before you arrived, about two months ago. She was the only one saved. Some Eschiras found her clinging to the hull. She was looked after and this evening she's being put up for sale.'

'For sale?'

'Whoever wants her must pay. If no one makes a bid, she'll be burnt.'

I was dismayed, deeply moved, disquieted. The big tom-toms thundered again and the music became livelier, no doubt to incite the purchasers and induce a decision. The woman stood as motion-less and distant as ever.

The witch-doctor rose to his feet from his throne of carved wood. The silence was interminable. No one paid the slightest attention to the cries of the monkeys in the distance. The witch-doctor's speech was rapid, his sentences abrupt. 'No one wants her for his wife? Then she'll be burnt.' Had she understood what he said? She didn't speak Bapono. She looked at the flames. She was far from beautiful, with her drooping breasts, her teeth filed to sharp points, her long skinny legs, her round shaven head; but her great big eyes, which seemed to be awaiting death, overwhelmed me. In a flash my mind was made up: 'Maila, what if a white man took her for his wife, here and now – myself, for instance?' He couldn't believe his ears; his eyes rolled wildly.

'It comes to the same thing, if you speak before the witch-doctor decides.'

'Tell him, Maila. Tell him I'll take her for my wife. After that, you'll let me know what's expected of me. I don't want to offend the Baponos or the witch-doctor.'

'It's very simple: you take her back to your hut with you. Once day has broken, she'll be acknowledged as your wife.'

'Go ahead.'

He rose to his feet and gave out the news. All eyes converged on me. The lumber-jacks palavered, but no one laughed. The woman couldn't have understood, for she remained standing in the centre and looking at the flames. The witch-doctor gave a signal with his fly-whisk: Maila rushed forward, dragged the girl back, thrust her against me and led us out of the clearing. I felt I had an automaton beside me. This woman seemed dead or drugged. Why had I done it? I kept asking myself the question. The spectacle had been un-bearable, I had made up my mind, that's all. And now here was this woman, in my hut, in the light of the hurricane-lamp. I could see she was bewildered; but after a moment or two she collected some logs, lit the fire, took up the pan which still contained a little rice, heated it and gobbled it up. I realized she was famished. She peered at the bunch of bananas hanging from the ceiling. I cut off a segment and handed it to her. I brought her some fresh water. Gradually she began to come to life, like a parched plant. Sitting on my bed, I contemplated her. She sat crouched on the floor, as calm as she had been in front of the terrible fire. She dipped into the food, raising the white grains to her lips with her fingers. She was really far from beautiful, but how resigned! What was I to do now? I felt no desire, nothing but immense pity, a deep undefined tenderness. I didn't even know her name.

Was she aware of my feelings? Was it instinct or fatigue that dictated her behaviour? She stretched out on the mat at the foot of my bed, as though she had always slept there. I put out the light and lay down. She murmured something I didn't understand: 'Nandipo'. Was it a word of thanks or a name? It was to be my name for her: Nandipo.

I was woken at dawn by the signal for work: a series of blows on a long hollow trunk. I loved the sound of this rich penetrating gong. I started to get up – in front of me, on her mat, sat Nandipo. Her great big eyes seemed void of all thought; yet she gave me a flashing smile which I have never since forgotten. I pointed at the bunch of bananas and handed her the big pan of sweetened black coffee. She immediately lit the fire and set to work. Now that day had broken, she was my wife according to the law of the clearing. We ate our first breakfast together, sitting face to face; then I went off to work.

On my return in the evening I found a neat little pile of grilled fish spread out on some leaves, my demijohn filled with fresh water, and a rice-and-fish soup. As a wedding present, Maila had given us another bunch of bananas. I also noticed that my mattress had been doubled in size. At the end of the meal Nandipo vanished into the dark and reappeared a long time afterwards dripping from a bathe in the river. She smiled again and lay down beside me. We had not yet exchanged a word since our 'marriage'. I took her hand in mine and we fell asleep.

Maxime didn't take a very favourable view of the situation; he himself had his native 'maid' but persisted in thinking, as she did, that I had been wrong to marry a 'foreigner'.

Work, however, prevailed. Thanks to Maila, we had marked hundreds of trunks and felling was about to begin in these new sectors of the concession. Maxime could not but acknowledge the excellent job we had done and the happy atmosphere that reigned.

Days and months went by. By this time I was supervising the calibration and transport of the trunks, at some distance from our base. I came back one evening to find my hut empty. Maila was waiting for me outside: 'Don't look for her. A pirogue came down the river. We heard some Pahuin songs. Nandipo spoke to her fellow-tribesmen. She came back here and told me. Look; she left you this. I thought it better for her to go off with men of her own race. She was happy.' I then noticed, on the floor, a larger pile of fish than usual, several bunches of bananas hanging from the ceiling and, on her half of the bed, a big forest flower. It was her farewell.

I picked up the flower and found beside it a little sliver of polished wood. Maila looked embarrassed: 'Keep it, Fernand. It's a greegree, and something else besides. Nandipo said so; she's happy because she's pregnant by you. She's going back home with a child. You must keep this piece of wood carefully, for it's your son.'

How to describe my joy and my sorrow? Gently I picked up the sliver of wood and held it in my hand for some time. Again I recollected the scene in the clearing, then I visualized the Pahuins' long pirogue taking Nandipo back to her tribe. Destiny had given her to me, destiny had snatched her away. And all that remained was this little piece of wood.

Why was it that one day, years later, almost on this very same reach, my pirogue turned turtle and I lost this little sliver – my son?

6

After Nandipo's departure my bamboo and palm-leaf hut seemed empty and forlorn. There remained the forest, my paradise. I would listen to its sounds, its music. First of all, our own voices, our singing and joking, while the birds and monkeys held aloof. Then the concert of axes and saws, punctuated by laughter and shouting. Finally, all of a sudden, a deathly hush, followed by the crash of a giant tree toppling and the thud as it landed on the ground. I pitied anyone who called this hell; I was oblivious to the bad food, the mosquito bites, the dysentery, the filthy water; I pressed on with my Baponos and Fangs; the trees kept toppling. Great shafts of sunlight suddenly appeared, splintering the glaucous and oppressive penumbra. Tons of *okoumé*, which I had discovered, located and marked, now lay cut into sections and calibrated at 3 metres or 3 metres 20. All that remained was to roll them down to a creek communicating with the river. We opened up several tracks for this task, starting from the stumps of the felled trees. To make the job easier it was necessary to study the contours of the ground and take advantage of the slightest slope. My blacks enjoyed rolling the logs by hand when the lie of the land had been exploited astutely. Some of them armed themselves with long levers made of a very hard wood, *mindoukou*, and raised the logs clear of the ground; the others then pushed from behind, singing and shouting. The creeks were often very far from the paths; a solution had to be worked out as and when each problem cropped up.

It was about this time that I undertook, on the advice of my blacks, to build a canal over five hundred yards long. Maxime had the necessary picks and shovels; the soil was kaolin, easy to dig. The canal would save us a lot of time; the logs would tumble into it and float gently down towards the river. They would merely have to be guided : no heaving or trundling required. Some of the blacks worked on the digging, the others rolled the logs; I supervised, exhorting them with my presence and high spirits. Maila occasionally reported some observation of theirs which encouraged me in my organization of the task. My other great friend by now, though not so close, was the witch-doctor. I was often conscious of his eyes watching a gesture of mine or looking out for a decision. I would glance back at him, and we would smile at each other. That was all.

When the canal was completed, there was another little celebration with tom-toms. The only white in the crowd of blacks, I felt I was less of a novice, more of a forester already. Maxime, meanwhile, began making delivery of the biggest logs which lay pointing towards the end of the canal. Maila ordered lianas of various lengths to be cut, which he kept in the water for several days until they were sufficiently supple. In those days iron crampons fitted with hoops didn't exist; the rafts had no steel cable to bind them. The logs had to be lashed together with lianas to form rudimentary platforms of floating wood until the proper rafts were built. I therefore had to divide my time between the forest strong-men, who rolled the logs as far as the canal, and the gangs lower down who heaved and trundled them down to the floating point, where the rafts would be prepared for the great descent towards Port Gentil. This absorbing work prevented me from brooding unduly over Nandipo's departure, but stories about me continued to circulate, as though by bush telegraph. I was conscious of this from the way the witch-doctor kept trying to tighten his bonds of friendship with me.

One night he came to my hut and spoke frankly. 'You are the first white we have seen who behaves like this, and with a black wife. Nandipo has gone for ever. She bears your child. You have our fraternal affection and many unmarried women in the tribe, outside the camp as well, desire you and want you to give them a child. I shall cast spells to this effect. Do you accept?' I was astounded, also disturbed, because I sensed the implicit snares and dangers. I heard myself reply: 'Come back tomorrow. I'll give you my answer. Thank you for your words.'

The night was short and restless. I turned the witch-doctor's incredible offer over and over in my mind: 'So many women in your bed, Fernand my lad, means so many fathers-in-law and brothers-in-law among the labourers. It's impossible. And what about Maxime and his Negress? They'd die of dismay. And your own reputation? You'd be a laughing-stock all the way along the Ogoué. A different woman every night, including week-ends. God, what an ordeal! And what if I grow bad-tempered, dim-witted, senile, washed out? You'd better push off, Fernand. No, that's out of the question. The rafts aren't assembled yet. You still have a lot to learn. You must stay here several seasons, get to know other species of trees, visit other concessions, go and see Jean, come back with some cash, float tons of wood down stream, explore other rivers nearer the rapids. That's worth a few sacrifices. Besides, many of the women are already married; there can't be so many in need of consolation. Anyway, to hell with it. Go to sleep, Fernand, go to sleep.'

By the time the early-morning gong issued its urgent summons, I had recovered slightly but had made no progress. That day I looked out for an omen in the crash of the giant trees as they hit the ground, in the black sky, the blinding flashes of lightning, the rain pouring down on our limp bodies. Everything seemed hostile. I came back soaking wet; the water channelled its way down to the canal. The *okoumé* trees floated of their own accord, providentially carried towards the river. I went back to my hut.

During the night the witch-doctor came back at the appointed hour; he was not alone; one of my black lumber-jacks accompanied him. His expression was forthright, his features in repose. He took my hands in his. His entire being seemed to be smiling; his powerful palms, his long fingers, stroked and fondled my hands and wrists. I didn't have to speak. He sensed I was not rejecting his offer, but accepting it. After a few moments I broke this pleasant silence:

'May I ask you a few questions, as a friend?'

'Yes.'

'These women – shall I have to accept them all, satisfy them every night?'

'I'll do my best for you. I'll see to the tom-tom of your nights myself. You'll do what you can. But, you know, when a woman desires, she desires.'

I persisted:

'Shall I have to accept them all ... no matter what their age?'

'I'll send you only those who can bear you a child. No one here is sick. You're in working order. When you get tired, you can have a rest. But you'll have to sleep with all of them, mind. There must be no jealousy or disappointment for any of them.'

I thought for a moment of my boss, Maxime. What a shambles! Meanwhile the witch-doctor went on: 'Here's your first father-in-law, Fernand. He has a daughter who's still young and beautiful and "in working order". She wants a child by you.'

I sat down on my bed. The lumber-jack gave a signal and I found myself alone. In the doorway a figure appeared: Nangha. Tall, slender, without an ounce of spare flesh or muscle, she stood erect as a statue. The sound of the cicadas was deafening. We gazed at each other. She took a step forward. I stood up. She drew nearer. I stroked her hair. Never, at night time, had I heard so many birds and cicadas. Nangha extinguished the hurricane-lamp. She preferred the native torch which exuded a scent of resin and swept us with flickering shadows. I felt I was no longer on this earth, but far, far away.

Next morning I noticed how greatly, in spite of myself, my authority over the black labourers had increased. That day the output almost doubled. Maxime himself, at the far end of the canal, was amazed to see the logs floating down so fast. He came to my hut to congratulate me. Nangha was waiting for me, proud and erect in the doorway. I went inside, feeling rather tired, and at once noticed how neat and tidy it was; inserted between the bamboos were dozens of freshly cut flowers. Maxime made no comment. His 'maid' no doubt put him wise about the whole affair; for next morning he seemed distant, ill at ease and vaguely envious: 'Good old Fernand! You do just as you please, don't you? Now that the rafts are progressing! ...'

The felling and floating went on in spite of torrential rain. I would come back from the hot-house atmosphere of the forest to raptures free from all sense of guilt. For several days I lived like this, on foot or in a pirogue, exhorting the log-felling athletes, then the acrobats down below, who skipped from one floating trunk to another, assembling the famous rafts. In the evening I went home to my dusky nymph.

One evening, less than a week later, when I got back from the river, Nangha was not standing as usual in the doorway of the hut. I heard a noise nearby. The witch-doctor appeared and ushered me inside: 'Don't wait for Nangha. She went down to the river to bathe. She stayed behind on the little beach of white shingle. Come.' He urged me out again.

Nangha lay stretched out on the glistening pebbles; her eyes were wide open. The witch-doctor said: 'She was bitten by a snake. We must leave her here till tomorrow.'

I had to touch her to convince myself that she was dead. It had stopped raining. Everything was washed clean; the sky had assumed a purplish tinge. The witch-doctor took me by the arm, for I could hardly drag myself away: 'We'll come back tomorrow to fetch her soul. It will be full moon.'

We were there again next night, both of us. The moon illuminated the reach; but Nangha's body and soul were nowhere to be found. The rising waters had swept away the shingle; there was nothing but a long white glow shimmering on the surface. I looked at the river in the moonlight. The birds had fallen silent, giving way to the mournful cry of the monkeys.

Next morning I flung myself frenziedly into my work. In the upper camp the last *okoumés* that had been marked came crashing down with a noise like thunder. Silently my lumber-jacks showed me their sympathy by working twice as hard. The witch-doctor did not let me out of his sight throughout the day. Down in the creek Maila pegged away at calibrating the logs so as to make the rafts fairly regular. He was also responsible, as a native of the river, for watching the level of the water. Maxime took his advice and told me: 'We have two months, perhaps, but not more. The water here is calm. We're going to be able to work. Thanks to you, Fernand, we're going to float a record amount down to Port Gentil. Last year I lost some logs right in the forest. My Negroes had run away, they were scared of the tsetse fly. By the time I had assembled a new gang, the water level had fallen. Nothing more could be done that season. The timber remained where it was.'

'Now we have the canal, boss,' Maila interjected, giving me a conspiratorial wink.

Yes indeed, we had the canal. Swollen with water, it continued to disgorge its floating logs. The most distant rolling camp was thus directly connected to the creek and river.

'Maila,' said Maxime, 'keep your eyes open for signs of the first spate.'

'The birds will tell us, boss. They know better than we do. In two moons' time they will arrive perhaps.'

The witch-doctor indicated that the sun was about to set and that he wanted to accompany me back to my hut. I noticed his determination not to leave me alone, as though he wanted me to renew my interest in life and keep my word.

40

But my heart wasn't in it. I felt I was an infinitesimal part of this Africa, where vegetable and human alike are swept up and carried away. Neither pride nor calculation, a strange sense of peace, an almost blissful surrender succeeded the fatigue of the day. In the end I yielded and there began a pathetic, trivial procession, a sort of dance conducted by my witch-doctor purveyor. At the appointed hours my nature would respond by means of sudden physical reflexes to the female appetite of this jungle village. I felt neither revulsion nor disgust. I merely obeyed. At night time I embarked on the saraband of brief ecstasy, and during the day, for two long months, I learnt the technique of raft-making.

Tornadoes, storms, tangled lianas, acrobatic performances on the logs, nocturnal raptures have remained intermingled in my mind ever since. 'Manioc' was the first candidate in this test series. In the morning the witch-doctor asked me outright what I thought of her. 'A man with an erection doesn't think.' It was a sort of proverb. Had I heard it on the lips of my friend Jean, a specialist in seduction? Had I invented it myself? No matter, I adopted it from then on.

'I've started with the ugliest,' said the witch-doctor. 'She's flabby and whinnies like a horse.'

And indeed, in spite of her round Bapono head, she had a heavy lantern jaw.

'She stinks of boiled manioc. If that bothers you, give her the child quickly,' he added.

I made no reply and thus achieved further distinction in his eyes. That evening I was in for another surprise. I, who had sworn to swallow everything, had to sample dear Manioc's favourite dish: termite pancakes. She concocted this 'caviar' in my best pan, chuckling as she saw the fat sizzle. To me it seemed that all food had acquired the taste of termites. I resolved to say nothing; I was stoical. She went off happy, taking her smell of boiled manioc with her and also, according to the witch-doctor, the gift for which she was hoping.

Down by the creek we were working waist deep in the water. The rafts were assembled, fifty logs at a time, secured by long rods and knotted lianas. Maila and some of the others lashed these platforms together so as to form a big rectangle fifty metres long and seven wide. At the four corners holes were drilled in the logs to receive four Y-shaped forks which were to act as rowlocks for the long oars serving as tillers. Maxime supervised this task and resumed his professorial manner: 'It's at this stage, Fernand, that you must check everything. During the descent you can't make any repairs apart from reinforcing a liana when it snaps. I'm going to take one convoy of rafts, you'll take the other. So make sure your tillers are good and strong. During the descent be careful not to run aground. Even with ten men, you're done for. You must tack about in time, keep in mid-stream, make for the bank before nightfall. You'll go ahead of me, I'll follow a day or two later.' For the lumber-jacks, working on the rafts was less arduous. An atmosphere of gaiety reigned; voices kept bursting into song; the hewing of the tillers and the weaving of the liana ropes proceeded apace. Maxime was infected by these high spirits; maybe he was also calculating how much he would be pocketing in a few months' time at Port Gentil. A thousand cubic metres at least, that was what he could float down this year.

'I say, Fernand, you must have a strong stomach to be able to look at your wife without feeling sick.'

'Yours must be feeling sick, anyway, judging by her face.'

And the king of liars would be off on his hobby-horse:

'My wife, if you'll pardon me, is a princess. She doesn't like the local riffraff. She's an aristocrat from the coast. Her father's a notable; he committed her to my care. Look at her bearing, her beauty – real breeding, Fernand, that's what. She hasn't the same fetishes as these round-headed savages. So she gives you ugly looks. She thinks you're being too familiar. Besides, she loathes your purveyor, as you call him.'

'What about you?'

'I have no objection. The work's progressing, that's all that matters.'

In point of fact the 'princess' was jealous and I had to be careful. Perhaps she couldn't bear being regarded – she, the boss's wife – as a despicable fancy girl, whereas my 'volunteers' were honoured like queens: Nandipo and Nangha had aroused the rancour of Princess Fouet. Yet this was only the beginning.

Maxime was right: my new 'fertile-night companion', as the witch-doctor called her, was subject to a slight but constant tremor. Her head looked enormous compared to her frail, slender body. She resembled the tree after which she had been named. Like the leafy-topped *kombo-kombo*, which is planted to provide shade for

42

the cocoa plants, she kept shaking her mop of hair. She would walk around like this, rapidly, intently, as though propelled by the wind. Her greatest pleasure was to forestall me when I felt thirsty. Graceful and agile, she would seize my tin mug, fill it with water and raise it triumphantly to my lips. Every evening she waited for my return, humming under her breath, with a little sliver of wood in the corner of her mouth; every morning she accompanied me affectionately to the door. She too eventually went off, happy and lighthearted like the *kombo-kombo* in the wind. It was she, I remember, who one evening held her two little breasts in her hands and, pointing them towards me, gazed at me earnestly. Then she seized my hand and swept it majestically over her erect nipples. Finally she showed me her bare stomach to indicate with pride that she had discerned the signs of fecundation.

Outside, we were busy reinforcing and checking every rope in our flotilla. Maxime had ordered some spare tillers to be made. I supervised the finishing touches, full of admiration for the primitive astuteness of Maila and his assistants. At the stern of each raft, a little cabin firmly lashed to the logs enabled the pilot to shelter from the rain or sun. It had a straw roof, no walls, and was open in front and behind. At the foot of this edifice the Baponos constructed a platform of branches into which they trod some clayey soil. 'That's for the cooking,' Maxime explained. 'You can light a fire on the clay without burning the logs. We'll set off with ten men each, we'll need as many as that for the handling. In the other cabin you'll keep the food supplies. For sleeping-mats, you'll take those from your hut. But we have plenty of time.'

'Another moon!' Maila shouted. 'The level won't fall until then.'

The witch-doctor was delighted because of the women and refused to tell me the number of his recruits: 'You've kept your word, Fernand. Women very content. Soon it will all be over. Only a few more. First of all "Dead Leaf" by way of a rest cure.'

'Dead Leaf' was flat-chested, and likewise afflicted with the shakes. She was a tom-tom dancer. 'She's possessed by the spirit that comes from afar,' the witch-doctor told me when I asked him why she shuddered like this during the day. It made me anxious. But as soon as she was in bed she lay motionless, inert, and quickly fell sound asleep. By the time she left I had had my rest cure.

I was reckoning without the wisdom and cunning of my witch-doctor friend. He had so far spared me the better to prepare me for the ordeal to come; in quick succession I was assaulted by a regular little ball of fire, then by two twin sisters. 'Mora' had escaped from a mission-house. She tore off her loincloth straight away, taking the initiative with a vitality that left me gasping. First in bed, first at table. She devoured almost the whole of every meal by herself. It was as though a tornado inhabited her chubby little body. She was always on the move, running down to the river, climbing trees, cutting bunches of bananas for me, and gobbling them up while waiting for me to come home. She was replaced, on the witch-doctor's orders, by the famous twins whom nobody wished to handle.

'They're nice girls, but in their life everything has to be fairly shared. Accept them, Fernand.'

How could I argue? I put the two beds at their disposal and pre-pared to doss down on the mat. A waste of time: I was promptly caught in a tangle of live lianas. Well might I struggle and defend myself, for two nights the twins indulged in a real acrobatic per-formance, each waiting her turn to launch an inventive assault. The mat, the floor, the beds, it was all one to these frenzied human whirlwinds. With a victim's resignation I pegged away at preserving my heroic and derisory reputation as a reproductive agent. After the third night I disgraced myself by falling asleep at work. This was indicative. When I woke I felt ashamed, but I saw that the witch-doctor was full of admiration and genuine respect: 'What a pity you're not black, Fernand! You'd be completely one of us. Your kinship is increasing. You're giving us coloured sons.' I realized he was speaking seriously. There wasn't the faintest smile on my lumber-men's lips, not a trace of irony in their expression. They had stood guard over my slumber and temporary exhaustion. What a sign of brotherly complicity! Yet I was very near to re-pudiating all black women for ever. The witch-doctor kissed my hand and assured me there were only two more: two gifts, two surprises. His manner, however, was most mysterious.

I rested that night; but at first light, before the wooden gong had sounded, I was honoured by a visit from a huge buxom woman, a superb, smiling force of nature. 'My name is Kapok,' she said in pidgin. 'I've come to see you.' At this I felt weak at the knees. I rushed off to work, thinking of the tree after which she was named, on the same principle as the tousle-haired Kombo-kombo, and as the day progressed I saw how closely she resembled the generous

44

kapok which scatters its flying seeds like dandelions. I tried to work out a plan for tackling this new tree of mine without making a fool of myself. Was Maxime in the know? Probably, because he leered at me and said: 'You look worried, Fernand. Never mind. A good cock is never fat.' He chuckled at his own jokes. To cut him short, I scooped some water out of the river with my hat and poured it over my head and shoulders. For the sake of appearances. We would meet again to settle accounts at Port Gentil; I must have earned a tidy sum by now, and I had the job at my fingertips.

I inhaled deeply for a moment or two, letting the evening air seep into me, then went home determined to put my puny energy at the disposal of my massive mate. I was surprised to find my hut increased threefold in dimension. Kapok was radiant. With the help of a female cousin, she had undertaken, machete in hand, to enlarge my quarters. She was just finishing the interior fitments and the huge bedstead. The little cousin vanished with a smile. I noticed some new cooking utensils. Kapok's bulk did not preclude nimbleness or rapidity. Her hands dealt adroitly with the dishes, the packing-case table, the grilled fish. I had a capable housekeeper in my service, no doubt about it. Ever since, I have retained a memory of unobtrusive comfort. She was silent and precise in her movements, soft to the touch and odourless. With her I spent nights of peaceful bliss. Her big eyes, her flashing white teeth, seemed to thank me for overlooking her bulk and weight. Then something astonishing happened; she became unexpectedly merry, started losing weight and had to leave me on the witch-doctor's orders.

'A seed germinates, Fernand. This will be the last time. Until you leave, you can keep the widow with you. I'll tell you more and you'll understand.'

I acquiesced. The work was now less arduous: the rafts were in place, the stores under shelter, ready to be loaded. The cooking platforms had been tried out and reinforced with clay; fires had been lit on it so as to form a layer of charcoal. Maïla had had additional liana ropes woven in case of emergency. Meanwhile he watched for the water level to drop. Everything was ready for the descent. Maxime and I had calculated the volume of the rafts. It was a big year for him; if the European buyers in Port Gentil offered decent prices, we were going to make a fortune. In those days there was no radio communication to enable the timber to be properly valued. Prices might suddenly soar, so it was necessary to reach the depots and not be in too much of a hurry to sell. Maxime was deliberately mysterious about this last phase of the operation: 'Careful! No false hopes, Fernand! There's a lot of competition. There are foresters all the way along the Ogoué. There are others at Libreville. The buyers gamble on that. The good thing for us is the growing demand. Europe is crying out for timber. In a few weeks we'll know what we're going to get for all our sweat and toil. You're young. Stay here a few years, keep your nose clean, and you'll leave, a rich man, Fernand! And to think you arrived here in a pair of espadrilles!'

'I don't own much more now. Like you, I'm waiting to be paid.'

'You won't regret it, Fernand. I've taught you the job, you have free board and lodging. You're living like a prince, moreover. Where else on the Ogoué would you live like this?'

High up in the sky some birds went flying past. From his pirogue Maila observed the creek and the approaches to the river, looking out for the slightest change in the current. Fishing with nets provided a clue. At this season the fish were likewise on the move.

'In two weeks' time we'll have to pay off the men who aren't coming down with us, Maxime.'

'I'll go to Lambaréné and organize the tug, so that we don't have to wait for weeks in the estuary.'

The first evening, the widow was graciously waiting for me outside my hut. The witch-doctor had come with her, either to assure her that I would keep my promise or because she herself was shy.

'This is Njapoungou,' he said. 'The last woman I have chosen for you. Her breasts are heavy, glorious, they have already given milk to three children. Three girls. She wants you to give her a coloured boy. I am working magic for her to be happy.'

I took her hand and led her inside. She disappeared for a moment and came back with a little tray surmounted by a pyramid of wooden platters covered in banana leaves. This set piece was rapidly spread out on the table. A meal awaited me, highly seasoned, varied, delicate. Millet, rice, bamboo-shoots tasting like wild asparagus. She went off again and I never understood how she was able to come back so quickly with a carboy of palm wine. Her eyes gently awaited approbation; her gestures expressed a touching refinement. Unlike Nangha, who was an early bird, she sat up late admiring my kerosene lamp and the magic light it shed. I turned the flame up and down, varying its intensity, which made her smile. The calculated half-light emboldened her, encouraged her to draw closer and hold my hand. An invisible power led us unconsciously to the natural gestures of love.

It was only next day that I understood why she had been so conscientious. At dawn three little Negresses, between three and seven at the most, arrived with some fruit and fish. And there they stayed. My life as a bachelor stallion was transformed into one of unexpected domesticity. Suddenly, while waiting for the births which my witch-doctor had promised, I was endowed with a trio of gleeful children who never stopped scampering about. When I called one of them, all three would appear as though by magic. I kept stumbling over them. Two of them would go fishing, dangling their legs in the water, delighted to be on the rafts beside an unhoped-for father; the third would come rushing down with a calabash of palm wine; their mother would suddenly appear with some fried lizards. I felt that all of them were confidently awaiting the arrival of a gingerbread-coloured baby boy. My last days were thus steeped in the natural joy of this happy brood who vied with one another to keep me amused.

The level of the river was falling visibly. The water had withdrawn from the edge of the creek and the clay banks of the Ogoué were laid bare. Clouds of conirosters and other birds gave us the signal by coming to seek their food in this sector and further north. We were going to be away for some time: it would take us several months to float the rafts down stream, sell our timber to the highest bidder, and reprovision ourselves on a massive scale for the next felling season. Maxime spoke of entering into negotiations, doubling his concession and engaging additional labour. He was in a state of euphoria. As for myself, I was neither cheerful nor sad. I was going to drift down to Port Gentil for three weeks. I prepared to load my old tin trunk on the leading raft. A cotton shirt for the journey, my gun, food supplies: these were the bare essentials.

At first light I left my hut; my little family vied with one another to carry my luggage and provisions. The sound of the tom-tom and shouts of farewell heralded the departure of my rafts. The pirogues acting as escorts guided us to the main stream. Maila directed the handling of the tillers so as to accelerate gradually up to a good floating speed. I fired a few salvoes with my gun and watched with emotion as the figures of Njapoungou and her little girls were reduced to dots and finally disappeared.

The banks of the Ogoué began to speed past. The Eschiras had divided themselves up between the two rafts, keeping only one pirogue afloat to act as a pilot and look out for any hazards such as submerged rocks or suspicious eddies. I was sitting on a fortune: a year's work. I took my matches out of a tin – one of those precious biscuit tins decorated with Breton girls in national costume – and started to make a fire on which to cook the rice.

Our descent took less than three weeks. I halted before five o'clock every evening to choose the best point for mooring that night, and starting again next morning. Maila and the boatmen were experts at handling. I merely had to let them guide me. My time was therefore spent in sleeping, doing the cooking, and plunging into the river every now and then in order to cool off. After Ngoumbi, other rafts replied to our salutations. They were emerging from the lakes of Ogonié and Mandjé; but, with the current in our favour, I thought it best to remain in the lead so as to spend less time waiting for the tug.

Long before we reached the mouth, the movements of the tide were apparent. The curlews were now more numerous and my Eschiras decided I ought to shoot these birds. I never liked to shoot without a purpose but, to my great surprise, they told me that curlews were a welcome addition to their diet. So right up to the estuary we had great fun and good sport; the Eschiras ate their fill, their morale remained as high as ever, and the time passed more quickly.

After waiting for two days, securely moored to the bank, we saw the tug that was to take us to the depot heading towards us. The skipper, René Prigent, was a Breton; his crew were all black. He flung out a line and asked me to come aboard.

'Where do you hail from?'

'From Maxime Fouet's, up north!'

'Must try to get up there some day. Nice place, isn't it?'

In a few minutes, glass in hand, we became close friends.

'A good hot Picon sets a man up. I'm taking you to Uncle Bert's depot. Will your fellows on the rafts be able to manage by themselves? Then stay on board and keep an eye on the cable. We're going to head out to sea.'

From the mouth of the Ogoué the tug got us safely over the bar, then entered a small cove on the far side of Cap Lopez. There was an iron chain across the entrance. The fellow in charge opened up. I moored the rafts, made fast, dismissed my Eschiras and arranged for Maila to report to me every day at Port Gentil; the rest of the food supplies would tide him over while he waited, like myself, to be paid. Then René Prigent and I made our way to Uncle Lan's hotel.

Still the same lobby, pitchpine furniture, massive wooden bar; and still the same clientèle. The merchants, buyers and representatives of European firms adapted themselves or not to this shabby dump, but most of them preferred to be put up by official friends or the Governor himself. The foresters therefore remained a closely-knit group and a round of drinks was enough to create fellow-feeling. Many of them had already sold their timber, and money was flowing like water. Some were even celebrating with champagne.

Uncle Lan's mulattoes were sweeping up the sawdust, when everyone suddenly rushed out of the bar to watch one of the Lafailles, dead drunk and miraculously clinging to the balcony railing, piss out of the window. 'Bravo, Lafaille! Another round!' We were youngsters, seized by a frenzy to live, to compensate for the tedious or dangerous moments through which we had passed. We were instinctively celebrating a victory. Jokes and yarns circulated at a cracking pace, laughter gave rise to more laughter, wild remarks provoked others wilder still.

'Who's coming to Sâo Tomé?' bellowed a ginger-haired man.

But no one replied; another forester had just arrived and was being given a boisterous welcome:

'Hi, Bilboquet! Bilboquet!'

And champagne corks started popping at every table.

'Well, have you still got that Negro of yours?'

'I'm married, you chump, and by correspondence. I'll be out of here in a month.'

The other Lafaille brother, half seas over and weeping with laughter, clutched at Prigent's sleeve to attract his attention:

'He's married, you bet! One night ... I was going up to my hut ... I had my hurricane-lamp. I saw a light flicker ... he was lying on the bed ... on his back ... having it off with his Negro, the old bugger!'

'Who's coming to Sâo Tomé with me? You silly sods! I've got my boat. What a lousy lot you foresters are!'

The ginger-haired man was still addressing the company in

general. I asked about him. His name was Le Hénaff. He was a
Breton sea-captain and was waiting at Cap Lopez for a shipment to
Nantes. Meanwhile he kept offering everyone a free trip over to the
island. But no one would listen.

Next day there were more high jinks. The door was pushed open
by a tubby, heavily whiskered little fellow, a total stranger. The
whole room fell silent. In no way embarrassed, the man stepped
forward. Instinctively the foresters scented a victim. He was well
equipped, with a brand-new carbine and big-game gun which must
have cost a fortune, and dressed like an illustration in a child's
adventure book. Bilboquet and Lacôte made the initial approach.
The fellow came from the neighbourhood of Cognac and was a big-
game hunter – especially in Asia, he said. Whistles of admiration.
Conspiratorial glances. A real godsend! He talked about clay-pigeon
shooting. His gun circulated from hand to hand. The Lafaille
brothers whispered to one of Uncle Lan's mulattoes who went off
chuckling. A few minutes later they turned to the hunter: 'There's
good sport here. It's not our job, of course, but for you ... Look!
Over there! Good heavens! A buffalo!'

Driven by a hail of stones from the mulatto, a wretched ox with
lyre-shaped horns came lolloping towards us. The Great Hunter
dashed out, took careful aim and shot the animal dead. Then he was
carried in triumph back to the hotel and everyone shook hands with
him.

Suddenly all hell was let loose. A huge Negro appeared and
pounced on him, yelling blue murder: 'You crazy! You kill my
meat! You puncture my ox! Me go police!' Apologies and explana-
tions – it was all a mistake. The Negro calmed down; no one could
have suspected him of being an accomplice. The ox became the
property of the Great Hunter who was only too delighted to pay
five times what it was worth, in cash.

Thanks to him, for the next three days all of us fed free of charge.
He had meanwhile disappeared into the bush with a couple of
shady-looking characters, the sort of henchmen only a sucker could
have chosen.

As can be seen, we were a rowdy lot. There was one exception,
however: Kléber Mangel, an elegant, distinguished-looking man who
played the musical saw every evening. Every now and then a beautiful Negress came in and brought him a drink. This was Azizie, his
wife. One day, when we were alone together, he told me more

about himself. Having neither the wish to be a bureaucrat nor the strength to be a forester, he had come out here to paint pictures, write poems and make love: 'But do you know how I earn my living? By baking croissants! Everyone wants them, from the Governor himself down to our black friends. They remind people of Paris.'

At this point, I remember, Maila came and notified me that Maxime had reached the depot and had already found a buyer.

'This calls for a celebration,' I said. 'I'm going to draw my pay.'

Mangel looked alarmed:

'You've been working for the Liar? And you haven't been paid? Poor fellow, you're going to be diddled. That apprenticeship trick! He played it again last season. The boy died at Libreville three months later. Fever, frustration, God knows what.'

When Maxime came in that evening I went straight up to him:

'When are you going to pay me?'

'What?'

'My pay, when do I draw it?'

'You must be crazy. I never pay an apprentice.'

'You're going to pay this one!'

'Bugger off!'

I was not foul-mouthed by nature and had to search for a word ... I must have called him a 'dirty cunt', or something like that, for he sprang to his feet and punched me on the jaw. I recovered my balance, swung my fist and dotted him on the nose. He grabbed hold of me and bent me backwards over a table. I felt I was going to pass out. Mangel came to my rescue. He picked up a heavy chair. Crash! Down it came on Maxime's head. He was out for the count. But I never saw the colour of my money.

7

Next morning Mangel introduced me to a friend of his, a forester from the Val de Cherrense, who had heard about my plight and offered to help me:

'You're going to get what Maxime owes you,' he said, 'or my name isn't Georges Siccard. I've calculated your pay and I'm willing to advance it to you as soon as I've sold my timber.'

'And how am I expected to reimburse you?'

'We'll get it back with interest this time next year, mark my words. I'll talk it over with Cerutti ...'

'Who's Cerutti?'

'A land-surveyor who got fed up working in the forest for a lot of dirty swine. He came to Port Gentil and now helps himself from the depots. One log here, another there. Very clever. He has two or three henchmen, expert divers. One word from him and down they go, knives clenched between their teeth. And in due course – fancy! – the lianas on that raft snap after crossing the bar! Disaster! Alarm! Emergency! Logs bursting in every direction like fireworks! Dangerous. The hazard must be removed. Cerutti turns up to lend a hand, offers his breakdown service, or buys the wreckage at a rock-bottom price.'

'He's a gangster?'

'No, a dispenser of justice. He keeps an eye on each boss who arrives, and makes enquiries. If the man has behaved decently in the forest, he lets him off and waits for the next. If he hasn't, then he goes into action. So, you see, Fernand, this time next year Cerutti will be on the look-out for that swine Maxime and we'll be amply repaid.'

Le Hénaff came in:

'Hi, you forest rats! Who's coming for a free trip to Sâo Tomé? I'll go by myself if you don't fancy the idea.'

'What's the great attraction?' Siccard asked.

'I've heard tell they sell gold dust there. I leave for Nantes next week. I want to have a bit of fun first. Besides, who knows? ...'

All of a sudden we were seized with gold fever. Next day, haversacks slung, we boarded Le Hénaff's old tub.

'Gold, you'll see,' he kept doggedly repeating.

'You're going to be in the money again, Fernand!' Siccard ironically remarked.

The island was a total disappointment. A few modern houses, some old Portuguese walls, a straw hut or two, then nothing but deserted beaches. We sailed right round it.

'The place to go to is Spanish Guinea, I'm told,' said Le Hénaff.

'So long as you don't take us all the way back to Concarneau!' Mangel chuckled. 'I'm a married man, you know!'

All of a sudden we caught sight of a propeller impaled in the sand. We landed with our equipment: shovel, axe, tool kit.

'We've found gold, my lads!' said Siccard. He tapped the propeller, picked up a rasp and started filing one of the blades. 'Look. It turns to gold.'

The dust trickled through his fingers. I humoured him.

'Wait, I'll help you.'

We toiled away like a couple of knife-grinders and soon produced a big pile of copper dust. We mixed it with the greyish sand and poured it into bottles.

On getting back to Cap Lopez, we saw the familiar silhouette of the *Tchad*. This gave us an idea. 'The Gold! Let's make it up into packets, into twists, then we'll go and call on Carriou.'

Carriou was a hospitable skipper. He enjoyed the company of foresters and was happy to welcome them on board whenever he put in. He met us at the top of the gangway and escorted us to the bar himself. Albert the barman was likewise pleased to see us: foresters were good business.

After a few drinks I fished a twist out of my pocket.

'What's that?' Albert asked.

'Gold dust,' Siccard casually replied.

'Put it away!' said Albert.

'Why?'

'Let's have a look, but come round here. You're crazy to flash it about in public!'

We joined him behind the bar.

'What price are you asking? How much have you got?'

'Three packets and six bottles. We haven't thought about the price. All we know is, it's gold dust and must be worth a hell of a lot.'

'Two thousand francs, is that enough?'

'If you say so. Gold's worth much more, but we don't know about dust. We get it from the blacks of New Guinea.'

'It's a deal. Go and fetch the bottles.'

We took the money and treated ourselves to a hilarious evening. On stepping ashore we were still laughing at the mercenary glint that had come into Albert's eyes.

A few days later Jean turned up. We celebrated his arrival with Albert's money. Siccard sold his logs, gave me the advance he had promised, and set off again for his concession. 'Come and work with me if you don't find another job,' were his parting words.

One evening, in the middle of the usual hullaballoo at Uncle Lan's, a seaman appeared in the doorway and announced:

'He's dead!'

'Who?' we asked.

'Prigent, the tug-boat skipper. He cut his hand on a loose strand of cable. Just a scratch, not worth bothering about. But tetanus developed ...'

An embarrassed silence ensued. Foulon, known as the 'Human Dog' because he was so hairy, sat scratching his head in perplexity. People never know what expression to assume at the announcement of a death. Gloom was about to settle on the company when an element of comic relief was miraculously provided by the unexpected reappearance of the Great Hunter. He looked so down in the mouth that merriment broke out again at once.

'The swine, the dirty swine! What a country! Worse than Asia ...' he spluttered. Apparently his two henchmen had abandoned him in a swamp and disappeared with his kit.

Foulon nodded:

'Cheer up, old boy, and have a drink. You at least haven't got tetanus, have you?'

Next morning, while the Great Hunter was enjoying a little snack, a superb white egret alighted right in front of the hotel. This bird was in fact half tame; it often landed on the bedroom balconies and disturbed the inmates at siesta time. Miquette, who had just arrived from Lambaréné, remarked: 'That pest! If only I had a gun ...'

The Great Hunter rose to his feet, carbine in hand:

54

'What kind of bird is it?'

'The kind that ought to be stuffed.'

'A rare species?'

'I should say so. Absolutely unique.'

The Great Hunter fired, shot it dead, and went out to retrieve it. Some time later a lady turned up, escorted by two blacks in *chéchias*. Uncle Lan greeted her: 'Madame Lamy, what an honour! ... The bank manager's wife,' he whispered to us in the same breath.

Madame Lamy glanced round the room, caught sight of the Great Hunter and cried: 'You swine, you've killed my dear little bird!' Then she slapped his face and added: 'Now we're quits!'

One fine morning Jean announced:

'My boss has gone back, he wants you to join us and has paid your fare on the *Alembé*.'

'I'd rather go up by pirogue with you.'

'Then we'll sell the ticket to the next greenhorn we see.'

And we did.

My first trip up the Ogoué had been a voyage of discovery. The second was more in the nature of a joy-ride, maybe because of Jean's itinerary – by way of Lake N'Gome and the Ouango – and the frequent halts we made. As we approached each stopping-place he would pick up my gun and fire a salvo to announce our arrival. The colonials or foresters would then come down to the bank to meet us.

The Lafaille brothers gave us a particularly boisterous welcome. They had several cases of Pernod with them and had evidently decided not to stop drinking until they had drained the last bottle. They had also brought a phonograph and any amount of discs.

In a short while we were all in an advanced state of euphoria. We flung an empty bottle into the shallows, where it floated like a target, and then took aim with the discs. Some of them landed on the bottle and smashed to pieces. The rest skimmed over the water and were finished off with a carbine. By the evening there wasn't one left.

At Lambaréné there was the mission. Papin had briefed us: 'The building on the left, just above Schweitzer's, is the Catholic mission. You'll be welcome there. As for old Sawbones, frankly, he's not very affable.' And indeed I noticed that the local foresters were disappointed in the doctor who already had the reputation of an apostle. I won't say any more. I met him only once, the following year. Personally I didn't find in him the great man I had been led to expect. But, after all, we had our job to do and it was not for us to destroy the legend that was beginning to emerge. The old Gabon hands will realize what I mean. As Papin had told us: 'The Catholics have had Joan of Arc; the Protestants, in their jealousy, are busy manufacturing Schweitzer.'

We eventually reached our logging camp, and work started straight away. I found the boss even harder to take than Maxime Fouet. He was an alcoholic and from time to time used to break out and go literally raving mad. He also had a phobia of venereal disease. Maybe he had dipped his wick not wisely, but too well, for he had a large supply of antiseptic ointments and especially permanganate. He couldn't do anything without washing his hands in it, and all his towels were stained that colour. He came into contact with a Negro? Permanganate! He pawed his native maid? Permanganate! There were traces of it on his fingers, and even on his face.

One Sunday, unable to stick it a moment longer – the boss was again dead drunk – Jean and I went off in a couple of pirogues to call on our nearest neighbour, Big Marcel. We found his camp completely deserted. 'I don't like the look of this,' said Jean. 'Let's go on to Mbilantem and see the Galipeaux brothers. They might know what's happened.'

They did know:

'Big Marcel came to grief under a raft. He was assembling the logs, slipped and fell in. But some people say he treated his blacks so badly that they pushed him under and held him down. He was a strong swimmer, remember.' They pointed to a pile of belongings in a corner. 'They're all his: a tin trunk, some khaki drill suits. He also left those filthy things.' They showed us some wooden stakes, carved in the shape of a human head. 'He filched them from Eschira tombs. A rotten thing to do, and anyway fetishes bring bad luck ...'

I found these objects impressive and beautiful; and, since the Galipeaux were only too eager to get rid of them, I took them away with me. Some time later I heard that both brothers had likewise died in mysterious circumstances.

In due course the rainy season arrived and the great descent to Port Gentil took place again. Jean and I were glad to get away and we celebrated more boisterously than ever at Uncle Lan's. One evening Siccard came in, beaming all over his face:

'All right, Fernand, you can stand drinks all round. Cerutti has done the trick. Maxime got his timber to the depots all right, but he can't understand how there's now at least half a raft missing.'

'What about Cerutti?'

'Don't worry about him. He's already cut up the logs and loaded them on to his boat. They have his mark on them, and the bills of landing are in order.'

Then Miquette arrived, accompanied by a greenhorn called Guillaud who had come out here to make his fortune with a metal tugboat. 'He wants to treat us all to a maiden voyage.'

'Then he can take us up to my place,' said Durix.

Durix's camp was not far from the River Abando. We stayed with him until we had drained his last drop of liquor. Then we approached Guillaud:

'Are you sure there's nothing to drink on board your boat?'

'Nothing, I swear.'

'Let's go and see.'

We went.

'These are bottles, aren't they?'

'You're crazy! It's eau de Cologne.'

'It's alcohol all the same! Come on, open that case.'

During the evening a forester whose name I can't remember passed out. No one paid any attention at the time. It was only later we discovered he was dead. But no one seemed to know him.

'Why did you go and die, you silly bugger?'

'Hey, what's-your-name, say you're not dead!'

We spoke to him. We shook him. To no avail.

'We'll have to bury him.'

'There's no priest.'

'There's no coffin.'

'But we can dig a hole.'

'Yes, we can dig a hole.'

'There are no planks.'

'Well, we're not going to cut down a tree in the middle of the night just to make some planks!'

'Must bury him properly.'

'Must make a coffin.'

'I can't find any nails.'

'Use some lianas!'

'Good, the blacks are digging the hole.'

'I've found an old packing-case.'

We ended up with a coffin that looked more like a child's mummy; the planks were too short and were held together by a cat's cradle of lianas. Fairly decently, considering our condition, we formed a procession behind the black pall-bearers. Just then the devil of a storm broke right overhead. The downpour transformed us into dripping scarecrows and by the time we reached the hole it had filled up with water. We were about to lower the coffin into it nevertheless, when one of the blacks stumbled and the lianas snapped. The planks floated on the surface, so did the corpse.

'What about holy water?' Miquette asked.

'Don't you think there's enough water here as it is?' retorted Siccard.

'It's not proper without holy water,' Miquette persisted.

And with the utmost solemnity he blessed the grave with eau de Cologne, while the rest of us shovelled back the earth which promptly turned to mud.

When we got back to Uncle Lan's, Siccard offered me a partnership. I accepted, and a few days later we embarked for Libreville together.

8

Libreville was a large trading-centre, but without a harbour. The ships anchored off shore. Siccard had done well for himself. For two thousand five hundred francs a year he and his other partner, Letourneur, had inherited an area of six thousand acres at the far end of the estuary of the Gabon. Right next to it was the concession he had earmarked for me:

'It's good land, thickly planted with giant *okoumés*, but uninhabited. There's not a single black in the area. This means you'll have to go up north and engage a hundred Pahuins as lumber-jacks. If you manage to win over the local chieftains, well and good; but you might just as easily get killed.'

'And even put in a pot and boiled, I know. I once had a Pahuin wife.'

'All the more reason. It wouldn't be the first time a white man vanished mysteriously up there.'

'So what do you suggest?'

'I'll give you four of my Pahuins as escort. One of them, Bakala-Bendé, speaks pidgin-French. He's tough and reliable.'

As soon as I had organized the equipment and stores – two sacks of rice, cooking-fat, salt, sugar, coffee and tobacco – we set off. For several days we travelled by pirogue, but after Kango, the last little French outpost, the foot slogging began. We headed north, through dense forest obstructed with lianas, then up the steep track leading to the Crystal Mountains. It was hard going. Day after day we had to cross rivers and rapids, and once we even had to repair an old liana bridge which otherwise would have given way under our weight. The clear streams were believed to have curative properties, and occasionally we came across small groups of sick people bathing in them. One day we even saw a witch-doctor who had set up shop at the foot of a cascade tending his patients by lowering them into the water in a wicker basket.

Up on the plateau we had an unexpected encounter with another white escorted by a small group of blacks. He was tall and handsome, and I took him to be some sort of official until he stepped forward and introduced himself: 'Marquis le Destrayat, I own a saw-mill near Libreville. I came up here to recruit labour, but I'm returning empty-handed. I took my revenge on a gorilla. I wounded him at least; but he scampered off after gashing one of these imbeciles in the calf.'

He went on his way, lordly and arrogant. Bakala-Bendé wasn't at all impressed: 'He bad white, foolish hunter; gorilla dangerous and not allowed.' All the same, the marquis had been unable to find any labour. Would I be any luckier? Bakala-Bendé read my thoughts: 'You different, we understand. You love us, he no.'

We eventually reached Oyem, where a nice French merchant put a spare hut at our disposal. I had the stores brought in and the tobacco prepared. It was packed in 'heads': five loose leaves rolled up in a sixth. Each was worth one franc fifty and made an acceptable gift.

Next morning, accompanied by an escort over whom he towered, a magnificent Pahuin in full regalia called at the hut. 'Him big chief Ovendo from River Nye,' Bakala-Bendé explained. My arrival had been announced by tom-tom, apparently, and the chief knew I wanted to recruit labourers. He therefore invited me to come and palaver with him that evening. I accepted with a smile and presented him with a whole sack of tobacco.

Torches and bonfires illuminated the big clearing in which he received me. A giant tom-tom started up in my honour and frenzied dancing began. Never had I seen such leaps and bounds. Like antelopes, the performers sprang into the air, quivering in every muscle. The noise was deafening. Meanwhile we were served a fermented brew that was unknown to me but extremely potent. Ovendo's countenance remained calm and affable throughout.

Next day, on returning to the hut for my siesta, I found three young black girls waiting for me. 'Gift from chief,' Bakala-Bendé explained.

'One would be enough,' I told him, 'what am I supposed to do with the two others?'

'Me cut down branches, make beds,' he replied with a wink.

In the evening there was more dancing and drinking to the sound of the giant tom-toms. My three women participated in turn, taking a swig from the calabash before coming back and flinging their arms round my neck. Glistening with sweat their bodies exuded a provocative, musky odour. I thought apprehensively of the night to come. I needn't have worried, however. By the time I got them back to the hut they were so drunk that I merely had to deposit them on the beds Bakala-Bendé had made. I slept apart, alone.

In the morning, so as to avoid all misunderstanding, I took the matter up with Ovendo:

'Great chief of the Nye, I thank you for your gifts. These women are very beautiful, but my religion allows me only one wife.'

'Then take your pick. I'll keep the others for the next white who comes this way.'

I chose the youngest. Her name was Mengoa; but I christened her 'Nye', after the river.

The palavers were successful. Ovendo promised to let me have at least fifty Pahuins and Fangs as labourers, and told me I would be able to recruit others if I went further north, to M'Bitam. Meanwhile he sent the tom-tom to notify the local chief, Elendaman.

The tom-tom worked wonders. By the time I reached M'Bitam, the whole of the frontier region had heard of my arrival. Regal in his ceremonial robes, Elendaman welcomed me and showed me into the vast guest hut in the centre of the clearing. I presented him with a sack of tobacco, some sugar and coffee. He spoke a little pidgin, which helped us to exchange a few simple words. Next day he gave a feast in my honour.

It was full moon. He received me under the porch of his hut, where some massive wooden benches had been placed, and invited me to be seated by his side. Several enormous bonfires were burning, casting flames over six feet high; the smoke coiled upwards in a dense cloud and melted into the darkness of the jungle.

All at once, with unexpected intensity, the tom-toms sounded and a crowd of dancers poured into the clearing, leaping into the air as though trying to cross an invisible obstacle. It was another antelope dance, even wilder than at Ovendo's, and it continued until the performers fell down exhausted. Some women came in and revived them with a brew they had poured into tiny calabash goblets. Elendaman handed me his own: 'Drink, it's *iboga*.' I gulped it down. It tasted very sour.

Presently my mind began to wander and my body seemed to take wing. I was in the air, in the smoke, in the flames, in the dancers' limbs, in the dancers' flesh, in their sweat, in their blood, in the moon. When I got back to the hut I found Nye in the bedroom. She stood naked, superb, but her eyes were glazed. I went up to her and took her hand; it was icy. She too had drunk *iboga*. I led her towards the bed of branches and mats. I stripped naked. My penis felt as though it was on fire and looked inordinately large. I seem to remember copulating all night, without a pause.

Waking in the morning, I had a curious impression: neither fatigue nor pain but a clear image of a magical and diabolical night. Another strange impression: the sensation of having no sexual organ. *Iboga* revealed new realms to me, to which I have never returned. I tasted the bitter exciting root this once only.

On Elendaman's advice I visited the frontier region of South Cameroon, and came back with another thirty blacks who were happy to join the rest of my prospective labour force. Then I returned to Oyem.

It was a joy to see Ovendo again. We spent the evening together. No tom-toms. Peace and quiet. He had a huge dish of grilled warthog served, which his servants sprinkled with throat-searing condiments. After the meal another servant came and placed a strange gift at my feet: a cylinder of bark, about thirty centimetres in diameter, fitted with a pierced lid. 'Open it. It's a *m'biery*.'

Inside I found a fetish: a male figure carved out of a single piece of smoke-blackened wood, the arms and wrists held flat against the chest, the knees tucked up towards the body. Under the buttocks was a hole to receive the stick which pierced the lid.

'It's yours. While you were at Elendaman's, another white came here to recruit labour; he said he was felling *okoumé* on the coast. I was on my guard, his porters spoke ill of him. I wanted to wait for you to judge. But next day all our men went hunting. The white sent his Eschira porters to steal this *m'biery* from a hut. A woman saw and told me. It was true, the fetish was found in his luggage...'

Ovendo peered at me, watching for my reaction: I did not bat an eyelid, I knew how to listen. Africa had taught me her law: in grave circumstances, the fewer words the better. So I kept silent. Ovendo seemed satisfied and gravely explained: 'The *m'biery* caused his death. He and his Eschiras fell from the liana bridge which you crossed on your way here – the one you repaired yourself. It gave way. Since this *m'biery* has been "touched" by a white, it has lost its power. I'm giving it to you as a memento. It no longer brings bad luck, but will grant whatever you wish.'

Everything was now ready for our departure, and I had already started mustering the men, when Bakala-Bendé came bustling into my hut.

'You remember bad white, foolish hunter? Wounded gorilla now dead. No female. Infant alone. You come see.'

So I postponed our departure and went to have a look. The body was in a state of decomposition, but near it was a little baby gorilla who at our approach rushed away screaming and beating his breast. Then he crept back to his dead father, uttering heart-rending cries. I felt I ought to do something about him.

'Catch him, but be careful not to hurt him,' I said.

My Pahuins started closing in, but the young gorilla kept escaping or biting them to the bone. They eventually cornered him, however, and I stepped forward, looked him straight in the eye and, before he could bite me, gave him a couple of slaps in the face, as though admonishing a cheeky brat. Then I grabbed hold of him, and fastened him by a leash made of lianas and brought him back to Nye. We attached him to a stake in front of the hut and gave him some bananas, cabbage palms, water, sugar and boiled rice, but he rejected this bounty, flew into a rage and whimpered like a child. I made him a longer leash and he eventually calmed down.

During the night, still half asleep, I felt a faint pressure on my arm. I thought it must be Nye. But my hand encountered a small hairy arm. I heard a faint whimper. The little gorilla was lying on my chest. I shook Nye and she lit the hurricane lamp. The infant's lips were clamped to my breast and I couldn't loosen them. 'Never mind, let's go back to sleep,' I said. Nye extinguished the lamp. In a few seconds I was drenched in urine and something more besides. We relit the lamp. Nye burst out laughing. I scraped away with a knife, washed myself all over and tried to clean up the culprit. He was not very co-operative, but didn't resist. Finally all three of us went to sleep.

Next morning I set off at the head of my troop, with the baby gorilla clinging to my bare chest. After a few days I was able to let him off the leash and taught him to cling less closely. Three weeks later I triumphantly reported back to Siccard and Letourneur. I had come back with one hundred men, a Pahuin wife and a baby gorilla whom I had meanwhile christened Toto.

On the march I had spotted a good-natured muscular black by the name of Koulibé. I appointed him cook to the concession and we started to clear a big space for the huts. Bakala-Bendé directed the work. It augured well. I was my own boss for the first time in my life.

My concession began to take shape. I had a big hut made of bark, and equipped it with two packing-case tables, two benches, blankets, two camp beds, mats and a mosquito net. Nye was happy in her new home, and the little gorilla continued to make progress. I trimmed his hair and taught him to sit at table more or less correctly. He ate a lot of bananas and made regular raids on the little hut next door where Koulibé the cook lived. When punished he would jump up and down whimpering piteously, and the blacks whom he never bit, would plead in his favour. I also taught him to walk upright (gorillas walk with a stoop and are inclined to support themselves on their knuckles) and we went around together hand in hand.

The climate was even more trying than on the Ogoué. In the evenings, with the point of a needle, Nye would dig out my ticks, those blackish bug-like insects that insert themselves under one's toe-nails. Every day five or six of them had to be dislodged and the blood allowed to flow. If this wasn't done, a sort of canker would form and there was a danger of blood-poisoning. There was no penicillin in those days; no iodine or peroxide, either. More often than not we invented our own remedies.

That year, despite all my efforts, I produced only 650 cubic metres of timber; but since I was my own boss I felt like a millionaire. We floated the rafts down to Libreville and spent a few days carousing at Costes's, a little hotel with a bar-room like a Wild West saloon. My colleagues would try to drown the memory of their hard life in the tropical forests and it was not uncommon to see a forester, in a spirit of mockery, provocation or bravado, wash his feet in champagne. Letourneur and Siccard got so drunk every evening that they became obsessed:

'Fernand, lend us your wife.'

'Nothing doing!'

'She's nice, your wife.'

'Exactly!'

'How did you manage to find her? You're no pal, you're no partner, if you don't lend her!'

I got a bit fed up with this and decided to do something about it. Not far from Libreville there was a village inhabited by ticket-of-leave Pahuins. I went there one afternoon and took the necessary steps. That evening Siccard as usual yelled:

'Well, Fernand, have you brought us your wife?'

I promptly replied:

'Of course, old boy. She's in the little shelter outside. You speak Pahuin, so you'll have no difficulty.'

The little shelter was nothing more nor less than the outside lavatory. It was built on stilts and to reach it you had to climb a wooden staircase. Siccard went up and parleyed through the door. The door suddenly opened and he drew back in alarm. For inside, gap-toothed and with drooping breasts, was the ugliest Pahuin woman I had been able to find in the village I had visited that afternoon!

One evening Durix arrived with his rafts, had his luggage brought in and, in front of us, unpacked some curious objects: Eschira masks and a fetish statue. All the lumber-men started teasing him: 'What horrors! Where did you find them? Shame on you, Durix! Put them away!'

I looked at the statue: a superb wooden head. The carving was simple, subtle, beautiful.

'It's a *m'bouiti*,' said Durix. 'If you want to buy the whole lot, masks and all, it's yours. Since you like this sort of thing you can have it.'

All my pals laughed at me; one of them even tried to smash the head with a machete. I stopped him and it ended in a fight. My friend was blind drunk and dealt me a nasty blow on the skull with his machete. (I still bear the scar to this day.) The sight of the blood calmed him down a bit. An emergency dressing for me, and brandy all round. It was high time to get back to work.

Shortly after getting back to the concession, I went down with a violent attack of malaria. I was absolutely bludgeoned. Nye sent for help. A few hours later Siccard was bending over me. I saw him through a haze. 'Are you pissing Picon?' he asked.

'Yes, I think so.'

Tropical fevers, being often bilious or haematuric, turn the victim's urine the colour of Picon. You don't suffer much, but you die. 'What am I to do?' I asked.

'Stay in bed, eat nothing. Drink plenty of lemon juice and don't worry. If you get better, fine. If not, I'll send for someone from the Institut Pasteur.'

My temperature was over 104°F. Some people, with these fevers, grow dull-witted; others, short-tempered and grumpy. I was merely delirious. I fancied I was in a circus-tent, with its big top and poles made of jungle trees. I was the lion-tamer and cracked my whip ... But after a time I began to recognize the people round me and recovered my wits. Within a month I was on the mend.

A few weeks later, however, the little gorilla died, laid low by an attack of enteritis. Nye and I buried him in the forest, weeping as we covered the hirsute little body with earth. To console us, Letourneur gave us a young cercopithecus monkey. 'Have you noticed?' he said. 'It's not the 14th July, yet he's wearing the tricolor on his private parts.' It was true. Like all cercopithecus monkeys this one had blue testicles, a white penis and bright red glans.

That season I managed to produce 900 cubic metres of timber and after the sale, though I was in rags like every other lumber-man, I had a small fortune in my haversack. But the strain had exhausted me and so I decided, with my partners' agreement, to relinquish the management of the concession for a while and go home on leave. It was 1925.

9

The boat took almost twenty days to reach France. This particular line of the Chargeurs Réunis was not designed for the fastidious; but for us, after all the discomfort we had suffered, it was sheer luxury. If only because this was the dead season, I was not the only one going home; Jean was on board as well, and also Soulié, Papin, Miquette and other old hands on leave.

Bordeaux at last: the harbour, the church steeples. Most of my pals had only one idea in mind: to hop into a cab and buy some smart new clothes. For my part, I had decided to wait and order my suits from a Paris tailor.

We arranged to meet all together on the terrace of the Grand Café opposite the theatre and I went and saw to my luggage. To impress my parents, I had brought home my tomb stakes, Bapono masks, the Oyem *m'biery*, and a lot of other odds and ends. The Customs man insisted on opening my tin trunk and was horrified to discover the fetishes:

'What are these beastly things?'

'They're for my grandmother. She's in her second childhood and likes to play with dolls!'

On the terrace of the Grand Café everyone admired one another's natty outfits, greeting them with ironical whistles of admiration. Suddenly a huge open Renault, with a chauffeur at the wheel, drew up. Out of it climbed an odd-looking fellow dressed in kilt, tam-o'-shanter and brogues, with a piratical patch over his eye and a heavy stick in his hand. A really splendid turn-out. All of a sudden someone yelled:

'It's Miquette, the old sod! Here, come and sit down. Since when have you been a Scotsman?'

Miquette had a passion for disguise and, though he couldn't speak a word of English, was annoyed at being recognized. After a few drinks, however, he forgot he was a Highlander until several hours later, when he drove off again.

I left Papin at the Gare d'Austerlitz. He had five million in his pocket and was planning to buy a big garage. I wished him luck and we exchanged addresses. Far from having his fortune, I was resolved to blow the contents of my haversack, then start off again from scratch. Meanwhile all I could think of was getting back to Le Vésinet.

I hadn't notified my parents of my arrival, because I wanted it to be a surprise. I entered the drawing-room just as I was, in my jungle togs. My mother wept with emotion and hugged me. My father said: 'You're safe and sound. You're thin, but you're back. Good.' His joy manifested itself in a squeeze of the arm, a wink, a quip: 'You stink of Negress, Fernand.'

I brought out my treasures: the tomb stakes and fetishes. My father nodded his head, my mother merely said:

'My poor Fernand, you shouldn't have gone to so much trouble. These things have no merit.'

Despite the warmth and joy of our reunion, I was aware of the gap between us. I came from a world in which the harsh realities I had encountered made Le Vésinet seem singularly small. The chick had broken out of its shell and I couldn't re-adapt myself to the dimensions of this cosy little universe.

I had a wash and brush-up, and stacked my luggage in my basement workroom. I saw my father come in from the street with a couple of sky-blue pails and a coal shovel. He was wearing his frockcoat, an overcoat, a gardener's apron, a bright blue silk scarf and, on his head, an old straw sun-bonnet of my mother's which she must have thrown away.

'How can you appear in public dressed up like a clown?' she sighed.

'It amuses me. Fernand's back and I like old togs.'

He gave me a conspiratorial wink. He had no complexes and, at home, liked wearing the shabbiest clothes in his wardrobe. He had gone to the butchers for some clotted blood, then into the street to collect some horse-dung. Now, seated on the kitchen steps, he proceeded to roll blood and dung together into pellets which he considered unbeatable as bait for fishing.

In the evening, after dinner, it was touching to find myself in front of the big fireplace and to see my parents still holding hands as in the old days.

Next day I went to Paris to order some clothes. I had a sudden urge to change my personality completely. Unfortunately a made-to-measure suit required several days, so it was still in my forester's togs that I went to Sir Robert's in the Rue de Richelieu to buy myself a pair of shoes in the latest style, with vamps of the finest black leather, dark red tongues and laces. For one of my suits I chose a splendid hound's tooth tweed and ordered a hat in the same material. I asked for all these things to be delivered to the Hotel Saint-Lazare Terminus; for it suddenly occurred to me that I had to have somewhere in Paris to stay. Still in my old rags, I looked rather conspicuous when I went round and asked for a room, but the manager, seeing that I had just arrived from Equatorial Africa, gave me a comfortable little suite.

That night I had the sort of longing that a child might have for a Meccano set at Christmas: I wanted a motor-car. The manager recommended a dealer in the Champs-Elysées. I went round there at once. Without knowing it, I had come to Labourdette's, the Hispano-Suiza coachbuilders. I had the money; why not make my dream come true? The director himself came over with a catalogue. I chose a long, luxurious roadster.

'I must tell you that we fit our bodies on to new chassis. To build you this splendid model, we'll need from six to eight months.'

'Out of the question, I shall have left again by then.'

'I don't see any solution, unless ... wait a moment ... We have a client in the suburbs who's leaving for Mexico and is probably going to sell his Hispano. It's a remarkable vehicle.'

I took the train, located the sumptuous villa with the big iron gate and porter's lodge. I rang and a footman appeared. I mentioned the name of Labourdette and asked about the Hispano for sale. The man went off to fetch someone else. Presently a tall fellow in chauffeur's uniform arrived. I came straight to the point:

'How much do you earn? I'll pay you the same, and even a bit more. I'll buy the car if you drive it for me; I don't like driving myself.'

'But ... but don't you want to try it out first?'

My dream was coming true. Luxury roadster, chauffeur ... Despite my rags, I felt stinking rich. The vehicle seemed to glide along the road. I could hardly wait. I signed the papers and handed over the cash, without even entering the property. I negotiated the whole deal in the chauffeur's quarters. His name was Bastien.

He was torn between apprehension and envy on discovering my

age. To be so young and to have done so much overawed him completely. I told him I wanted to cut a dash and that part of his job was to humour me by driving stylishly, with distinction, and showing due deference – I even told him, when drawing up anywhere, to wait a few seconds, until I tapped on the glass partition, before coming to open my door, cap in hand. 'The fun's only going to last six months, Bastien, but I want it to be real fun. Drive on!'

One evening we decided to hold a dinner for all the foresters from Gabon, Cameroon and Indochina. We chose a big table in an expensive restaurant on the Champs-Elysées. We ordered all the things we were unable to find in Africa: oysters, rare meat, a variety of cheeses, elaborate confectionery. The other customers raised their eyebrows at the succession of dishes that were carried to our table. Suddenly Miquette had a bright idea:

'Let's order some grilled lobsters. They taste good, they look expensive, and they smell to high heaven.'

'Let's have them grilled here in front of us.'

'You bet!'

We devoured half a dozen lobsters each, in an absolute cloud of smoke, and in no time the restaurant was deserted.

Another evening, when it was raining hard, we went along the boulevards and hired every cab until midnight. 'Draw up here under the trees and wait. Here's your fare.'

When the theatres emptied there was no cab available within miles. Men in evening dress ran about shouting and cursing; their womenfolk joined in; and we looked on while our cabbies imperturbably repeated:

'I'm hired, I tell you. Till midnight, damn it all! I've already been paid, damn you!'

'But what's going on? It's a scandal. Police! They're all hired. This is a stunt!'

Papin rang me up next morning: 'Go and see Durix. I can't, as I have to go down to Marseille. It seems he's at the Salpêtrière, poor fellow.'

I recalled with gratitude how he had made me a present of the Bapono masks and the *m'bouiti* one evening at Port Gentil. I set off at once, determined to do my best for him.

He was in bed, in the incurables' ward. The sturdy young man I had known only a few months ago, I now saw lying inert, hair and beard quite white. He was practically incapable of speech and could only signal to me with his eyes. I couldn't understand what he was trying to say but he recognized me, I think. I felt helpless and asked to see the doctor in charge.

'This man has just got back from Gabon,' he said.

'I know, but what's wrong with him?'

'Some disease we know nothing about. Blood sound; pressure reasonable. We've made every analysis. Nothing abnormal. At thirty, he looks like a man of ninety. I'm beginning to wonder if he isn't the victim of some evil spell cast by those savages in his employ.'

I suddenly thought of the *m'bouiti*. Had he stolen it, like the Marquis who had gone up to Oyem and met his death there? An evil spell perhaps, but accompanied no doubt by some *bilongo* or Gabon poison.

A week later Durix was dead.

A few days afterwards, on the Boulevard de la Madeleine, I ran into Guy Boucheau, whom I had last seen on the rafts at Libreville.

'You're looking splendid, Boucheau.'

'Don't speak too soon, I'm just out of the Institut Pasteur where I spent three months. I had sleeping sickness. They inoculated me, looked after me. I was cossetted. Fresh milk galore. I've only just been released.'

We arranged to meet two weeks later for a reunion of the lumbermen. He didn't turn up at the rendezvous. I went round to his mother's and found her in tears; he had just died. Gabon, plus the Institut Pasteur, had killed him.

One evening a stranger came into the hotel and greeted me with these words: 'You're a forester, I know. An adventurer, I know. I know everything. My name is Carthis. I'm a private detective.'

He was an odd, attractive character and I asked him to my table. I thus discovered he was well educated and was new to the profession. He seemed intelligent, cool-headed, sharp-witted, methodical, and I noticed that he managed to eye every woman who passed by without losing his train of thought. 'There's one thing wrong with you pioneers: you don't know how to handle money. You all end up in the soup; European life is beyond you. I'm on the look-out for hard cash. I want to get my business started, and later expand it. I'm opening a little office near Montparnasse: investigations and shadowing. I work on my own or almost. I need a backer, a shareholder. Come and see me tomorrow evening.'

Next day Bastien dropped me at the address he had given. The place consisted of only one room and a lavatory, but what a set-up! A book-case which swung open to reveal a bed. A kitchen in a recess, concealed by a folding door. A huge safe, full of bottles of champagne.

'This is my den,' said Carthis. 'With twelve thousand francs I can start up. I'll do you a favour if you lend me that sum. I'll introduce you to Paris life, believe you me!'

I produced the money because I had it on me – besides, for some unknown reason, I trusted him. He gave me a receipt and cooked a sumptuous dinner. After this I didn't see him again for some time.

Next day, just to have a look round and see if I could make up for my loan to Carthis, I asked Bastien to draw up outside a modest shop specializing in tropical handicrafts. My enquiries revealed that Negro art had become very popular with certain millionaires who were titillated by the exotic. I was given the address of Paul Guillaume in the Rue La Boétie who was said to be the king of Negro art.

I arrived in the Hispano, so naturally I was first shown the most expensive items. And then, surprise! The saleswoman's slim fingers drew back a red velvet curtain to reveal a *m'biery* standing on a pedestal in a niche.

'It's an admirable piece of sculpture and extremely rare.'

'How much?'

'Forty thousand francs.'

'Thank you very much.'

It was almost the price of a new Ford roadster. I was put in touch with another dealer in Negro art to whom I mentioned the *m'bouiti*. He was keen to buy, I could feel it, but intuition also told me he would offer ludicrous prices.

'If it's authentic and as big as you say ... five thousand francs.'

Remembering the *m'biery* at Paul Guillaume's, I refused his offer and said I would think it over.

A few days later I went and had a word with the nice little woman in the tropical art shop tucked away under the arcades of the Palais Royal. She told me that a rich American collector of Negro art was staying at the Ritz: 'He pays well and knows his subject.' I rang him up at once, arranged to meet him at Carthis's and dashed down to Le Vésinet to collect my fetishes. Next day, to the detective's astonishment, I displayed the 'horrors' saved from stupidity, destruction and the customs.

The American was astounded. He couldn't keep his eyes off the Eschira tomb stakes and was enthusiastic about the *m'biery* and *m'bouiti*. I threw in the masks as well. Since he appreciated the authentic, I decided to sell him the lot and waited for him to name his price.

'Ninety-seven thousand francs.'

Why haggle? Carthis was dumbfounded. I was as pleased as Punch as I took the cash and stowed it away in my money-belt. It was almost what my Hispano-Suiza had cost me. We opened a bottle of champagne to clinch the deal.

When the American had gone Carthis asked me why I had suddenly taken back a tiny packet, namely a wad of newspaper. I noticed yet again that nothing escaped his eagle eye and unfolded the crumpled sheets for him to see.

'It's the only thing I wanted to keep,' I said.

He stared in surprise at the charming necklace made of cowrie shells, which at one time used to serve the blacks as coins.

'Souvenir or superstition, I'm keeping it,' I went on. 'Nandipo, my Ogoué wife, gave it to me to bring me luck. I'll never sell it.'

One evening, about five o'clock, destiny guided me to the big boulevards. There were no radios or tapes in those days, but you could listen to recorded music in certain shops where you sat down in a comfortable armchair with some counters and your individual ear-phones. I selected my records and sat down to listen to them, immersed in my thoughts, carried away by the music, losing all sense of time. I was preparing at last to leave, when I noticed an elegant young woman sitting opposite me. I still had some counters left and spontaneously offered them to her. Our eyes met.

Who was this stranger, I asked myself, whose beauty moved me so deeply and directly? I wanted to know what lay behind this face. As she in her turn prepared to leave, I went over and asked if I might drive her home. Suddenly I felt on top of the world; everything seemed easy. I found myself taking her by the arm and helping her into the car. As we drove along, I told her who I was. And she replied that her name was Rica, that she was a foreigner but of Corsican extraction, that she was twenty-seven years old. I clasped her hand, inhaled her perfume. Then I told her – and what an effort this admission cost me! – that in a few months I would be going back to Gabon. She looked grave yet at the same time radiant, as though determined to make the best of things.

By the time I dropped her home it was obvious to both of us: we were in love. We arranged to meet again next day in a café on the Boulevard des Italiens. For several days running we repeated the meeting. Then, one evening, almost in spite of ourselves, we spent the night together and exchanged our hearts, our souls, our bodies.

Through Rica I discovered the deep, calm love of which I had always dreamt. In her I found my ideal woman. I revelled in her tenderness and delicacy of sentiment: a far cry from the physical excesses or casual carnality of my black wives in Africa. The Hispano-Suiza enabled us to travel wherever we liked – the Riviera, Italy, Rome – and these journeys drew us even closer together.

Thus several months went by. I was getting through my money, but still had enough to carry Rica back to Africa with me and build her a splendid hut out there. I dreamt of making our own furniture, planting flowers all round our jungle home. The day of my return was rapidly approaching; I therefore told her what I had in mind. She looked abashed: 'Fernand, I wanted to keep it from you until you left ... I'm married. My husband is in Switzerland, bedridden, consumptive. I've been to see him twice since meeting you – a few paltry days, which I certainly owed him. I must put up with it. If I went off with you for ever, it would be the death of him. Forgive me.'

Rica married? I felt utterly crushed. I knew I was going to lose her for ever. In the morning she rushed off without turning round, so as not to show her tears. I watched her until she disappeared out of sight. We never saw each other again.

After that, there was no point in lingering. I left Paris for Bordeaux, alone. No more Hispano, no more chauffeur. The luxury motor-car, sold for a song, paid for my third-class fare. All I had now was a smart suit and a few banknotes in an envelope. But what did I care? Carthis was right: we foresters didn't know how to handle money.

10

I couldn't get Rica out of my mind. I kept hearing her voice. Her scent, her funny remarks, her mischievous expression, her charm continued to haunt me. I recalled my last sight of her as she rushed down the corridor of the hotel. By the time I got back to Libreville, however, I began to recover my spirits; and thanks to my partners, Siccard and Letourneur, who had looked after the concession in my absence, my taste for adventure revived and I was eager to pit myself once more against the forest.

My first task was to improve the network of channels and dams. I wanted to produce a thousand cubic metres a year, and to achieve that target I knew there was only one way: to get everyone, down to the humblest lumber-jack, personally interested. Thus the job assumed the aspect of a game. We played with the water, vied with one another in speed and efficiency. Yet nothing in the nature of the climate or the soil made life any easier. First thing in the morning, we had to wade up the channels working waist-deep in the water, climb out again on to the bank, reinforce the lianas, step back into the water, and so on until nightfall, alternating between constant hot and cold, for the water felt almost icy in comparison to the temperature of the ground and the air. No matter: day by day we made further progress.

My only recreation was a weekly visit to Siccard's. Nye and I would stroll up there hand in hand every Sunday and Letourneur would drop in with his Pahuin girl. The card table would be brought out and the two foresters and their black wives would play belote, insulting each other in no mean terms: 'You shouldn't have played that card. Now you've lost a trick, you jack-ass!' Far from getting angry, our three Negresses would roar with laughter, happy, even under this barrage of sharp words, to be among the pasteboard kings, queens and knaves and with their lumber-jack lords and masters. Meanwhile I was busy building a poultry run to prevent Siccard's hens from fouling our mats every morning. They perched, squawked and left their droppings everywhere, but he did nothing to stop them. 'A hen must be allowed to run free,' he would say.

One day Bakala-Bendé came back with an unwelcome gift, Siccard's cercopithecus monkey: I decided to bring it up at liberty. That very evening our hut was reduced to a shambles. Set free in the dining-room, the monkey had managed to squeeze through the bamboo partition. The mosquito-net was in shreds, the bed and the floor covered in broken eggs. He had located the poultry-yard, released the chickens, stolen that day's laying and made a giant omelette.

'That swine Siccard, he wanted to wreck my house. Bakala-Bendé, take the monkey back!'

'Dark now, boss.'

'So much the better. Put the monkey in the poultry-yard I built last Sunday. Also leave this message.'

And, on the spur of the moment, I scribbled out an invitation to a party purporting to be in honour of the administrator's visit. I let Nye into the secret, then went off to a Pahuin village that had come into being on the edge of the concession. The inhabitants had come down from the North and settled here. They kept to themselves and never worked with the whites. In fact, though without being in any way hostile, they held aloof even from my labourers. They were therefore no worry to me. I had heard that in this village there was an albino woman and, personally speaking, I can think of nothing uglier than a white Negress. I therefore gave the necessary instructions.

During the week Siccard sent a note to accept the invitation. The fish was hooked. He duly arrived.

'Georges, you're in luck. That silly administrator isn't coming after all; he's too busy, he says. But as a gesture he's sending us his daughter. The blacks tell me she's wonderful: bright as a button and mad for a man.'

'You don't say? And how is she getting here?'

'In a *tipoi*, old boy. Carried by four porters. She's bound to come through the Pahuin village. We'll be notified. So get ready. If you manage things properly, you can take her off with you and maybe keep her. It seems she's hot stuff.'

'Good heavens! An administrator's daughter, are you sure?'

'What do you risk? They say she's mad keen. Comb your hair and don't look such a ninny. Make yourself presentable.'

76

'And afterwards?'

'Whisper sweet nothings in her ear. If she doesn't respond, get down to brass tacks. Lift her veil, for instance, and kiss her hand.'

He went off into a corner and slipped into a smart white suit, then came back and accused me:

'Admit it, it's you who returned the monkey, eh! You sod! He put paid to several hens, the brute. I had to tie him up again.'

'Look, don't worry about the monkey. The procession's arriving. Can't you hear the singing? It will halt at the entrance to the village and wait to be welcomed in. You go and see to it, it's up to you.'

He rushed out, impeccable in his white pith helmet, and snapped to attention:

'Georges Siccard, at your service, mademoiselle!'

Total silence. He went on:

'I've come to welcome you to Fernand's concession.'

The albino Negress moved behind her veil.

'Allow me to express my pleasure ...'

And, emboldened by the supposed coquetry of the young lady, he lifted the veil ...

One morning, after working in the water for several months, I felt a strange pain in my kidneys. I went home and lay down. The pain was so violent and so sudden that I sent Bakala-Bendé to warn Siccard that he might have to convoy the rafts I had just assembled. My obsession with the rafts kept me awake; I could think of nothing else.

I had no proper medicine and could discern none of the symptoms of malaria. For three days and three nights, I writhed in agony. I consumed litres of water and kept tossing and turning under my mosquito-net. My temperature soared and I became delirious. Nye was at her wits' end.

Bakala-Bendé came back and, on seeing my condition, took the responsibility of constructing a litter on which to transport me. He cut down a couple of bamboos and made a rectangular frame, then stretched some lianas across it to form a mattress. I was laid down on this makeshift stretcher, then four porters lifted it on to their shoulders and set off at a jog-trot. It wasn't long before the lianas began to cut into my flesh. Each jolt, however slight, seemed to tear my muscles apart and grind my bones together. I kept asking for water, even the muddy water of the streams and swamps. My faithful Bakala-Bendé trotted alongside, urging on his troop, relieving each of the porters in turn. I could hear his voice, feel his hand, though I was almost unconscious and half dead from the pain.

After four days I heard the word 'Libreville' and saw we had come to a halt by some straw huts on the outskirts of the town. I have a faint recollection of being transferred to a bed made of foliage and matting. Bakala-Bendé came in with a wizened old hag. Her crinkly hair was white; her eyes looked huge; she was nothing but skin and bone. Her horny hands kneaded my body. I felt I was dying. Then I was left alone, submerged in my fever. Some time later Bakala-Bendé came back and handed me a rather bitter drink. I took a gulp and at last fell asleep.

When I woke, Bakala-Bendé was lying on the ground by the little fire he had kept alight. He looked at me curiously. I tried to smile but my muscles refused to respond. The old hag arrived and made me eat several calabashes of mash. I was too weak to fight back. I slept again.

On the fourth day in the hut I woke, incapable of uttering a word, but above my head I was able to distinguish the face of a white man: 'I'm a French doctor passing through Libreville. My boy told me there was a white man in this village dangerously ill.' I felt him examining me, then he went off. In the evening he came back with some medical orderlies and, against my will, against the advice of my porters and Bakala-Bendé, I was transported by force to the Libreville hospital. I was conscious of lying in a real bed. I thought of Durix, but didn't have the strength to struggle against the injections, blood tests and medicines.

Next morning I felt I was really on the verge of death. I could no longer move at all. I tried to remain conscious; even my fingers no longer responded.

'Sleeping sickness,' said the doctor.

My eyes alone betrayed my agony. I had neither the strength nor the will to resist. I endured the barrage of hypodermics, blood tests, a lumbar puncture, an analysis of the glands in my neck. I had only one flicker of desire left: to get out of this place, escape. I was in prison, trussed up in sheets. I tried not to surrender to delirium. Escape. Escape ... I relapsed into a black abyss. This was the end. I was locked up in a cell, held incommunicado. The orderly, my warder, was constantly on watch. I felt myself sinking.

One evening I thought I saw a face bending over me. It seemed vaguely familiar. I surfaced for an instant, intrigued by the eyes, the colour of the skin, the aquiline nose ... Bodman ... Yes, it was Bodman, the lame mulatto from Costes's. He begged me to pull myself together and listen to him:

'Boss, in two days you'll be dead. The doctor says so. Bakala-Bendé and the old woman think they can cure you. Do you want me to get you out of here?'

I must have succeeded in saying yes or nodding my head, for shortly afterwards I was again woken by stealthy movements and whispering voices. In my coma I could see several shadows, enormous shadows, which must have been real. Desperately, I tried to struggle to the surface. The pain felt as though I was being sawn in half. I was rolled over, lifted up. I tried to speak – impossible. At one moment I saw my orderly in his loose white smock; he was shouting and gesticulating and looked as though he wanted to kill me. He seemed to have a huge mouth as white as his smock. (In point of fact, as I learnt later, he was being tied up and gagged before being laid down on the bed I had just vacated.) Then I felt myself being carried away and I relapsed into my abyss.

I emerged again to feel the leather of a car seat behind my neck: Costes's old rattletrap, driven by Bodman who was smiling at me. We drove on. I didn't care where. I had escaped.

At dawn I found myself back in the little hut on the outskirts. The old hag sat beside me. I trusted her. She massaged my body with leaves soaked in luke-warm water. She kneaded my feet, my thighs, my back. She gave me injections with long palm needles. I didn't feel a thing and offered no resistance. I fell asleep and slept like a log; my first real sleep since I had been taken to hospital.

After a week of this treatment I was able to wiggle my fingers. Then I managed to move my legs and arms. I was saved.

At this juncture two white men succeeded in locating the village. The tallest, an athletic type, was the elder brother of the lone yachtsman Alain Gerbault. His friend was a forester. I had never seen him before. He introduced himself.

'Célier. And I'm Robert Gerbault. What can we do for you?'

'Nothing. I'm on the mend. A Pahuin sorceress cured me.'

'We heard about you from Doctor Husson. He had given you up for dead.'

'What did Husson say?'

'That he had examined you and couldn't account for your paralysis.'

'Why not?'

'The analysis didn't reveal sleeping sickness or syphilis or anything. But he was sure you were going to die. We wanted to help you after your escape from hospital.'

'I don't need anything. Thanks all the same. Don't come back here, I beg you, and good luck to you both.'

Good old Robert Gerbault! He was to disappear a few years later in the jungle up north, near the frontier of Spanish Guinea, and I never saw him again. As for Doctor Husson, I met him many years later in Cannes. He had left Gabon a long time before.

'What, you're not dead!'

'No.'

'What was wrong with you?'

'It's not for me to say, I'm not a doctor. But an old sorceress must know, it was she who cured me.'

'It's unbelievable. Nothing can ever happen to you again after that ...'

A month later I was back at work. I tried to exorcize my demon, push further into the forest, open new rolling tracks, clear more ground, press on in my pursuit of exotic woods. I had almost ten years' experience behind me. In that short space of time timber had risen from forty-seven to seven hundred and fifty francs a cubic metre. But I began to dream of other adventures, other species of trees, other territories to discover. Gabon seemed too small all of a sudden, the big companies that were being formed were bound to destroy everything and eventually exhaust the forest.

And so I decided to go home, follow my instinct, unearth something else. I sent Nye back to her village with a substantial dowry, treated all my blacks to a cinema show every night for a whole week, bade my former partners farewell and boarded the *Tchad* with a cercopithecus monkey over sixty centimetres tall. I was never to see the sandy banks of the Gabon estuary again. I had arrived there a callow youth. When I left I was a mature man.

11

Coming back to France for the second time, I said to myself:
'Fernand, watch your step; you have enough dough to live like a
king for a year: fashionable hotels, luxury motor-cars. But money
doesn't last for ever. And when it runs out, what then? You're no
longer a child. Use your noddle.'

In a few days my mind was made up: 'Think it over, Fernand.
You're a tropical forester. You've sold your rafts. Your timber has
been exported to France. So there are firms dealing in timber at this
very moment. Find the biggest, or the one that appeals to you most,
and introduce yourself. You'll discover the other end of the chain:
the factory.'

Without wasting a moment, I settled the preliminaries that I
considered indispensable: three new suits and a car. A little Eau
de Lubin to drown the smell of monkey, and I was ready to drive off!
Not quite, for since my arrival at the Terminus Saint-Lazare the
manager had received several complaints about my cercopithecus
'compatriot'. He was fairly big, admittedly, scared and therefore
dangerous. I decided to board him out. But where? As usual, in
Paris, the answer was to be found in a bistro. 'Go to the Rue du
Renard,' I was told. 'Ask for Bibi; he's a butcher.'

I went.

I found Bibi, in a shed at the back of a courtyard. He wasn't a
butcher, he was employed at the slaughter-house and his hobby
was taxidermy. He dealt particularly with the animals that died in
the zoos or the Jardin des Plantes. He was interested in every species,
and also in my description of wild life in Gabon: 'You've actually
seen a gorilla? Now there's an animal for you! I should love to
study an anthropoid one of these days.' In the meantime he gladly
agreed to keep my monkey in exchange for visits from me during
which I promised to talk to him about Africa.

It was during these visits that I, in return, learnt something about
the incredible life of the denizens of Paris. And this reminded me

of Carthis's promise: 'One day I'll show you what real Parisian life is like!'

So I called on him at Montparnasse. After all, I was a shareholder in his detective business, and had every right to be solicitous about his welfare. No sign of him. The bird had flown, the office was let to someone else. No forwarding address. Nothing. From which I concluded that he had come a cropper and my money had gone down the drain. Never mind, it was all part of the game. Meanwhile it was time to embark on my rounds of the factory managers.

I refused the first job I was offered: 'You're a forester, fine. I need a buyer. I'll send you back to Gabon.'

'No, I want to learn this end of the business. I want to see how the factory works.'

My argument fell on deaf ears.

This happened again and again until, one morning, I walked into Luterma, 4 Rue du Port, at Clichy, and found a manager who was willing to listen – Monsieur Grünwald, a thickset, dynamic Lithuanian: 'We'll try you out. Since you want to see how a factory works, go to Le Bourget. That's where ours is.'

I went to Le Bourget, and I was surprised and intrigued by what I saw. Everything was mechanized: the timber was hoisted, transported and deposited by mechanical monsters. Log after log, over three metres twenty long and with a minimum diameter of seventy centimetres, was grasped in the jaws of a giant clamp as though it was a mere play-thing, and then whittled down by a long, well-directed blade to emerge as thin layers of wood. A fascinating sight.

'Well, forester, how do you like that stripper?' Monsieur Grimault, the assistant manager, asked me.

Without thinking, I replied: 'I want to learn everything and I'll start at the bottom: sweeping out the factory and any other menial job. I'll bring my overalls with me tomorrow.' From the expression on his face anyone might have thought I had made an improper suggestion!

For several days, however, I turned up for work with my overalls and plied my broom. In due course I progressed to the presses and giant trimmer. For the first time I saw the pattern made by the internal veins of an *okoumé* and was able to appreciate the beauty of the very heart of the tree. I was happy in my work, and an idea started germinating in my head: 'One day I must go and look for other forests in the world. One day timber will be in short supply ...'

Meanwhile, every evening, I dressed up in my best suit, hopped into my Ford and drove off: to the theatre, or to have a drink with Georges Siccard who now ran a little bistro, or to meet other former colleagues. For, one by one, the old Gabon hands were coming home and Paris, like a great maw, engulfed them all.

I also called regularly on Bibi the taxidermist. One evening I found him quivering with impatience:

'It's about your monkey. I saw a fellow today ... Doctor Voronov's assistant.'

'What about him?'

'You ought to accept. It's in the cause of science.'

'Accept what?'

'Well, Voronov uses monkeys' testicles for grafting. In this case it's for an elderly senator.'

'Do you expect my monkey to sacrifice his balls for a senator, Bibi?'

'I'm serious, I tell you. It'll be no worse than leaving him alone like this for the rest of his life, without a female.'

'But he's my pal. What about selling your own balls instead?'

'It won't hurt him. He'll be given an anaesthetic. And the professor will look after him afterwards. I saw the last volunteer, he was spoilt and cossetted no end. For a monkey, it's a wonderful life.'

He was so insistent that in the end I agreed. I sold my monkey to Voronov for ten thousand francs. I didn't need the money; I was earning a good living. But why make a gift of anything to a senator?

My apprenticeship in the factory eventually came to an end. I must have made a good impression, for the manager now offered me a well-appointed office and a secretary of my own at Clichy. I was to be responsible for sales promotion.

'It's a new department,' he told me. 'We're starting from scratch. Let me have a report in due course.'

I knew nothing about sales promotion, but once again I was eager to learn. And the best way to learn, I thought, was to go out and meet the clients themselves.

For my first tour of duty I chose Beauvais and Chartres, and at once realized there was something radically wrong with our methods. Our customers were worthy little carpenters who ordered in minute quantities – parcels of a dozen or even half a dozen panels had to be made up for them – and paid as and when they saw fit. This was clearly uneconomical. I therefore had some order vouchers printed at my own expense – Société Luterma France, name of client, quantity, dimensions, price – and called on the clients in person, one after the other. I would introduce myself and suggest a drink in the café opposite. Then, I would start talking about Gabon, the jungle ...

'So cannibals really exist?'

'Yes. Now what about this order? How much? Sign here.'

The system worked. Within a couple of weeks I had collected enough orders for a wagon-load of six or eight tons. But on my return to Clichy I found there was hell to pay. Little Grimault was waiting for me with an odd expression on his face:

'Don't you know the regulations? Our representatives are meant to submit a report every evening and come back here at the end of a week. You've been away over two weeks, and without giving a sign of life! Do you think you're back in the jungle, or what?'

'Monsieur Grimault, I don't like paper work. I can't sit down every evening and write an account of what I've done during the day ... I've had ten years in the jungle, I'm a forester, not a pen-pusher.'

'Then you'd better go and see Monsieur Grünwald.'

Grünwald didn't appear to be unduly worried by my alleged misdemeanour. He asked me to sit down and said: 'Tell me about it.' I showed him the results – the sales book, the number of orders – and suggested a repeat performance in the west of the country. He agreed at once, and so I set off for my second tour of duty.

At Saint-Nazaire I found the Penhoët shipyards working at full capacity. One of the vessels under construction was a quick-firing gun-boat. This gave me an idea. Luterma had just invented a metal-backed veneer patented under the name of Plymex. The process was still secret and the sheets, which were absolutely rigid, offered additional protection, especially against fire. I thought it would be good publicity to offer one of these sheets to the gun-boat's engineers. 'We're not authorized to buy,' they replied, 'but if it's a gift we could use it for the instrument panel.' I reported back to Grünwald. He was delighted that one of the first modern gun-boats in the French Navy should have an instrument panel made of

Plymex. Subsequently seven other gun-boats were similarly equipped, and a few years later the same material was used on the *Normandie*, to the pride and profit of Luterma.

On returning to Paris from one of my tours in the provinces, I remembered that I'd had no news of Papin or his garage in the Avenue de la Grande Armée. Since my car needed an overhaul, I naturally decided to take it to him. I found he had sold out and was now living at Reuilly Diderot. I ran him to earth there. He was as affable as ever, but had taken to the bottle: 'I got fed up with the garage and put the proceeds from the sale into "Ozone", a gadget for purifying water. But I came a cropper; the shares fell, I sold too late. The Stock Exchange is worse than the Port Gentil rafts; you have to know the ropes. I was practically cleaned out and now I'm living on my last few pennies. Here, have a look.'

He opened a huge creaking cupboard. His wife, a sprightly little woman who had been a schoolmistress, watched him closely. He lifted a pile of sheets, and suddenly there was a superb diamond cradled in the palm of his hand: 'You see? That's all I have left. It was a present to Josephine. Now I'm going to sell it and get out of here.'

I spent the whole evening with him. Next day I had to get back to work. When I returned three months later, the place was closed. He had died of angina pectoris.

Gradually my sales methods began to bear fruit, though I still had difficulty in convincing certain wholesalers and even certain architects that the days of massive woodwork were over and that the future lay in veneers. This was obvious, yet they refused to give up their old habits. I would say, for instance: 'Look, here's a model of a modern door. Mahogany veneer, invisible lock and hinges.'

'Good for poultry-yards!' they would reply.

I would point out that at Rockefeller's and almost everywhere in America ...

'We're not in America,' they would retort.

'But Bailly's, in Paris ...'

'We're not in Paris.'

And instead they would suggest 'some nice oak doors with mouldings', massive and heavily carved — real wedding-cake decoration! 'Now that's what we call beautiful, monsieur.'

Beautiful, my foot!

During one of my tours, in the Bordeaux district, I acquired a splendid stick, a forester's secret weapon which a craftsman still made by hand. (He has since died, and his secret with him.) It had a T-shaped handle which could be unscrewed like that of a sword-stick but was fitted, not with a blade, but with a kind of corkscrew spike. I learnt that it was used mainly in Périgord, where certain unscrupulous dealers were buying up the last good walnut trees. The fellow I bought it from was only too happy to show me how the dodge worked.

He drove me to Périgueux in his superb American roadster. 'You know, I bought this car with the proceeds from only three up-rootings.' According to him there were still any amount of bump-kins who owned walnut trees, but the sale of the nuts didn't even cover the harvesting costs. 'The peasants still have no idea of prices, which helps no end. Take the gypsies, for instance. They get hold of lovely old hand-woven linen sheets in exchange for double the quantity of coarse sheets. These are shoddy stuff, and after three washings fall to bits; but they also throw in a free gift, a tapestry with a picture of a stag, a big doll, or a bedside mat … Look, do you see those trees by that farm over there? Wait for me in the car.' He climbed out, went up and saluted the farmer's wife: 'Good morning, madame, what a pretty little girl you've got. And what a pretty farmhouse. A sight for sore eyes … Are those fig trees over there?'

'No, walnuts. They're hundreds of years old,' the poor woman replied.

'Walnuts? They're worth a lot, I know. I have a friend who buys them from time to time.'

'We're not selling; we inherited them from our forefathers.'

'Quite right too. What's more, I believe their price is falling and hasn't reached rock bottom yet. Don't sell. Good-bye, little girl.'

He climbed back into the car and waved farewell. 'It's in the bag,' he winked, as he jotted down the name of the farm in his notebook, and off we drove again. In due course we reached another farm, and from the back of the car he produced an overcoat, a black homburg and a small parcel: 'I'm going to get the stick ready. My partner has already reconnoitred this place and he'll be calling in a couple of weeks at the farm where we've just been, just as we're now calling here. Look: three more walnut trees.'

He got out of the car and with great self-assurance approached the farmer's wife: 'Good morning, madame. I was just driving past. You must have seen one of my friends the other day. He told me about your adorable little girl. I've actually brought something for her, I can't resist children – look, take this, my dear, it's for you. Tell me, are those the walnut trees you didn't want to sell? Do you mind if I look at them more closely? I may be able to give you a word of advice, you never know!'

There he stood, with his stick, while the little girl unwrapped a lovely doll. Confused and embarrassed, the woman wiped her hands on her apron and led the way towards the trees. 'You know, they're not at all bad, seen from here,' he went on. 'I can even tell you if they're sound inside: I happen to have my instrument with me.' And he plunged the stick deep into one of the trunks. The woman was impressed and intrigued, as he examined the slivers of wood which the spike had extracted.

I realized the value and the danger of this remarkable instrument; the tree was liable to die from such treatment, but an experienced dealer was thereby able to get some idea of the design and conformation of the core. The value of the veneer could then be estimated with very little error. Meanwhile the voice continued, unctuous, impeccable: 'I'll be quite frank with you, madame. If you won't sell your trees, it doesn't matter. Walnut's no longer very fashionable as a wood. But think it over. Your trees are worth more now than they will be later, and I'll assess the volume to your advantage. You couldn't do better. Otherwise you might have to deal with bunglers who'll try to saw the trunks or cut them down with an axe, and you'd lose on the transaction. What time does your husband get back?'

'Midday. Why don't you stay to lunch?' the woman said.

'I don't want to disturb you; I only want to see that you're not diddled. In your own interests I'm going to tell you how you can gain half a cubic metre. Mark you, a tree like that is worth forty thousand francs if it's properly uprooted, but one has to know how. For that sum you could buy yourself a sewing machine, a car or whatever else you fancy ...'

We stayed to lunch and my 'colleague' clinched the deal with an argument that was bound to appeal to the farmer: 'If my partner does the job himself, he'll have to deduct the cost of his work. Now you're a hefty fellow, you're not pressed for time, and you have day labourers who are already paid in any case. So here's a word of advice; dig round the roots. Once these are exposed, cut them with an axe. The tree will fall more gently and it's certain not to split. I shan't say a word; what's more, I could measure the circumference right down near the roots. You'd gain six or seven thousand francs. So think it over. You know, I was only driving past. But you're not likely to see me again for a couple of years or more.'

In the end they sold, in front of me. What could I say? I was merely a witness. My 'colleague' was delighted as we drove away: 'They're very fine, those three trees. The pith rays reveal some pink and purple designs that are really worth while. What do you think?'

'I think you've taught me a lesson,' I replied. 'I'd like to do you a favour in return. Can you drive to Mussidan?'

At Mussidan I asked after Letourneur, who had also recently returned from Gabon. Though he had since become a market gardener, he was still the same comrade in adventure: muscles of steel, angular face, aquiline nose, dark piercing eyes. He told me: 'I left on the crest of the wave. I'd had enough of the forest, the blacks, the paperwork, the taxes, the red tape. So I cleared out. Now listen. I've been invited to a colleague's wedding in four days' time. I insist on taking you both with me. No one will mind. I'll pass you off as cousins of mine. You can stay with me till then.'

He had a cellar, and had just brought in his first harvest. We drank, first to please him, secondly to celebrate our reunion, finally to get in training for the wedding. This proved to be a memorable party. On arriving at the big farmhouse where it was held, I threw several handfuls of pepper into the flames of the giant stove. No one noticed; but in a few minutes all the guests were coughing, weeping and laughing; the kitchen was full of tear gas; and Letourneur, who was already rather tight, apologized: 'You must make allowances: they're my cousins from Gabon.' This appeared to excuse our behaviour. I took the arm of the bride's mother who was glowing with pride and almost bursting out of her corset. 'I warn you,' she said, 'with all this excitement, I forgot to put on my knickers.' Things had got off to a good start. I had lost contact with my 'colleague' who was devoting his attentions to the bridesmaids. Meanwhile Letourneur was making advances to the bride.

Towards the end of the meal things grew even livelier. The bride's mother kept repeating more and more loudly that she had no knickers on, and the man sitting next to her said he could feel something. 'Pull!' she screamed, quivering all over. And he flung a handful of pubic hairs into the dish of stewed pears. There was a wild scramble. Everyone wanted to taste this strange dessert. I never saw my 'colleague' again.

Whenever I got back from the provinces I used to spend some time at Le Bourget to keep abreast of the latest processes. At Nancy I also had occasion to visit the famous Ecole des Eaux et Forêts and exchange ideas with the engineers there. 'We have a little office in the Rue de la Paix, and a larger establishment at Vincennes,' they told me. 'Drop in whenever you like.' For I still had the same idea in my head: to set off again one day in quest of new species. Meanwhile I awaited the right moment, the signal that would tell me when to go.

12

I was having dinner at the hotel one evening, when a dazzling figure appeared: Panama hat, white linen suit, shoes to match. A picture of prosperity.

'Fernand, I knew I'd find you here one day.'

'Carthis! I thought you were ruined. I called on you at Montparnasse. No one there.'

'Those days are over.'

And he told me the unexpected turn his affairs had taken. Business was booming. He had opened a big office near Les Halles; there was no shortage of clients, even though competition was keen. He hadn't forgotten his promise or my financial backing and, to prove it, insisted on ordering a bottle of champagne.

'Come on,' he said, when we had drained it, 'I'm going to show you the seedy side of Parisian society.'

That evening he was on a case: searching for a missing girl. As we walked along, he told me about her: she was over twenty-one and used to live with her parents, in the suburbs. One evening she failed to come home after work. There was no sign of her for three months. Then she suddenly turned up, smartly dressed, with plenty of money. Shortly afterwards she disappeared again. Her mother was worried and had asked Carthis to investigate.

'Do you think she's on the game?' I asked.

'Of course. But where?'

He had made enquiries, she was not a registered prostitute. There was therefore a pimp involved, and he had to be found. All of a sudden Carthis stopped dead: 'Well, well. Look, over there.' I couldn't see anything, only two old greybeards shaking hands, two shabby old Jews from Central Europe.

'Didn't you see?' said Carthis.

'No.'

'You must learn to use your eyes, Fernand. I'll teach you. One of those fellows slipped a little packet to the other: a ball of tissue paper. An old dodge! They're selling diamonds. I'll follow it up one of these days.'

He strode on down the street, peering, sniffing. I had difficulty in keeping up with him. 'Wait here,' he said at one moment.

He went into a bistro from which a strange-looking woman was just emerging: purple cape and long cigarette-holder. I had never before seen a transvestite close to. An odd impression. After a quarter of an hour Carthis came back in high spirits; it seemed he had a clue.

It led us from Montparnasse to Les Halles, and finally to an alleged clinic which in point of fact was a house of ill fame. The investigation was over. The wanted pimp was the girl's own father!

Another evening, Carthis turned up and said: 'Fernand, your shoes need cleaning. Follow me.' He led me down an alley where a couple of shoeblacks were at work. 'See that character over there?' he said, indicating one of their clients. 'He's the queen of the fairies. Thanks to fellows like that, there are fewer cuckolds. And that other character, look, I bet you he's going to go into that ice-cream shop – what did I tell you?' The man disappeared and presently Carthis glanced at his watch. 'But if it's just for an ice-cream, he's taking his time about it, don't you think?'

I had no idea what he meant.

'Fernand, you're a numbskull! In this alley there are two specialist shops. I've been watching their little game for months. Over there, on the right, you go in and ask for a bra for your wife. You're shown into the back parlour, and once you're there, Fernand, look out for your virtue! If you ask for a heel-piece, be sure what you're saying if you don't want to get more than you bargained for. Over there, on the left, they sell ice-cream cones – vanilla, chocolate, pistachio, everything to suit all tastes. There's even a girl who dances stark naked with a game-bag slung on her shoulder. Personally I don't give a damn, but I'm on the tracks of a big financier who might be a thumping crook.'

I accompanied him on this case for several weeks and thus made the acquaintance of some extremely odd specimens of humanity, together with the girls who catered for them. Finally, one night, in hiding behind a curtain, I witnessed an incredible performance.

'Now I've got him, the old bastard,' Carthis said.

And together we watched a nice little girl, who had first stuffed herself with sugared beans, get down on all fours and loose off fart after fart right into the face of the famous financier who inhaled in rapture.

Months went by like this ... Well might I say to myself, like Carthis, that 'personally' I didn't give a damn and it was none of my business, in the long run, hell, Paris stank of corruption and I was nauseated. I began to long for fresh air and wide open spaces. Suddenly I remembered the words of the engineers in Nancy: 'Call in one day at Vincennes or the Rue de la Paix.'

The director, Monsieur Guillet, was interested in rare woods and eager to locate every species of tree that was in danger of dying out. He mentioned in particular the white gum-tree and told me it was still to be found in Martinique and Guadeloupe. 'And that's French territory. Why not go and see? We can't guarantee anything, of course, but keep in touch all the same.'

This was all I needed. I went to say good-bye to Monsieur Grünwald: 'I've worked here for five years. I've lived well, I've learnt the job, I've had a lot of fun. Now I'm going off again, this time to look for white gum-trees in the Caribbean.'

So farewell, Paris! Once again I found myself back in Bordeaux, ready for adventure and determined to select my boat carefully so as to get the utmost out of the voyage.

I was wandering about the harbour studying the shipping when I ran into Marc, a forester I had known in Libreville. I agreed to sell him my car and he took me back to his place. At his feet lay a pedigree mastiff bitch, four or five years old, in perfect condition. I admired her girth, her smooth coat, the folds round her muzzle and neck. Marc shook his head: 'She's going to die. It's sad.'

I learnt that she belonged to a neighbour, an old farmer, who was himself at death's door. He had made Marc promise to have her put down as soon as he was dead, so that she wouldn't suffer from losing her master. 'I gave the old man my word. I'll do it,' Marc assured me.

I knew he would. I remembered how determined he had always been. I tried to argue him out of it. A waste of breath. Suddenly he said:

'You know what happened to Miquette?'

'Never saw him again.'

'You ought to go and see him, he's now a landowner. He didn't know what to do with his money, so he bought a château with a park. It's on the Arcachon road.'

I decided to go there next day, a Sunday. My boat wasn't leaving for Point-à-Pitre until two days later. I was happy, in high spirits. After paying for my first-class ticket, I still had a hundred and fifty thousand francs in my pocket. I could go and give Miquette a surprise.

The surprise was mine. I left the car outside the big iron gates and started off on foot towards the château. In the distance, on the lawn, I saw a number of people gathered together and also a portable altar, a priest and some choirboys. 'Hell, poor old Miquette must be dead,' I thought. 'Just my luck! I've come in time to attend his funeral.'

I drew nearer and found myself in the middle of a service. But there seemed to be something odd about it: the priest's speech was dreadfully slurred and he was singing off-key. I looked at him more closely. It was Miquette! Dressed up as a priest, saying Mass on the lawn! And dishing out a *vobiscum* here, an *amen* there. And not only that, but also ogling the choirboys. Odd-looking choirboys, furthermore. I took a closer look at them as well. They were buxom young girls, bursting with health and laughter.

Back in Bordeaux, when I delivered my car to Marc, I made another attempt to persuade him: 'Look, you'll never be able to bring yourself to kill this mastiff bitch, so I'm taking her with me.' In the end he agreed. And so, on the morning of my departure, he brought her on board and installed her in a cage on deck. Her name was Bill. When the siren sounded and Marc went ashore, I went and sat beside her to show her she wasn't alone.

THE AMAZONIAN JUNGLE
1935-1942

13

During the voyage my main distraction was giving Bill her food and talking to her through the bars of her cage. This daily occupation attracted the attention of one of my fellow passengers, a young Guianese girl whose parents were in business in Cayenne. Her name was Sylvia. What with the dances and parties on board, we were on mildly flirtatious terms by the time we reached Guadeloupe. Sylvia had relations there, with whom she was going to stay for a few days before going on by another boat to Guiana.

Our innocent flirtation continued. She introduced me to the Creole community and I was thus able to take her to a *doudou* dance. I was the only white man present. There was frenzied dancing to the sound of oboes, clarinets and drums. The tune we liked best of all was called *Cheese Rind*. When I saw her home she thanked me profusely: 'You're the only white I've known who has ever dared to go to a Creole dance-hall.'

Meanwhile I started making enquiries about the famous white gum-trees. The local experts laughed me to scorn:

'A hundred years ago, perhaps, monsieur. But today there's only a handful left.'

I was soon convinced I had better give up the idea, and made up my mind then and there. Sylvia was going on to Guiana; I decided to follow her.

I was thirty-five years old when I landed at Cayenne. It was the beginning of July and everything was a novelty to me: the little steamer, the wooden jetty, the main square with convicts in spotless pyjamas and straw hats tending the lawns ... they looked like placid gardeners. I was enchanted and felt ready for anything.

Sylvia had given me the name of a Frenchman, Merlin, who ran the Hotel des Palmistes where I decided to stay. He was a charming character, extremely friendly, but when I told him what I was planning he did his best to discourage me: 'My dear fellow, this place is the end of the world. I've seen other characters like you come out here and try their hand at forestry. They left again, absolutely cleaned out, or else stayed on and were reduced to human wrecks hanging about the street corners. There was a man called Talbot, for instance. His timber ended up rotting on the Approuague. And he himself came to grief – murdered – for he was also looking for gold. The murderer was never found. Take my advice, get out of here as quickly as possible. A fine young man like you has no business in a country like this.'

I retorted that the example of Talbot wouldn't deter me, since it was obvious the poor fellow knew nothing about wood. Merlin then started outlining all the difficulties I was bound to encounter over recruiting labour. The only labourers available were the convicts – good-conduct men, at liberty but under supervision, like the gardeners in the square. But even they were not to be trusted. Finally, seeing I was still adamant, he put me in touch with an engineer in the Water and Forestry Department: a Polytechnician by the name of Gruther who had come out to Cayenne the year before.

Gruther was enthusiastic:

'It's a miracle! You're the first forester to come my way.' He told me that every tree out here had a vernacular name: 'There are "cod trees", so-called because they smell of cod; "shit trees", because they exude a foul stench. You also have "pig wood", "egg-yolk wood", "hard crust" and "crazy crust". You'll have to prospect.'

'When and where do you think I ought to start?' I asked.

'Wait for three days; you'll have to anyway. The 14th of July is a holiday and I can recommend the parade.'

I've never liked this celebration. Even as a child, I hated the procession of decapitated heads carried round on the points of lances. The commemoration of the bloody capture of the Bastille nauseated me. I said so to Gruther.

'At Cayenne it's a big joke, you'll see. The blacks dress up and march past in their own fashion. I'm going to watch it with my Guianese secretary. Why don't you join us?'

The parade was indeed worth seeing. Troubadours, noblemen, princes, jugglers, minstrels, jesters and musketeers filed past. The uniforms were impeccable and the Guianese wore them with exceptional dignity. The procession was long and majestic, culminating in fifty or so pretty Creole girls dressed up as marchionesses, duchesses, ladies of the Court.

'There's Madame de Pompadour!'

It was true! Towering head and shoulders over her ladies-in-waiting, Madame de Pompadour advanced on the arm of a superb d'Artagnan, followed by a Richelieu-like cardinal brandishing a tall cross. The history of France with its principal characters unfolded before us ... The band paused and suddenly the master of ceremonies raised his long beflowered cane. The couples, hitherto so dignified, were instantly transformed. The musicians had broken into the tune which was all the rage, and I roared with laughter:

'*Cheese Rind!*'

To hell with the Bastille! The trumpets and clarinets pointed to the sky; the history of France went haywire; faces beamed with gaiety; the supple and inspired Guianese bodies quivered, writhed and revolved.

Gruther's secretary asked me back to lunch in his beautiful palm-leaf hut and gave me a few tips that were to prove extremely useful.

'Merlin knows a lot. If he has faith in you, he can help you.'

'You mean about the labour question?'

'He ought to be able to find you some escaped prisoners. It's tricky. But if anyone can do it, he can.'

'What about the blacks?'

'The locals won't venture into the jungle. It's too dangerous, it has a bad reputation. You'd have to engage *saramacas*.'

'*Saramacas?*'

These were blacks from Dutch Guiana, he explained. At certain seasons they infiltrated in groups, crossed the Maroni and took jobs. Some of them arrived regularly by sea. They had special permission to leave their own country for two years and were then free to be employed here.

'Where do I find them?'

'You don't. They find you. They're very proud; they're the descendants of Negroes who fled from the Antilles in the days of slavery and eventually reached this coast. Since then they've been known as "those who are not for sale".'

By the evening my host and I had become firm friends and we went to the *doudou* dance-hall together. He introduced me as a forester and found me a pretty partner to dance with:

'You have permission from her brother over there who greets you.'

We took the floor, but after a few dances my friend saw fit to warn me:

'You're dancing with a well-bred young girl, Fernand, so don't expect anything from her. I'll introduce you to another. You'll be able to go outside with her.'

'Go outside? What for?'

'Don't play the innocent. You've seen what the couples are up to. Outside there's a full moon. The ground's clean, the leaves are soft. No one's afraid of anyone looking. No peeping Toms. Only the sound of the crickets. So you can make love during the interval between dances. I'm going to fetch you a jewel. If she finds you attractive and begins to look dreamy, don't bother about me.'

The girl arrived, and the waltzes, polkas and local dances started up again. During each dance her hand rested in mine and clasped my fingers. She did indeed look dreamy, but I couldn't bring myself to take her outside. I never liked furtive love-making.

I was more than ever determined to chance my luck. The agent of the Compagnie Transatlantique promised to contact Paris and do his best to ship whatever timber I produced. I still had to choose the area and find the labour. And I also needed a reliable assistant. Gruther and Merlin said they would try to find me someone suitable.

One fine morning they both appeared together:

'Fernand, I think I've found someone.'

'I've thought of someone as well.'

'Who?'

'A convict; he's working as a servant.'

'So is my fellow. He's employed by the governor of the prison.'

'Camara!'

Both of them had independently thought of the same man – a good sign. But the governor himself was loth to part with him, but in the end relented: 'It'll do him good to get out of Cayenne for a while.'

Camara was thirty years old, handsome, tough, and spoke French perfectly although he was of Spanish extraction. Through him I learnt more about the escaped prisoners to whom Gruther's secretary had alluded. There were several groups of them hiding out in the interior, even whole villages founded and populated by convicts. If I wanted to get in touch with them, Merlin would help me.

Merlin did help me. One evening he arrived in triumph:

'Fernand, I've arranged a meeting for you with the banker of one of those clandestine settlements. Go and see her tomorrow.

She's been warned of your visit.'

'A woman banker?'

'Yes, a Negress. Pretty hefty, but not bad looking.'

I had no alternative, I went to the rendezvous: a modest straw shack with a palm-leaf roof. In the middle stood a four-poster bed with a spotless mosquito-net. A buxom Negress appeared, smiling, waggling her hips, rolling her eyes:

'Come and sit down. Are you hungry? Would you like a drink?'

'I'm not an escaped prisoner.'

'I know.' She gave a great guffaw. 'I know all about you. You can have some men. Only you'll have to pay.'

'How much?'

'A hundred and fifty francs for each man, every month. Merlin told me you were aboveboard, I'm trusting you. I'll give you some contacts, you can take your pick. If you manage to obtain a concession or a legal permit, I'll provide you with any amount of labour.'

I was on to a good thing. I went back to Gruther and asked him for a forestry prospection permit. By now he would have given me the moon. We shook hands and I embarked with Camara and Bill, my dog, on a little coaster bound for Regina.

Camara looked years younger; the sea air was like a breath of freedom for him. Bill, too, sniffed inquisitively as she scrutinized the coast. We sailed past the swamps of Béhague Point, started upstream towards Guisambourg and finally reached Regina, perched high above flood level on the right-hand side. In a village to the north-west there were some ex-convicts who had never been denounced. They were considered more useful than dangerous by the measly little merchants who were thus supplied with cheap labour. Some worked as sweepers or served at table; others fished the rio or made furniture. I made contact with them and also started prospecting.

With Bill at my heels I went off every morning to explore the virgin forest, returning to the village in the evening to find Camara still recruiting: 'On the spot we give you food and work. At Cayenne you draw your escape fee: a hundred and fifty francs. That's the figure the banker fixed.' The news spread all the way along the rio and westwards to the River Kouroi. I plotted my expeditions on a sketch-map and began initiating Camara into the various species of wood which we would soon have to fell. I had to take risks, produce timber that was still unknown on the world market. I was aware of the difficulty: even a wood of superior quality can't be foisted on buyers abruptly. The factories are geared for such and such a species; customers are creatures of habit.

In due course I found an area which looked propitious, and decided to start felling at once. My savings would be enough to feed the convicts. I gave Camara instructions to buy the cooking-fat and rice in Guisambourg and Regina, so as to keep in with the local merchants. Meanwhile I set off for Cayenne to collect money, provisions, medical supplies, tools and the felling permit.

When I got there I found cause for celebration. Gruther was more enthusiastic than ever. My felling permit had been issued. The promise of a boat had not yet been confirmed but the Transatlantique agent said he vouched for it personally. I had the labourers. All that remained was to clinch the deal with the Negress and thank Merlin for putting me in touch with her.

'Ah, Fernand!' he said. 'She has come to see me at least five times. You're handsome, she says, she finds you attractive, she wants you. Don't hesitate.'

'I don't do that sort of thing on the sly or to order, Merlin.'

'It's a diplomatic move, you idiot. You must do it.'

'I'll try.'

I called on her that evening:

'I've come to thank you, but I don't yet know the number of men. Here's a list.'

'Never mind, I like you, take the men; you can pay for them each time you come back. I hope you'll come back often.'

Well might I force myself to put my hand on her knee and stroke her thigh, my heart wasn't in it. Merlin protested:

'You *must* do it, Fernand, you *must*. I'm going to give you something to put lead in your pencil.'

'I don't want any of your filthy concoctions. It's not a drug, is it?'

'No, it's a secret.'

He broke an egg, whisked it up with something or other and added a little white rum. I drank it, and felt blind drunk at once. I went back to the Negress, staggering from side to side, struggling to keep upright. I arrived at the big hut. I aimed myself at the four-poster. The effect of the concoction was unexpected: I passed out like a light and slept for ten hours. My hostess must have dossed down on the carpet; I found her there in the morning, smiling and affectionate, delighted to have watched over my slumbers. Despite her tenderness, her solicitude, the charm of her big black avid eyes, I was never able to gratify her with anything more than a polite kiss on the hand.

When I got back to the village I found the number of my convicts had increased to over thirty. Just in case they regarded me as a softy, I took a firm line with them straight away: 'You'll have to do better than this. The present huts are filthy. You'll start off by building some proper straw shacks.'

After a month it was like paradise, although there was a certain amount of petty thieving. One day my Parabellum and knife disappeared. I realized I was in for a trial of strength. I mustered the whole gang and said quite calmly: 'One of you has robbed me. I'm not asking who. But I want to find my knife and pistol back in my hut tomorrow.' By noon next day, the weapons had been returned.

One morning some *saramacas* appeared. I remembered Gruther's secretary telling me how proud they were, and treated them accordingly. I gave them permission to settle on the opposite bank and establish a new camp of their own. That evening their chief asked me to come and sit with him by the fire. He flung some herbs into a cauldron steaming over the flames, and contemplated the smoke. Then he declared: 'We are going to work for you; the cauldron says you are a good boss.'

The *saramacas* were fed in camp, but I kept them apart from my own men and paid them in kind, not in cash: an axe, a couple of machetes, a knife, or whatever else they needed. One day they went off again, as abruptly as they had arrived. But by this time all the rafts were ready and I made a flying visit to Cayenne to arrange for them to be towed down.

Through Gruther I found a Breton skipper by the name of Mercier and a week later his tug took my convoy in tow. Once again I saw Guisambourg, the swamps, the coastline of Cayenne. I parked my rafts tidily at the end of a creek and had the softer woods put under cover. Nothing remained but to wait for the Transatlantique Compagnie.

But in spite of the promises of the local agent, the head office in Paris refused to send it. I never discovered why. A misunderstanding? Faulty communications? Whatever the reason, whoever was to blame, I was the loser. I had wasted my time and toiled in vain.

14

I was practically cleaned out. After a year's toil a thousand cubic metres of timber lay idle in a creek. But I had proved my point and was determined not to let this blow affect me. Camara was more downcast than I, so, to cheer him up, I suggested going to the cinema one evening. Merlin held regular film shows to supplement his meagre income and his customers consisted exclusively of blacks.

The film was *The Life of Beethoven*. No sooner had it begun than the whole auditorium was in fits of laughter. The more the wretched Beethoven grimaced and postured, the louder the blacks guffawed and slapped their thighs. 'Silly buggers!' Merlin grumbled. 'This is supposed to be a tragic story ... !' But I realized these people looked upon any kind of emotion as a sort of disease. Jealousy, passion, infidelity seemed ridiculous. At the sight of reactions so alien to them how could they help laughing? 'Don't tell me they're normal,' Merlin went on. 'The other evening they roared with laughter when a jaguar gobbled up the hero who was an explorer!'

But the show did Camara no end of good. Next day he was his old self again, full of energy and determination. 'We must recoup somehow,' he said.

'What have you in mind?'

'Contraband. I knew a fellow in prison who used to write letters in invisible ink made from onion skins. He's sure to have contacts. He knows a cobbler who smuggles gold. He hides the nuggets in the hollow heels ...'

'Think again. That's small-time stuff.'

'There's also contraband beef. Mercier with his tug is bound to know about it.'

Mercier did know, and told me more:

'You know how bright and clever the Jesuits are. For a long time they tried to acclimatize cows, oxen, long-horned zebus. They reclaimed the forest, grew elephant grass, experimented with cross-breeding. The animals did quite well, even belly-deep in mud. They bore up against the flies and all that muck, but not against the vampires. You know what vampires are?'

'I've seen them on stage at the Grand Guignol.'

'They have two little incisors in their jaws, and they can kill an ox. The herds are in constant danger. So the Brazilians from the frontier zone ship live oxen up the Oyapok to be slaughtered by the local butchers. It's a nice little racket, thanks to which you're able to eat a steak now and then. If you waited for meat from those sodding warders, you'd die of hunger! If you like, Fernand, I'll take you up the Oyapok as far as Saint-Georges. You'll see some lovely forests. Who knows, you might continue with your prospecting?'

The name 'Oyapok' was music to my ears. 'Did you say something about a frontier?' I asked. He explained. The right bank of the river belonged to Brazil; the smugglers crossed from the Amapa territory to the French bank, and the police on both sides turned a blind eye. The contraband animals had been acclimatized for some time and came from the Jari, the Araguari, or even the borders of the Amazon. The Amazon! All of a sudden Guiana seemed too small and ill-equipped for me. I wanted to leave. The great river, still unknown to me, seemed within easy reach. Why hadn't I thought of it before? I longed to drop everything and chance my luck there, yet I heard myself replying: 'Mercier, I'd like to go to Saint-Georges with you and see the forest.'

And so I left Cayenne on the tug, parting company with my faithful Camara at Guisambourg after giving him a 'good conduct certificate' and some money to share out among the convicts at Regina. Then I sailed on towards the mouth of the Oyapok. As we made our way upstream, Mercier drew my attention to the trees: 'Look at that timber, it must be worth a fortune.' I didn't reply. My thoughts were winging across to the Brazilian bank, and beyond it I pictured the Sierra Lombarda and Tumuc-Humuc. Only a few hundred miles from here, the Amazon split up into countless branches to reach the Atlantic. Meanwhile the lovely trees on the French bank stood out against the setting sun.

I disembarked at Saint-Georges and stayed there for several days in order to think things over. A little further south, on the other bank, I could see the town of Oiapoque. Beyond it the river assumed a different aspect; much rougher, punctuated by falls and dangerous rapids. A new landscape revealed itself: an inextricable tangle of tall grass, drooping lianas, luxuriant vegetation. I couldn't resist it. Then and there I made up my mind to go further upstream and explore these lesser-known areas of the country. My plan was to set off on foot towards the south-west, make for the lower branch of the Approuague and then come back down the Oyapok by pirogue.

'It's a long way round, but it's feasible,' said Mercier, when I told him.

'I shall need a guide, or even two.'

'I know a couple of down-and-out *seringueiros*.'

Thus Pablo and Pedro entered my life. My first impression was not particularly favourable. They looked rather shifty and I felt I had better not enquire too closely into their background. They spoke Portuguese, with a smattering of French, and were obviously Brazilians, so I assumed they must have fled to Guiana as a result of some misdemeanour. I told them that as far as I was concerned their past was a closed book and that if they gave me satisfaction we would land up one day – I drew a sketch for their benefit – in the pretty little harbour of Belem do Para. I had never seen this town, nor had they, but their eyes sparkled with pleasure.

And so, with the faithful Bill at my heels, I left Saint-Georges in the company of my two shady henchmen. The *selva* stopped abruptly and was succeeded by desert-like country. We found ourselves advancing through a sort of lunar landscape consisting of low hills and gorges blocked with landslides, in the lee of which we sheltered at night.

One morning I woke early and climbed a hill to scan the horizon. I hoped to see the bed of the River Approuague, some fifteen miles away according to my calculations. Pablo and Pedro were still fast asleep, guarded by Bill. On my way back I noticed something glittering on the ground. I bent down and picked it up: a nugget – a nugget of gold! I couldn't believe my eyes. I started scratching at the soil with my nails. My hands were trembling, my heart thumping. I scratched still deeper and several more nuggets appeared, unequal in size but not widely dispersed. It was gold all right. Within a few minutes I had unearthed ten kilos of it! An absolute fortune.

Dizzy from the dreams and projects whirling through my head, I decided to stay here, explore this ravine, and reconnoitre the neighbouring gorges. But this wasn't so easy. I had to keep my discovery secret. However trustworthy Pablo and Pedro might be, gold might turn them into murderers. Every morning I had to think of some new excuse for wandering off by myself. I sent them out hunting or to collect firewood. I had no pick or shovel. How could I tell that I was scratching up the earth with a machete, after saying I was interested in trees?

But after a week I realized my efforts were in vain. There was no gold mine here. The nuggets I had come across were no doubt the cache of a former prospector or the treasure-trove of an escaped convict. I therefore struck camp and made a bee-line for the banks of the Oyapok, where I bought a good pirogue for the return journey.

I felt relieved to be on the river again. Pablo was an expert helmsman and seemed to detect intuitively any invisible hazard such as a submerged rock or water-logged tree-trunk. Negotiating the eddies and bends in the river was child's play to him, but even he was no match for the deadly 'falls'. The only way to avoid them was to jump ashore, hoist the pirogue on to our shoulders and launch it again further downstream. These rapids were sufficiently numerous to make my two henchmen grumble, but they knew the danger and preferred acting as porters to running the risk of being dashed to death on the rocks. Pedro, clever fellow, stowed our food away in bags covered with several layers of raw rubber so that in the event of an accident they would float. It was he who did the cooking when we stopped for the night, using a rudimentary pan made out of a five-kilo bully-beef tin. He was rather heavy-handed with the spices and tapir fat, but I devoured his concoctions all the same.

On the last part of its course the Oyapok grew wide and majestic; we were able to sit back and merely drift with the current. The banks went flashing past until we reached our point of departure opposite Saint-Georges. We re-sold the pirogue and I started looking for a boat.

On the Brazilian bank lived a certain Thomas, an ex-convict who had made a fortune from commerce and no doubt contraband as well. He advised me to buy a *tapouille*: 'An ideal vessel: sea-worthy and handles well. If you fit her with a jigger, you can manoeuvre in the slightest breeze.' Needless to say, he had one for sale: 'A ten-metre in tip-top condition, equipped with a mainsail, jib and stay-sail. Her deck's hermetically sealed: for the sea she's perfect, and you have nothing to fear when it rains.'

Thus I acquired my first Brazilian boat.

Pedro and Pablo set to work on her, making the hull spruce and painting the name I had chosen for her on bows and stern: *Helena*. Thomas then delivered the stores I had ordered: two drums of sweet water, sugar-cane made up in bundles, two cabbage palms, two bunches of bananas, hundreds of green oranges, two live pigs, one hundred kilos of rice and several quintals of salt to preserve the fish we hoped to catch. All was now ready. At ten o'clock in the evening we cast loose.

The moon flitted rather sadly in and out of the clouds. We had covered only a few miles, following the dark line of the river, when a strange music reached my ears: a muted chant, a discordant chorus coming from the Brazilian bank. I manoeuvred to get closer and suddenly felt a lump in my throat, for I recognized these gruff, disturbing voices and presently distinguished a number of ragged figures advancing along the bank: my former convict labourers singing the *Marseillaise*. This was their farewell. How had they managed to get across the river? From whom had they heard that I was going to sail that night? No doubt Camara had made enquiries and informed them. The singing stopped, the voices called out: *'Bon voyage!* Good luck!' I was deeply moved.

Our voyage lasted twenty-nine days. The wind bore us towards the Amazon. Bill indulged in lengthy siestas. The navigation was simple and trawling afforded us a profitable pastime. During the day I studied the coast, as luxuriant as ever. At night, stretched out on deck, I observed the strange brightness of the tropical sky, milky and balmy, with thousands of stars twinkling through a veil of mist.

One morning we landed at Belem do Para, the only seaport in the huge Amazonian basin. In our hold we had over a ton of salted fish, which Pablo and Pedro received by way of salary. As for me, within a few hours I had re-sold *Helena* for twice the amount I had paid for her. No doubt about it, this was my lucky day!

15

Belem had two faces: the American city with its broad avenues and handsome apartment houses, and the overcrowded slums. The population was extremely mixed. I noticed lovely young Brazilian girls with big black eyes and sallow complexions, *cabocios*, strange half-caste women designed for love-making, men as spick and span as bureaucrats, and also prospectors, ragamuffins, half-breeds, slaves. For the first time in my life I found myself in a land that was not under French rule. I decided to spend a few days in the best hotel to take stock and collect my thoughts.

My luggage consisted of a big canvas hold-all and the haversack in which I kept part of my money and my nuggets; hanging from my belt was my inseparable machete; my Parabellum was within easy reach in a special pocket of the hold-all. Thus accoutred, in working clothes, with Bill at my heels, I entered the Grand Hotel. 'This establishment is not for the likes of you, monsieur,' the manager icily announced. Without thinking I fished out some banknotes, which made an even worse impression on him. 'It's not a question of money,' he said. I felt I was about to lose my temper, so beat a tactful retreat.

Outside the front door I was accosted by a sprightly fellow in polished riding-boots, well-cut breeches and silk shirt:

'You haven't just arrived from Guiana by any chance? You wouldn't happen to be a forester?'

'Yes, but how ...'

'I'm Jack Gelle de Francony. I've just come from Cayenne. I'm a pilot and my friend Gruther told me about you. Come along. I'm going to introduce you to another friend.'

Thus I made the acquaintance of Paul Lecointe, the honorary French Consul. He greeted me with a broad grin and showed no surprise at my turn-out. His eyes were bright, direct, sparkling with intelligence. He had the sturdy figure of a peasant, tall and broad-shouldered. His white hair and thick moustache toned down the strength of his features. He, too, had led an adventurous life. Posted to Brazil as a young man on behalf of a big firm, he had conceived a passion for the country, its natural resources, its immense areas of forest. A chemist and botanist, he had explored the basin of the Amazon on foot and by pirogue, observing the jungle, the flora, the minerals. He had reached the region of Lake Titicaca in Bolivia, collected specimens of unknown plants, enquired into the pharmacopoeia of the Indian witch-doctors. He had been one of the first to point out the importance of curare and was now investigating the extraordinary properties of ayahuasce.

His encouragement was spontaneous, his enthusiasm contagious. 'You're right,' he told me, 'you must go deep into the jungle. It holds all the secrets. You'll discover fresh resources, but above all keep your eyes open for plants, stones, insects. Collect samples and specimens.'

He insisted on accompanying me back to the Grand Hotel and derived a malicious pleasure from teaching the manager a lesson by testifying to my respectability. The wretched lackey was forced to apologize profusely and say he was delighted to receive me.

At last I was back in civilization, with a prospect of hot water, a soft bed, decent drinks. I had a leisurely bath, a haircut, a manicure, then went out to buy some clothes. I came back to the hotel in triumph, transformed: polished shoes, silk socks, white flannel trousers, expensive shirt. But I hadn't been able to find a ready-made jacket. Even the largest sizes were too tight across the chest, and the sleeves far too short. So it was in shirt sleeves that I entered the dining-room. Bill lay down under the table and I attached her leash to one of the legs. I consulted the menu, determined to have a good blow-out. A waiter stepped forward:

'Regulations, monsieur.'

'What regulations?'

'In the dining-room one must wear a jacket.'

I tried hard to keep my temper:

'Tell the manager it's over 100°F and I couldn't find a jacket to fit me in the whole of Belem.'

'I'll ask him to come and see you himself, monsieur.'

Was it that he slung his napkin over his shoulder too abruptly? Or that he exuded an aura of hostility? Before I could stop her, Bill had gone for him, sending the table, table-cloth, glasses and plates crashing to the floor. The manager arrived white in the face and pursing his lips:

'Regulations are regulations.'

'Then I'll have lunch in my room.'

I went up, stripped naked and rang the bell. The manager himself answered it, escorted by the head waiter. He looked as if he was going to choke. 'I'm in my own room. May I have lunch dressed like this?' I said, and proceeded to order a large steak and six mango ices. My reputation for eccentricity was now established.

Meanwhile I continued to work out my plans. I had another long talk with Paul Lecointe and decided to push as far as I could into the interior, heading in a westerly direction, and make a rapid reconnaissance of the big tributaries which flow down from the cordillera of the Andes towards the Atlantic. The only way to get there was by steamer plying up the Amazon. And so, on the 15th August 1936, with Pablo and Pedro and Bill, I embarked on the *Adolfo*, a charming old tub bound for the river port of Iquitos in East Peru, some three thousand miles away.

No sooner had the little vessel left the wooden jetty and slowly started across the huge estuary than the skipper came up to me and introduced himself: 'I'm Don Adolfo. Peruvian. Make yourself at home on my ship. I've been in command for thirty years and I'm also the owner.'

Unfortunately he knew hardly anything about the forests of the higher tributaries: 'At Iquitos you'll find some rickety old saw-mills, that's all. In the whole of my career I've known only three pioneers in the timber industry. They all pushed off, fed up with the bureaucratic procrastination.'

This was not very encouraging. I watched the banks glide past. The landscape scarcely varied. Every now and then a couple of straw huts overlooking a wooden jetty stood out against the monotonous background. I was impatient to reach Iquitos and continue upstream either by pirogue or *lancha*, a local flat-bottomed vessel, for beyond Iquitos the Amazon was no longer accessible to boats of any size and the river even changed its identity, assuming the humble name of a delicious wild fruit: the Maranon.

At last, after twenty-one days, Iquitos came into sight. The harbour looked quite big for a river port: Peruvian warships, tugs and launches were moored cheek by jowl with Indian pirogues and mahogany rafts. A few miles away lay the *selva* of my childhood dreams, that new jungle which I seemed to know already. Further, much further off, I could see the first foot-hills of the cordillera of the Andes. A flying-boat passed overhead.

'There's an air base here, and an up-to-date hospital and cinemas. Good luck, Don Fernando,' said the skipper.

This was the first time I heard the Spanish version of my name. I felt as though I had been christened anew. Don Fernando! It was music to my ears.

It was 5th of September. The *Adolfo* was returning to Belem on the 25th. 'Will you be coming with us?' Don Adolfo asked me.

I decided I would. I therefore had twenty days in which to explore some untouched country and, with a bit of luck, apply for a concession. Gabon, Guiana were over and done with! Millions of acres, stretching as far as the eye could see, unfolded their virgin luxuriance. My brain was suddenly working very fast: 'Don Fernando, you have twenty days to discover some new species. But this time no nonsense. You'll go straight back to Europe with your samples. Not wretched little slivers like the ones you used to show at Luterma's, but logs, real logs, on which the stripping process can be carried out. Then they'll be able to compare the quality of Amazon timber with that of African.'

As soon as we were ashore, I sent Pablo and Pedro off to reconnoitre the town, while I moved into the hotel. Leaving Bill there, I then went back to the harbour where I had seen a number of rafts moored together. In my espadrilles I leapt from one to another, examining the logs. Darkness was falling, the jetty appeared to be deserted, yet I was suddenly conscious of someone standing behind me. I turned round and saw a little shrimp of a man: white, young, with a sickly complexion. He addressed me in Spanish:

'You're not from here, are you?'

'No, I've just arrived.'

'You speak Spanish like a Frenchman!'

'I am a Frenchman.'

His attitude changed at once. He smiled, a sparkle came into his eye and he broke into French.

'My name's Paul Lescuyer. My parents and I came to Iquitos seven years ago. My father was a war invalid; he hoped to make a quick fortune here. He hasn't succeeded; the climate doesn't suit him. He's taken to drink. So has my mother, in desperation. I work as an overseer in a saw-mill. Are you interested in timber?'

'What makes you think so?'

'I saw you examining the logs.'

I had a sudden feeling that this lad had been sent to me by Providence. He was in the timber industry. He had been out here since he was a boy. His father, a wretched pioneer, must know all the difficulties from personal experience. I couldn't overlook such an opportunity and therefore asked him outright:

'Do you know where I can buy or hire a pirogue?'

'You want to go up the Maranon?'

I disclosed my plans.

'I know some thick stands of cedar and mahogany a few days away from here. You have to go up the Rio Ucayali, the Pachitea and the Rio Pichis.'

'Do you know of a reliable guide?'

'There's an Indian who'd be perfect if he accepted. Unfortunately he only speaks a few words of Spanish.'

'Never mind. My first job is to find that pirogue. It must be big enough to take four men and stores for several weeks.'

'I know someone who might have what you want.'

'Can we go and see him right away?'

'Why not?'

By now it was pitch dark. After passing the warehouses and some ill-lit shacks, we plunged deeper into the slum area. Eventually we reached an isolated hut. The moonlight shone on the straw roof.

'Hans! It's Lescuyer!'

An old man opened the door and showed us in. His pale blue eyes contemplated us listlessly. But, as he listened to Lescuyer, they began to gleam: 'Yes, I have a big pirogue. With an outboard motor. I'm too old for it now. Just imagine, monsieur, I was a surveyor. I explored the Rio Pichis for years. I was married to a splendid Indian woman, a *Campa*, who bore me ten children. My wife is dead, my children grown up; they're roaming about the upper Amazon, half Indian and half German ... But come and see the motor.' He picked up a lamp and led us out to the shed: 'It's a Johnson, in perfect condition. Try it out if you like. The petrol's over in that corner.'

I heaved it on to my shoulder, took a can of petrol and we made our way down to the river. Soon the motor roared. I headed towards the eddies and whirlpools to test the pirogue's stability. It behaved perfectly. There was nothing more to do but go ashore and clinch the deal.

Next morning I gave my two henchmen some money, and instructions to buy the stores. Instead, they got dead drunk. So I locked them up in my room to prevent them from escaping and went off to make the necessary purchases myself. 'Now let's go and see the Indian,' I said to Lescuyer.

An old rattletrap deposited us outside a tiny hut an hour away from Iquitos, tucked away in the greenery at the foot of some huge trees.

'His name is Kenou,' Paul whispered to me. 'I'll go in first and speak to him. He's very proud.'

Presently he came out again. The Indian was with him. He was about thirty years old, with lean, supple muscles and slanting eyes. His reddish, sun-tanned skin was enhanced by two bracelets of seed pearls. He stared at me intently, scrutinized me, summed me up. He spoke to Lescuyer for a good quarter of an hour without taking his eyes off me.

'Kenou accepts,' Lescuyer finally said. 'For his fee, he wants an American axe, a machete and a knife.' Paul went on. 'He's at your disposal.'

'We leave at dawn tomorrow. Tell him to join us at the pirogue.'

I was up and about well before dawn, dragged Pablo and Pedro to their feet, and gave them each a nip of *aguardiente* to clear their heads. Kenou was already by the pirogue when we arrived; without being told, he had slept there to guard the stores. We set off.

Civilization stopped abruptly on the banks of the Ucayali. The river was like a huge rift, a liquid thoroughfare running through this luxuriant vegetation, this vast cauldron in which billions of leaves exuded their humidity under the blaze of the sun. Kenou drew my attention to an inlet tucked away in the bank. Low branches and tree trunks obstructed the entrance. Pablo and Pedro were accustomed to dealing with this sort of 'palisade'; in less than an hour we were able to creep into the narrow channel. The water was deep, and dark with humus. Kenou motioned me to go ahead. The motor gave a reassuring roar. The channel wound its way into the *selva* and eventually emerged into a vast *concha*, a sort of lake or watery clearing, swarming with alligators. We decided to land and make camp for the night. With Kenou and Bill I went off to reconnoitre.

I had an impression almost of holiness. I was carried away, enchanted, spellbound. Here at last was the great Amazonian forest, sombre, dank, majestic. I kept my eyes skinned. Kenou advanced steadily and soundlessly ...

And suddenly I was bowled over. Right before my eyes rose a stand of giant cedars! I rushed up to them, made a notch in the bark to reveal the wood underneath. *My* trees. I started counting them like a miser counting his gold. Three hundred soaring majestic cedars! One thousand five hundred tons at least! Millions of francs!

I sat down on a stump and pondered: if I managed to discover three stands of this size within a radius of a couple of days' march, I would have discovered the basis of a substantial development. Kenou had guided me straight to the spot where he knew I would find what I was seeking.

It was almost dark by the time we got back to camp. I saw Bill stop dead in her tracks, her eyes fixed on the shelter under which Pablo and Pedro had made up my bed. She dashed forward and worried my old cotton shirt for a moment, then came back with a tiny snake in her jaws. It was still struggling. By a stroke of luck she had picked it up by the neck, thus incapacitating it. I too gripped it firmly by the neck, ordered Bill to let go, and cut its head off with a knife. Bill was no longer indebted to me; she had just saved my life.

The fire blazed, the crickets chirped, the monkeys yelped, the birds uttered their various songs. I fell asleep, lulled by the music.

The first gleam of daylight was our signal to wake. After reloading the pirogue we set off again. From time to time I landed and reconnoitred the forest. At dusk we made camp. This became our daily routine. Another prize revealed itself: eight hundred cedars grouped together in a single stand! And on the 11th September, in the afternoon, I finally located six hundred mahogany trees, of which I took two samples. I could now turn round and go back; I knew enough to chance my luck.

Four days later we tied up at the Iquitos jetty. Kenou seemed very proud to have brought the expedition to a successful conclusion and my two henchmen's eyes glinted at the prospect of a spree in town. But no sooner had I climbed out of the pirogue and set foot on land than a couple of policemen came up and arrested me.

16

I was hauled off:

'Why are you arresting me?'

Neither policeman seemed willing to answer my question:

'*El Señor* Prefect desires to see you.'

If the Prefect 'desired' to see me, why pick me up like this? 'Listen, Fernand,' I said to myself. 'It's a misunderstanding for which you alone are responsible. In your haste and simplicity, all you thought of was your forests! You didn't report to any authority on arrival. Silly ass! Colombia and Peru are in a permanent state of tension. Spy mania being what it is, you must have raised any amount of suspicion.' I remembered the way I had hung around the harbour examining the rafts, opposite several warships. I had even waved at a flying-boat, just for fun. Then I had vanished into the jungle with two Brazilians and an illiterate Indian. I suddenly realized I had got off to a bad start.

We reached the Prefecture. I was locked up at once in a sort of basement. An hour went by. Through the skylight I watched night fall and began to feel worried. I gave an occasional cough to draw attention to my presence. No result.

It was pitch dark by the time the policemen came back and summoned me to follow them. We ascended a splendid staircase and I found myself in a big room in which a distinguished-looking elderly man was writing at a mahogany desk. Eventually he looked up and I contemplated a well-bred European face. I started talking as eloquently as my command of Spanish would permit:

'I meant to come and see you tomorrow, *Señor* Prefect. Your policemen have expedited our meeting.'

'I'm sorry,' he replied in excellent French. 'Only an hour ago I was not only going to arrest you but also fling you into prison. This telegram has saved you.' He brandished the document and asked me to be seated: 'I've only just been told you were here, at the Prefecture, and I received the telegram too late to countermand my orders for your arrest. We had received a report on you from Omaguas. I apologize again for this misunderstanding. But you must admit your behaviour was bound to appear rather strange. You made no official contact and we were notified only by grapevine telegraph.'

'Grapevine telegraph?'

He explained the situation: aware of the constant danger of war with Colombia, the Peruvians saw spies everywhere. He therefore had to exercise the strictest vigilance and interview all suspects himself, to avoid any blunder.

'You now realize I bear no resemblance to a Colombian spy?'

He said he was entirely reassured on this score, the French Consul at Belem having vouched for me, and even went so far as to express his delight at meeting a forester. 'What do you think of our *selva*?' he asked.

I saw at once that the situation was redeemed. The prefect was open-minded and intelligent and seemed to enjoy seeing someone from 'abroad'. On the spur of the moment I asked him if he could spare half an hour to listen to my views on the potentials of his province.

He stood up to offer me a cigar, hesitated a moment, then grinned and said: 'My work's over for the day. Go ahead.'

I told him that in a few days' time I would be going back to Belem on the *Adolfo* with two samples of the local wood. I added that I had prospected the Ucayali and was also thinking of visiting other places in South America. I gave him to understand that I was representing an important financial group who had given me carte-blanche to negotiate and deal in my name.

This was hardly an exaggeration, for I was convinced that once I had my concession it would be easy to find the necessary backing.

'You know what businessmen are like,' I went on. 'Those I represent are no exception to the rule. They're always impatient and their usual method is to reconnoitre several countries simultaneously. Another colleague – why hide the fact? – is at this moment prospecting in Colombia. He's an old Africa hand like myself. That's why I'm in such a hurry to get back to Paris with my samples. I want to clinch the deal before he gets back himself. I have a slight lead on him, but I'm afraid of the slowness here. Is it true that in Peru? ...'

He replied that President Benavides had managed to rouse the administration from its torpor and that he himself was trying to get things moving more quickly in his own district: 'But there's still a lot to be done. My father always said that our greatest riches are in the east, in our huge slice of Amazonia. You confirm his opinion. So submit your application for a concession. I'll back it for all I'm worth. But the final decision, of course, depends on Lima.'

'I'm only interested,' I said, 'if the concession is for a substantial area.'

'How many hectares?'

I had thought this over on the spot and had decided on 100,000 hectares for a period of ten to fifteen years. Yet now I heard myself saying: 'It won't be an economic proposition unless I have 350,000 hectares made over in my name for a period of twenty-five years.'

He didn't bat an eyelid: 'All right, I'll draft the application for you. It'll be ready for you to sign in the morning. I'll forward it to Lima with my personal recommendation.'

I thanked him and was about to take my leave when he offered me another cigar: 'You're in no hurry, are you? Let's go on chatting for a bit. When will you get back from Paris?'

'Early spring.'

'I think everything will be in order by then.'

'Thank you, Monsieur le Préfet.'

'One more word of advice. Foreigners in Iquitos are not always viewed with a favourable eye. Some people here resent their competition. This is just a friendly warning. I must draw your attention, for instance, to the enormous political influence which a certain Maltese exercises over the town and the whole province. He's extremely rich and I have to reckon with him. His wholesale grocery business is no doubt a cover for other activities. Between ourselves, I have every reason to think he was responsible for spreading the rumour that you were a Colombian spy. His henchmen must have reported your arrival on the *Adolfo*. He certainly had you shadowed afterwards. I'm pretty certain he'll have his knife into you.'

'What do you intend to do?'

'For my part, I have this telegram from Lima which officially covers me as far as you're concerned; but unofficially I'm going to submit a short report about you. It will appear in the local paper and put an end to all these rumours.'

I was preparing again to take my leave when the sound of a violent commotion reached our ears. The prefect leapt to his feet and dashed out. I had a bit of a shock when I saw him reappear with the policemen who were struggling with my two *seringueiros*: 'These men are the Colombian spy's bodyguard!'

'Leave them alone,' the prefect said curtly. 'This gentleman is neither Colombian nor a spy. He and his men are to go free.'

The policemen snapped to attention while the prefect and I shook hands. Pablo and Pedro were all at sea but tried to smile winningly, which to my mind made them look more unprepossessing than ever. 'I congratulate you on inspiring such devotion,' said the prefect. 'Those fellows look as though they'd willingly die for you. Bravo. See you tomorrow.'

My two henchmen accompanied me to Paul Lescuyer's house where Kenou was also waiting for us. Then I went back to my hotel, invigorated by the *aguardiente* we had drunk to celebrate our reunion.

Next morning I sent out for the local paper. The prefect was as good as his word and had written a very circumstantial article enjoining the inhabitants of Iquitos to distinguish between spies and respectable foreigners. A paragraph was devoted to me specifically, requesting all and sundry to ease my task. If the Maltese really existed, this article must have spoilt his breakfast; for the paper was circulated along even the smallest tributaries of the Amazon.

I spruced myself up to go to the Prefecture and sign my application. The prefect had had a memorandum prepared for me on the various methods of development. All that remained was to load my logs on to the steamer. They weighed over two hundred kilos each. The skipper shook his head in awe as they were lowered into the hold.

As soon as we got to Belem I made enquiries about cargo boats bound for Europe. 'There's a German freighter, the *Attika*,' I was told, 'but she never takes passengers. That's a rule.' Rules are made to be broken, as far as I am concerned, so I went off to find the captain.

He was a charming, chubby little man, but a stickler for rules and regulations. I couldn't see how to win him over, until he himself unconsciously suggested a way:

'So you're just back from the forests of the Upper Amazon? What did you see there? What did you bring back?'

His eyes suddenly gleamed, his face betrayed childish curiosity. 'Fernand, the termitary!' I said to myself. 'That'll do the trick!'

I told him about the splendid termitary I had placed for safe-keeping in a tin trunk.

'Could you show it to me? I've never seen a termite.'

'I have lots of them, and probably the queen.'

'*Prima*. Would you sell it to me?'

'I'll show it to you. Nothing could be easier.'

I stepped forward to the rail and called to Pablo and Pedro who were taking Bill for a walk along the jetty. Half an hour later they were back with the trunk. The captain gazed in awe at the termitary, viewing it from every angle, stroking its rough surface with his plump little hand: 'I've seen photographs, but never this! ... What a magnificent specimen!'

'I'll be only too glad to give it to you, if you'll make an exception and take me as a passenger.'

He hesitated only for a second. 'To hell with my first officer! I'll give you his cabin.'

I bade farewell to Belem, found a room for my two henchmen in the old town, and gave them a sufficient quantity of milreis to tide them over until my return.

Three days later I was on my way back to Europe. The high seas, the wind, the clouds, heralded the approach of autumn. I was torn between two conflicting desires, between two continents. A figure I had thought of on the spur of the moment in a prefect's office had transformed my life: three hundred and fifty thousand hectares!

17

Though the *Attika* was bound for Genoa and Naples, the skipper did me the favour of putting in at Marseilles and shortly afterwards I was heading north with Bill in a truck I had hired to transport my logs.

With such luggage there was no question of staying at the Terminus Saint-Lazare. I therefore telephoned from Auxerre to book a room in a more modest establishment near the Porte de Saint-Cloud. When I drew up outside, the manager almost had a fit!

'This is a hotel, Monsieur, not a saw-mill. And what a weight! How do you expect us to deal with it?'

I brandished my wad of dollars. This did the trick. He turned to the porter: 'Send for Lucien and the cellarman. Don't worry, Monsieur, we'll find a corner for you. Now then, you two, get moving!'

Next morning another truck came and took the logs to a factory in Saint-Maur-les-Fosses which had agreed to test them. Within a few days I knew my samples competed favourably with African woods. I now had to compare the respective cost prices, and therefore paid a series of flying visits to Belgium, Holland, Germany and England. Within a few weeks I knew what the cost of delivery would be to London, Le Havre, Antwerp, Rotterdam and Hamburg. My calculation was correct: I could sell at a lower price.

Meanwhile I was also busy nursing Bill. The poor bitch was still covered in sores caused by ticks burrowing under her skin during our expedition in the jungle; and though I dabbed her regularly with tobacco juice, she didn't respond to the treatment. Eventually I took her to the Institut Vétérinaire. 'Leave her with us, she's in very poor shape,' they told me. Twice a day I went to see her. She grew worse and worse, and in the end could hardly move. 'There's no hope for her. The ticks must have given her some fatal disease. She'll have to be put down.' Sadly I bade her farewell.

I decided to give myself a short holiday before going back to the

The starting point: a wonderful family from Le Vésinet.

My paternal grandfather. A blacksmith in the Var, he eventually settled in Paris and became a jeweller.

My family at Le Vésinet for my First Communion, 1912. From left to right: my sisters, my father, my mother, my two brothers.

Almost overnight I turn from a young playboy into a lumberjack in Black Africa.

Before my departure: the young playboy at Deauville.

In North Gabon I rescued and brought up a baby orphan gorilla.

Soualaba. One evening my black lumbermen thrust her into my hut: 'Here's a wife for you, Fernand.'

Nandipo. I saved her from the sacrificial pyre. One day, on the river, she heard the singing of her cannibal kinsmen and was gone by the time I got back.

In Gabon, on the River Ogoué, my first descent on a raft of *okoumé* trunks.

Adventure is a paying proposition if you put your back into it:

1925, my first return to France. On the proceeds from my African adventure I was able to afford a Hispano and chauffeur!

Southern Amazonia. One of my countless Indian friends, the unspoilt folk of the *selva*, who still use bows and arrows for fishing and hunting and, only when they are attacked, for defending themselves.

The hammock: the Indians are born in it and die in it, more peacefully than in any hospital.

When I first saw this couple I thought: 'Adam and Eve.' The jungle called the 'Green Hell' is in reality Paradise.

Seringueiros or rubber-tappers, tough little Indian and European halfcasts, who roam the jungle, machete in hand.

In the jungle a horse is a rare possession, requiring special adaptation to the climate, the food, the insects.

Rosita: she was sent to spy on me but love turned her into an ally. Thanks to her I was able to frustrate the schemes of my enemies in Lima and beyond the Andes.

At Satipo, my headquarters built of solid mahogany, with my horse and my Harley-Davidson on which I crossed the Andes to put paid to 'the Tyrant' who was terrorizing the neighbourhood.

Napoleon, my valiant and loyal henchman in the jungle.

Kinchokre, my 'brother', a pure Campa Indian, chief and witch-doctor – nobility personified.

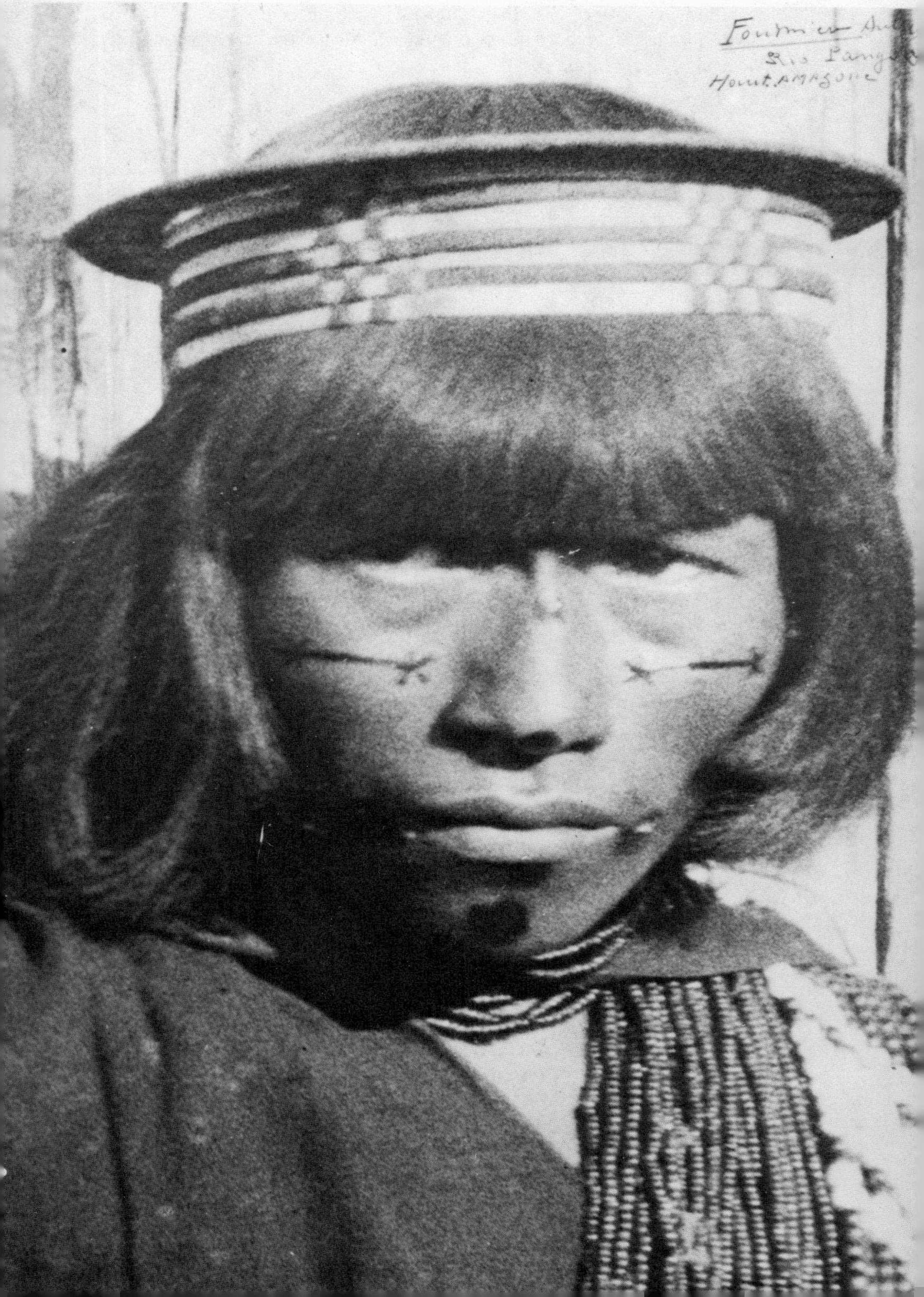
Fournier
Haut. AMAZONE

Standing in front of me, Pangoate, my wife according to the law of the Campa Indians. She bore me two children. All three of them were shot dead, victims of 'civilization'.

'Horse', my horse at Satipo. I rode him without spurs. I taught him to salute by raising his hoof and wagging his tail.

1943: I became a 'vitamin fisherman' and my catch saves thousands of human lives.

Ecuador, 1943. My first base for my shark-fishing expeditions in the Pacific. I provide tons of shark livers which save the lives of thousands of wounded and sick.

My first boat, the *Pelicano*, and my first catch: shark livers rich in Vitamin A, bonitos yielding Vitamin D2.

Myself with Victoriano Suarez, an Indian from Ecuador, my henchman on the high seas.

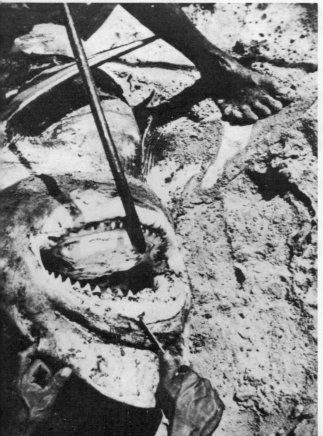

My crew. They were unpaid but, apart from the sharks, everything we caught was theirs. This suited them better than trade union rules and regulations.

A shark's jaw: twelve rows of razor-sharp teeth.

No launch on the *Pelicano*, only a balsa raft from which to spot the sharks.

A shark's liver, loaded with vitamins, a quarter of the total weight of the beast.

My first refrigerator ship, the *Cecilia*. Things are looking up!

Myself during the war, when I was known to all and sundry as 'Captain Shark'.

Ayde: her image was engraved on my mind during my shark-fishing expeditions.

Ayde: before the end of my shark-fishing days. Parting from her almost broke my heart.

Tierra del Fuego, the tip of South America, not far from the Straits of Magellan which my father knew.

In the Guaytecas Archipelago, on my initial reconnaissance of the area.

At Chiloe. Carmen in the centre. Working on a fishing-boat, she disappeared at sea one night in a storm.

My four *sufridos*, cheerful rascals in spite of the harsh living conditions in the worst climate in the world.

Our 'castle' in the Guaytecas, built with the only materials available.

In the harshest climate in the world I break my arm and leg.

The longboat turns turtle, I break my arm and leg. No doctor. Home-made splints of planks and cords. But never say die!

On the opium and gold route in the north of Afghanistan. A forbidden zone controlled by the big contraband tycoons. The motor road ends here. No more jeeps, only camels.

At Kabul. To film this *buzkachi* of Uzbeks (the best horsemen in the world) I had to kneel down with my camera in the path of fifty horses at full gallop. This gesture served as an open sesame enabling me to penetrate into Forbidden Asia in 1955.

With my guide and 'brother', Cheul the Terrible. Thanks to him I was able to advance, lap by lap, along the track leading to the secret gateway of China. Using jewels as money, I buy my white horse and my camel. On the secret track there is no more day or night, time ceases to exist.

Azyade. Love, so pure and powerful that it transcends everything, even death.

Our first caravan. The tents are of raw camel hide. The wind blowing over these steppes, the *bouran*, drives the swallows towards the north. By day the reflection is blinding, at night it's icy cold.

Tachki, my friend and bodyguard, on guard at my door after Azyade's death. He shared my grief and my indifference to being still alive.

These walnut-trees in Upper Kashmir saved me. I insisted on uprooting them and rolling them up hill and down dale, without equipment, by manpower alone, as far as a Decauville railway.

1972: At the age of 71 I plan more adventure. . .

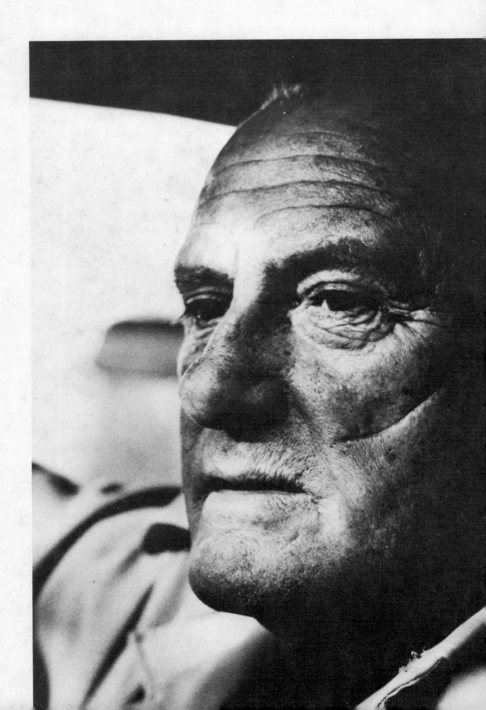

jungle, and was preparing to leave for the Côte d'Azur and Italy, when the fancy took me to have a watch-chain made with some of my nuggets. So I went into a bicycle shop and said to the mechanic: 'Drill a hole through these things for me and you can keep the dust. They're real gold.' When this was done, I picked up a spoke of a wheel and threaded the nuggets on to it. 'Now twist each end into a knot so that they don't come off.' I attached my watch to the chain and gave the mechanic a handful of loose change.

Delighted, I went into Weber's for a drink before lunch. An American sitting at the bar was riveted by the sight of my latest acquisition.

'That's a pretty little trinket. What's it made of?'

'Gold.'

He gave a loud guffaw:

'Have you got a lot like that?'

'Sixty-seven to be exact. The rest are in the bank.'

'If they're really gold, I'll buy them!'

I looked at him more closely. Realizing I was trying to assess how much he was worth, he took offence:

'Are you scared I haven't the money to pay you? Look ...'

And he produced a fat wad of banknotes from his pocket. How could I turn down a buyer who appeared so providentially a few hours before my departure?

'If you don't believe they're real, let's go to the jeweller's opposite.'

'Yes, Monsieur, they're gold,' said the jeweller, testing my nuggets with a sort of whetstone.

The American was mesmerized. He gazed at my watch-chain as though in a dream.

'I'll buy all you have.'

'I'll be back in an hour.'

I went to the bank and drew out the rest of my nuggets. In the presence of the American I had them weighed, and together we went to his bank. He drew out the money to pay me and we had a final whisky to clinch the deal.

After such a windfall there was no reason to pinch and scrape. I had a splendid holiday and lived like a king. Then I started making plans for my return. I ordered two of the latest outboard motors to be sent direct to Iquitos. I renewed my wardrobe, which included a couple of ties in the colours of the Deauville Yacht Club. Finally, with several crates of champagne, I embarked at Liverpool on the *Anselme*, a steamer of the Booth Line bound for Belem.

During the crossing I often thought of my two *seringueiros* and wondered if they would come down to the docks to meet me. But there was no sign of them when the *Anselme* eventually arrived and I had to see to my luggage myself. As it piled up on the quay, I noticed the head customs official peering at me intently. He was dressed with flashy elegance in a white flannel suit and wore a red carnation in his buttonhole. Suddenly, as though making up his mind, he came over towards me:

'Are you from Paris? What a town! I went there seven years ago. Your tie comes from there, doesn't it?'

So that's what had caught his fancy – the red, white and blue stripes of the Deauville Yacht Club!

'Do you like it? I have another exactly like it in my luggage. If you come round to the Grand Hotel in an hour's time when I've unpacked, I shall be happy to give it to you as a souvenir of France.'

He didn't wait to come round in an hour, but had my luggage loaded into his own car and drove me to the hotel himself. When I gave him the tie he looked more delighted than if I had given him one of my nuggets, and assured me that if there was anything I needed during my stay in Belem I could count on him as a friend and ally.

After he had left I jumped into a taxi and drove down to the harbour again. The *Adolfo* had sailed the week before; but there was another vessel, the *Comandante Macedo*, a luxury steamer of the Amazon River Company, leaving for Iquitos in two days' time. I booked three passages on her, then set off in search of my two henchmen.

I eventually located the wooden hut I had found for them before leaving, but no one in the neighbourhood could remember them and the hut had since been sold. It was as though they had never existed except in my imagination. I went back to the hotel, furious and disappointed. I had only one day in which to find them. But where was I to look? I saw myself having to do the rounds of all the low-dives in the dock area. What a sweat! Then I had a brain-wave. 'Why didn't you think of it before, Fernand?' I asked myself, and rang the head customs man.

'Only too delighted,' he replied. 'If your two fellows are in Belem I'll find them for you.'

I had lunch with Paul Lecointe who was delighted at the thought that I would soon be in possession of a vast expanse of forest. When I got back to the hotel there was still no news of Pedro and Pablo. The search must have come to nothing. I was extremely cross. How could I ever replace them? I was about to go round to my customs official when his telephone call came through: 'We've found them. They're working as waiters in a little café in the harbour: El Cabocio. Any taxi-driver knows it.' I thanked him and dashed off.

From outside El Cabocio looked like the worst sort of thieves' kitchen. The low wooden door was warped and peeling. I ducked under it and was almost suffocated by the reek of alcohol and tobacco inside. The men sitting at the grimy tables were almost invisible in the smoke.

As I came in they all stopped talking, stupefied at the sight of my shantung suit, Panama hat and white buckskin shoes. The silence was suddenly broken by two voices raised in unison – 'It's the boss!' – and I found myself clasped in a double embrace, with two pairs of hands patting me on both shoulders. Barefoot as usual, Pablo and Pedro had obviously forgotten what I had taught them, including their manners; they sat down at my table and yelled at the proprietor:

'A bottle of white rum! Three glasses! Don Fernando's back! Hurry! How was Paris, boss?'

'I'll tell you when we're on the boat. We sail tomorrow. Why did you change your digs?'

It was a whole saga. They had promised to behave themselves, but in a town like Belem this was easier said than done. They had started off by going on a bender which had lasted several weeks. Then they had thought of doing a little fishing or freight-carrying. But by this time their money had run out. They had found an old *tapouille* that had been abandoned and proceeded to repair it.

'When we had made it as good as new, the harbour police arrested us and accused us of stealing it. We showed the paper saying we were in your employ. They hesitated to put us in prison, but we had to surrender the *tapouille* and find a regular job.'

'So we ended up here. It's better than being stevedores.'

They were about to embrace me all over again, when they noticed the rum hadn't yet been served. 'What about that bottle?' they shouted.

The proprietor stepped forward. He was a giant of a man, and didn't seem to like what was going on:

'Back to work, you two, and make it snappy!'

'Shut your trap and bring us that rum!'

The giant was quick on his feet. He slipped behind Pablo and gave him an almighty sock on the jaw. Pablo keeled over. I managed to restrain Pedro who had meanwhile leapt to his feet. All eyes were turned in our direction. I felt it was advisable to get the other customers on our side. In a calm, steady voice I said:

'It's a disgrace to hit someone from behind! I'm the former employer of this poor waiter. He was absolutely entitled to have a drink with me.'

'Yes, it's a disgrace,' echoed a Negro standing by the bar.

He had no time to say more. The giant felled him with one blow. This was the signal for a general scrap. The giant tore off his shirt. His bare arms looked like legs of mutton. He made straight for Pablo, who had just struggled to his feet, and floored him again. Then he turned on me. Against this hunk of flesh I didn't stand a chance. He advanced towards me with a stool in his hand. I gave him a sharp kick on the shin. He dropped the stool and doubled up in pain. All I had to do then was bring my knee briskly up to his jaw. He swayed and finally collapsed under a table.

I felt it was time to call a halt: 'Stop it, everyone. Enough is enough. Let's all have a drink.' I ordered a glass of white rum, waved it under the giant's nose and shouted: 'Long live Don Pancho!'

He opened one eye, then the other, took the glass and drained it in one gulp. I earned a round of applause by filling it again. Thereupon he gave me a broad grin. Peace appeared to have been restored. No doubt he realized I would be a good customer. 'Pablo, fetch your guitar!' he said. The music started up, the rum flowed, the time flashed by. It was dawn, and a few stevedores had already dropped in for their first swig of rum, when Pablo, Pedro and I staggered out.

A few hours later we were on board the *Comandante Macedo*. Two days before we reached our destination we called at a tiny clearing hemmed in by giant trees. A pirogue set out from the bank. The two Indians paddling it brought it alongside to enable their passenger, an impeccably dressed white man, to cross the gangway. No sooner were the boatmen in full view than everyone drew back in horror. Their faces were lipless and noseless, or almost. The white man, Doctor Avecedo, was in charge of the San Pablo leper colony. He couldn't prevent himself from uttering a mild reproach: *'Caramba!* I'm not bringing leprosy aboard, Captain! No one need have any fear!'

On the 16th April we tied up at the long awaited jetty. A motley crowd had gathered to meet the handsome white ship. I had never seen such a mass of people. Ragged peons stood cheek by jowl with uniformed officials and colourfully dressed *Loretanas*.

I sent off my two henchmen in quest of Paul Lescuyer, who eventually arrived looking distraught:

'It's no good, Fernand. You've got the Maltese up against you.'

The article about me in the local paper had apparently caused a sensation, but the Maltese had responded by contacting the politicians in Lima. The prefect had been relieved of his functions and replaced by an official who was more amenable. My main support had collapsed. I tried to reassure Lescuyer: 'Never mind, we're not dead yet! Go down to the customs shed. There are two splendid Johnson outboards waiting to be cleared. Bring 'em back with you.'

But he came back empty-handed.

'Didn't you find them?'

'Yes.'

'Then what's wrong?'

'The cases were broken open, the motors are damaged beyond repair.'

I leapt to my feet:

'How does one get to Lima?'

'By military plane, if and when they're willing to take you.'

'Let's go to the base.'

I marched into the *comandancia* headquarters. A thickset little officer with hard, beady eyes turned round as I opened the door.

'Are you in command here?'

'I am. What do you want?'

I introduced myself.

'I want to get to Lima as quickly as possible.'

'Impossible, Monsieur.'

As a last resort I applied for an interview with the new prefect. For an hour I paced up and down the gallery, where a few months earlier his predecessor and I had shaken hands, before receiving the reply: 'The prefect is too busy to see you now. Call again in three weeks' time.'

The cards were stacked, the dice loaded. Fuming, I went back to the hotel and lay down in my room. Presently there was a knock on the door. I opened it, to find a shabby young Indian standing there:

'*El Señor Francés?*'

'Yes, what is it?'

He handed me an envelope. It contained an invitation from the Maltese to dinner that evening!

'Tell your boss I'm coming right away,' I said.

18

The invitation bore an address: that of a general store, which turned out to be a vast cavern reeking of kerosene, cheap scent, oil and spices. Against a background of flowered chamber-pots, bales of printed cotton, sieves and preserving pans, tinned food and lavatory paper, stood the owner himself.

He had the dusky countenance, oleaginous complexion and shifty eyes of a Calcutta pedlar. His mouth was pursed and, worse still, he sported a little toothbrush moustache like Hitler's.

'My dear friend,' he began, 'I'm extremely honoured ...'

'None of that nonsense, I'm no friend of yours.'

He gulped, then beckoned me into the back parlour:

'There must be some misunderstanding, *Señor Francés*. I ask you to dinner, and you come here and snarl. Let's talk things over.'

'There's no misunderstanding. The only reason I came here was to tell you that I don't like your ugly mug and it doesn't frighten me in the least. I'm not the sort of man you can intimidate, so you'd better watch your step.'

But he went on, smarmy as ever:

'Listen. I know you have a great project in mind. You thought you merely had to apply for a concession to obtain it. You want to work on your own. Out here that's impossible. I want to help you. I have lots of friends, in Lima and everywhere else. You'll get your concession if I see to it. I'm interested in big deals. Let's come to an agreement and everything will go smoothly. Stay to dinner. We'll work things out between us.'

I couldn't keep my temper any longer:

'My arse, we will! You and your dinner! You were hoping I'd do all the work and you'd take half the profits, eh? Not on your life, you reptile!'

This time he took exception:

'You think you can insult me, do you? You'll never get your concession, never!'

I grabbed hold of his sleeve:

'Oh yes, I shall. You'd better be careful. If I see fit, I'll put paid to all your rackets, and to you as well.'

I let go of him and he reverted to his wheedling tone:

'You're wrong, *Señor Francés*. I'm not as greedy as you think. Stay to dinner. I only want a small share. Let's shake on it.'

'Never!'

Lescuyer was waiting for me when I got back to the hotel.

'I've just come from the Prefecture,' he said. 'I saw a friend there. The prefect isn't against you, but he's scared. You must get to Lima. If you're successful there, he'll help you.'

'The commander of the base has already refused to fly me out.'

'He's not a bad fellow really. He must have been put up to it.'

'I'll go and see him tomorrow and have another try.'

I went back to the base next day, determined to stake my all. I scribbled a few words on my visiting card: *On urgent business*. The orderly reappeared within thirty seconds and this time I was shown into a huge dazzling-white office. The commander courteously offered me a chair and asked what he could do for me.

I told him everything: the former prefect's attitude, the sabotage of the motors, my visit to the Maltese. He remained inscrutable. As a last resort I appealed to his better nature:

'My project requires the support of all decent Peruvians, and I'm being torpedoed by grocers. Where are the patriots in this country?'

This did the trick. He confessed he had been mistaken and apologized: 'You can leave for Lima tomorrow. As for your motors, I'll have them dismantled at once and repaired in our own workshops.'

He invited me to dinner in the mess and gave me letters of introduction to his fellow-commanders at Pucalpa and San Ramon: 'You have to change planes there. I'm arranging for you to be driven over the Cordillera in a truck. At Lima the best thing would be to see the president himself, General Benavides. He alone rises above the petty conflicts and intrigues ... Now let me introduce you to your pilot: Lieutenant Baillarine.'

Next morning Baillarine lent me a spare pair of goggles and leather helmet: 'It's an open plane and you'll be in the machine-gunner's seat.' An Indian half-caste helped us into a pirogue and paddled us out to the aircraft. We climbed aboard and took off.

What a spectacle! As far as the eye could see, the forest unfolded its green astrakhan coat, and the river flowed in a long red ribbon punctuated by the white streaks of sandbanks. We flew at such a low altitude that the trees stood out in astonishing detail and I was even able to recognize certain species by their foliage and flowers. Here and there huge parrots suddenly took wing with a flash of brilliant plumage. The rain came hurtling towards us and I realized we would have to alight. Baillarine pointed out a little lake surrounded by huts: Contamana. We alighted on the muddy water, throwing up a reddish spray. A pirogue came out to meet us, while some men moored the aircraft to a huge balsa buoy.

A half-caste orderly ran up to us as soon as we set foot ashore. He snapped to attention: 'Lieutenant Perry very sick. Come quick.'

We entered an adobe building with a straw roof. Inside, a white man lay groaning and shivering under a mosquito net. I remembered myself writhing on the stretcher in the jungle of Gabon. 'He's got a hell of a fever. I'm going to try quinine,' said Baillarine, preparing an injection. There was a clap of thunder overhead; the rain poured down in sheets. The orderly suddenly came in. Though consumed with fever, Perry none the less sat up in bed: 'Ephilio, double the mooring lines, and stay on the buoy until the storm blows over. Thanks. *Dios mio* ... I'm cold!' Baillarine threw a poncho over him to make him sweat copiously and we waited for the storm to abate.

As the weather improved, so Perry likewise appeared to recover. Despite his fever and shivering, he cooked us an impromptu meal – roast haunch of ant-eater – before letting us take off again. Eventually we alighted at Pucalpa and I was allotted a room in the *posada*, a local inn which served as the officers' mess. It was stuffy and I had difficulty in getting to sleep. A sound like someone scratching at the window made me prick up my ears, then I heard a voice whisper:

'*Señor, Señor Francés.*'

'What is it?'

'*Señor*, a letter for you.'

I was immediately on my guard and raised the sash of the window cautiously.

'Hand it over,' I said.

'I'm not tall enough. Please reach down for it.' The voice sounded like a child's.

I was about to lean out into the dark, when suddenly I thought better of it. What instinct made me pause? What sixth sense commanded me to wrap a bath towel round my left fist before I thrust it through the opening? There was a whistling sound. I withdrew my arm in the nick of time, but even so there was a gash in the towel! The blow had clearly been intended for my head.

I lay down on my bed and tried to reason with myself: 'Only one person can be behind this: the Maltese. Impossible; he hasn't had time to notify a henchman here. Then who? One of the officers? Never; they've all been as friendly as can be.' I was about to give up when the answer occurred to me with blinding clarity: 'The plane! Maybe it brought some mail. The Maltese may have had time to warn a local henchman after all.'

At first light I set off to find Baillarine and questioned him tactfully. He had indeed brought a small mail bag from Iquitos to Pucalpa: 'Official documents, apart from one letter for the trading station.'

Now I understood. The Maltese had an agent here in his pay, a henchman disguised as a commercial representative. Within an hour I had discovered his identity and entered his shop.

He answered to the gentle name of Jesus Garcia and bowed before me like a flunkey. I walked past him, inhaling the smell of jaguar, ocelot and wild-cat skins, and headed for the alcove at the back which no doubt served as a bedroom. On the wall hung a machete which I noticed had been recently honed, for the cutting edge was shining. I asked the prices of various goods. They were steep. I grabbed hold of the fellow's hand and crunched his fingers.

'You're hurting me, *caballero*!'

'It's nothing to what I might do to you later. I'll be back. I'm thinking of settling in this region.'

'It's always a pleasure to see foreigners settle here. All I want is to help them.'

He had the same mealy-mouthed tone as his boss. I was determined to solve the mystery of last night, but couldn't afford to waste time at the moment. So, after crushing his fingers again, I left.

My pilot on the last lap to San Ramon, was Victor Gal'Lino. After an uneventful flight we landed at the foot of the sixteen thousand feet high Cordillera which I still had to cross in order to reach Lima. Next day, provided with a truck and a driver, a roast chicken and duck, a loaf of bread, some bananas and four bottles of wine, I set off; and twenty-two hours later drew up in front of the Hotel Bolivar in the Plaza San Martin. The streets were deserted. It was a warm, balmy night. I gave the driver a handsome tip and watched him set off, without a sign of fatigue, on his return journey.

I was able to sleep at last, confident that I was now within reach of the influential people I wanted to approach. I already had what I hoped would be an open sesame: a letter of introduction to Colonel Reccavaren, Supreme Commander of the Peruvian Air Force.

19

The early morning sunlight flooded my bedroom. I sent my letter of introduction round to Colonel Reccavaren, then strolled out into the street. Sentries in scarlet breeches stood guard outside the huge presidential palace, my final objective. There were flower-beds everywhere, trees, old Spanish houses ... I spent the whole day exploring the town. Next morning a despatch rider delivered a note summoning me to the Ministerio de Fomento.

Almost immediately the colonel gave me his whole-hearted support. So did his brother, Don Pedro, an expert in economics. Any mistrust they might have felt at first was quickly dispelled by a perusal of my file, my knowledge of the area I had already reconnoitred and the information they had received on my career as a forester.

'Will I be able to see President Benavides?' I asked.

'We'll arrange an interview for you as soon as possible.'

They were as good as their word. A few days later I was notified by telephone: 'The President will receive you at eight o'clock tomorrow morning.'

President Benavides looked more a senior civil servant than the soldier he was: stocky, thickset, with bright, slightly slanting black eyes. As he stood up to greet me, I saw he was wearing a plain grey dressing-gown.

'Forgive my clothes,' he said in extremely good French, 'I've been working since five o'clock and I haven't yet had time to get dressed ... Give me a brief outline of your plans.'

I did so, while he drew up the tray on his desk and proceeded to have breakfast. When I had finished he looked me straight in the eye: 'Clear, reasonable, accurate. But this development requires technicians and financial backing. What can you contribute?'

There was no point in bluffing, so I said: 'I've always worked without financial backing, preferring to prospect at my own expense. This guarantees my independence, so that I don't have to act as an executive agent for any national or international pressure group or power. On the other hand, with a concession in my own name, my order book will be quickly filled. Here's a report on cost prices for every big port in Europe. On this showing I'll be able to obtain all the funds I need.'

The President didn't bat an eyelid.

'Thank you for being so frank,' he replied. 'If you had told me you had huge funds at your disposal, I should have been extremely reserved. As it is, I'd like to see you again. I'll let you know.'

In due course an officer of the Presidential Guard called on me at the hotel to deliver an invitation to dinner, at the *Palacio del Gobierno*. Sentries in full dress uniform mounted guard outside the building. I produced my card. An officer showed me into a lift. To my surprise, it went straight down to the basement. A long vaulted corridor led to a small door guarded by two more sentries. The officer gave the password and one of the soldiers knocked three times with his rifle butt. The door opened and another officer ushered me into a small room with a low vaulted ceiling. I was bewildered by this curious ceremonial. Instead of the brightly-lit, crowded drawing-room I had expected, all I could see was a monastic table laid for two.

The President, who had been concealed by the back of a tall chair, stood up to greet me. This evening he was wearing a plain khaki uniform with miniature decorations. He uncorked a bottle of Châteauneuf-du-Pape : 'We're going to dine alone, so we can discuss business. It saves a lot of time.'

He rang the bell. An Indian appeared carrying a long silver tray laden with *alfajoles* : croquettes of maize flour, eggs and white of chicken, enclosed in aromatic leaves. These were followed by *seviché*, diced fish with lemon and pimento, and then the national dish of duck with rice.

We talked shop, but the tone was free and easy and I took the liberty of describing a few of my adventures. He told me that at one moment he had thought of giving me an official position : 'I now see it was a bad idea. You're not cut out to be a civil servant.' Instead, he had three tasks in mind for me : the development of a pilot concession, the establishment of a forestry school working in conjunction with the existing agricultural college, and perhaps an enquiry into the formation of a river flotilla : 'I'll give the necessary orders to Colonel Reccavaren. Your prospecting and travelling expenses will henceforth be met by the Ministerio. Don't hesitate to let me know if there's anything you need.'

I took leave of him, extremely pleased with myself but painfully aware that I would now be stuck in Lima for several weeks as a result of my commitments. Farewell for the time being to the forest, my two *seringueiros*, the provincial charm of Iquitos, my little pioneering world!

I rented a villa with a garden in the pleasant suburb of Miraflores, and engaged an Indian couple as servants. After my hotel room, it was pleasant to live in the midst of flowers and palm-trees. Yet within a few days I had the unpleasant sensation of being followed and spied upon. One evening I came across a suspicious-looking character lurking outside the gate. Before he could slip away, I went straight up to him and asked him for a light.

As he fumbled for some matches, I examined him closely. He was an Indian half-caste, with one very distinctive feature – there was no lobe to his left ear; it had been sliced off by a razor no doubt. This ought to make it easier to identify him. I hurried off to notify Colonel Reccavaren, who promised to look into the matter.

A few days later he confirmed my suspicions: 'You're right, you're being shadowed. Your work at the ministry has come to the notice of certain businessmen. No doubt they feel their interests are being threatened. We're keeping our eyes open. Don't worry, but take care.'

Mysteriously everything reverted to normal. Next day there was no sign of my shadow. I breathed more freely.

In the late afternoon, as I was leaving the ministry, a handsome Ford roadster drew up with a ravishing young woman at the wheel.

'*Señor*, aren't you going to Miraflores?' she asked.

'How do you know that?'

'I live there myself, with my mother.'

I could think of nothing to say and just stared at her. She burst out laughing:

'Why are you looking at me like that?'

'Because I think you're beautiful.'

'Shall I drive you home, then?'

I sat down beside her.

'I lied to you,' she said, as she dropped me at my house. 'I don't live at Miraflores; I merely have some friends here. You're not angry with me?'

'Not if you promise to come and see me again.'

'Here's my telephone number.'

Her name was Rosita. She came to tea next day; and subsequently I found her there every day, for since she seemed to enjoy my villa and the garden I gave her a spare set of keys. It was delightful, after a hard day's work, to be welcomed back by her kisses and to spend the rest of the evening in her arms.

One day, however, a small incident roused my suspicion. I had come home earlier than usual, because I wanted to give her a surprise and take her out to dinner. As I entered the drawing-room I saw her hastily close a big file of documents I had left on the table. I pretended not to notice but I was intrigued. Next day I came back with an even bigger file, marked 'Top Secret', which I purposely forgot in her car. She never alluded to it, yet she could not have overlooked it. What conclusion was to be drawn?

The newspaper *El Commercio* provided the answer ten days later with a report of the impending development of a large forest area. The zone illustrated was strangely similar to one of the maps in my 'secret' file. It was hard luck on my beautiful spy's lords and masters that they had had such a splendid fake document planted on them.

When Rosita arrived at the villa that evening, with her arms full of flowers, I thought I was going to explode. I allowed her to embrace me, however. I could not bring myself to believe in her deceit, to think that her lovely eyes were of a spy who had been foisted on me.

My expression must have betrayed my feelings, for she nestled against me and sobbed: 'Fernando, I can't go on like this. Listen to me, then do as you see fit ...'

As I listened I recovered my composure. What she said amounted to a total confession. Her uncle, a shady politician, had managed to convince her that I was a Colombian spy who had ingratiated himself with the President: 'He asked me to unmask you. But I've now seen through him and his cronies. They've got their knife into you. Fernando, I'm disgusted with the part they made me play. I love you and want to help you. Forgive me.'

I felt so happy that I forgot to tell her the file had been a fake – which she only discovered when the financiers of her uncle's group eventually came back from Iquitos empty-handed and furious at having hired two *madereros* to prospect a worthless area in vain.

One night I came back to the villa later than usual, and was surprised to see no sign of her. Then I noticed there was a light on in my bedroom. I opened the door and saw her sitting on the bed, half naked and white in the face, dabbing with a bloodstained towel at a wound in her thigh. I dressed it properly, while she told me what had happened:

'I wanted to give you a surprise, so I came in here to wait for you. Suddenly a man sprang out from behind the curtains. I picked up the bottle of eau de Cologne on the table and broke it over his shoulder. He lost his head and jabbed at me with a knife.'

'What did he look like?'

'A *cholo*.'

'With no lobe to his left ear?'

'I didn't notice, I was watching his hands.'

I had been in Lima for four months when, on 12th July, I was woken at seven in the morning by a telephone call from Colonel Reccavaren announcing the good news: my concession had been granted. I had my three hundred and fifty thousand hectares of Amazonian forest! I could hardly believe my ears.

By this time, however, I had spent all my money. Here I was, master of a vast area full of potential wealth, yet without the price of a ticket to Europe! And only in Europe could I find financial backing. What could I do? 'There's only one solution for you, Fernand my lad – the jungle. Alligator skins, jaguar skins – go hunting. There's no hurry; you have twenty-five years in which to develop your concession. Meanwhile Kenou and your two *seringueiros* are waiting for you at Iquitos.'

So farewell Lima, Miraflores and Rosita. Soon I was crossing the Cordillera again, but in the opposite direction.

20

I wanted to embark on my hunting expedition as soon as possible, and therefore stopped at Pucalpa to order food supplies and equipment. Thus I found myself once more entering the general store belonging to Jesus Garcia. The smarmy little rat greeted me effusively, for my return had set tongues wagging – I was the man with 350,000 hectares.

'I'm going to leave you a list of my requirements,' I told him. 'I want them to be ready by the time I get back.'

Then I went on to Iquitos. A few weeks later I was back in Pucalpa with my two *seringueiros*, my outboard motors which had been repaired, my cases of champagne, my forestry implements, and a pirogue big enough to transport six men and all the stores I had ordered: magnifying glasses, planes, binoculars, axes, rifles, powder, petrol, rice, alcohol and salt for treating the alligator skins. As they stowed them away, Pablo and Pedro checked each item on the list, then handed me the invoice and awaited my reaction. My reaction was immediate:

'The rotten thief! Not only a murderer but a shameless profiteer! I'm going to give him what for!'

I knew the prices, as the little rat was going to discover to his cost. I dashed into his shop. He must have realized I meant business, for on seeing me he immediately reached for his Colt hanging on the wall. I drew my Parabellum.

'That's enough, Jesus. It's high time. Own up.'

'No, *Señor*, it wasn't me!'

'Your gesture has just given you away. You were thinking of the machete that missed my head. Own up or I'll shoot you dead.'

'Don't kill me! For pity's sake! It wasn't my idea. I shouldn't have. I'll do anything you say.'

I stood motionless, pointing my revolver. He collapsed under the tension:

'I'm entirely at your service ...'

He was hideous to look at, white in the face with fear. I decided to settle the business at once:

'I'll let you off, Jesus, on one condition. And I'm doing you a favour. Reduce this bill by half and give me a receipt at once. It's a bullet you really deserve, but I'm going to pay you in alligator skins. Not until I get back, however. Sign and we'll say no more about it.'

His hand was shaking in his eagerness to sign; but he probably felt he was well out of it, for he smiled with relief as he handed me the receipt and said again: 'At your service, *Señor*.' I put my Parabellum away and marched out.

Two days later Kenou arrived in his tiny pirogue. As usual he wore his exiguous loincloth; but, for our reunion, he had adorned his face with designs in brick-red paint, and he showed me his American axe and machete. I put my arms round him and great was my surprise to hear him greet me in almost fluent Spanish. What an amazing fellow! His friendship for us had led him, during this long absence, to get a job on a coffee plantation near Rio Peréné in order to learn the language in which we would be able to converse together.

I presented him with a brand new gun, plugs, cartridge cases and a bag of shot. Many an evening afterwards I came across him gazing tenderly at the weapon or sleeping with it clasped in his arms like a toy.

And so we started hunting. Sometimes I would venture out alone, smiling at the forest like a faithful swain coming home to his beloved. Meanwhile the three others reconnoitred the grassy beaches along the river where the crocodiles lay in wait for the monkeys coming down to drink. At other times we went off together for days on end, following the dark *cochas*, building kilns in which to smoke the salted hides, storing our goods on makeshift balsa rafts.

At dawn one morning, as I was about to leave the shelter in which I had spent the night, I heard a little brass bell. I headed towards the sound and presently came upon a tiny chapel with a straw hut beside it. There were some two dozen Indians outside, surrounded by their dogs and poultry, and in their midst stood a white delivering a sermon. He was extremely old, bowed, bearded, white-haired; his old brown homespun habit was heavily patched and his hands and fingers looked deformed. At the end of the sermon I went towards him and saw that his face was aglow with inward joy; true humility marked his drawn features.

'Don't come near me if you're afraid of leprosy,' he said. 'Otherwise, welcome. I'm Padre Henrique.'

I stayed with him the whole of that day and night and the memory of those hours are still indelibly printed on my mind. He was a Basque and had lived in Paraguay and Amazonia before settling in this dingy straw hut beside his little chapel. He spoke to me of the forest, which he knew like the back of his hand, and also of his beloved Indians. I can still hear his quavering old voice: 'They listen to me, of course, but they quickly forget and revert to their own rites. They don't understand, and yet they're fond of me. No doubt I'm to blame for not going about it the right way, but I hope God will not disregard my good intentions ...'

He noticed me looking at his deformed fingers: 'I can still do a bit of mending, but I haven't enough strength to uncork the communion wine. My sacristan sees to it. Poor fellow! He's so primitive that he goes back to his tribe to have the cork drawn. He's devoted, but a rascal; he never comes back with more than half the bottle. But these are the minor drawbacks of life among the savages. I love them all.'

I fell asleep in his hut, as though on the threshold of paradise. Next day I went off to explore the *cocha* with one of his assistants and saw over a hundred saurians basking here and there on the banks. I returned at once to notify Kenou and my *seringueiros*. We jumped into the pirogue, started the motor and headed back, while clouds of mosquitoes attacked us. Kenou was afraid we might damage our propeller on a submerged root, so I took his advice, stopped the motor, and we paddled the rest of the way.

Every now and then we glided past enormous anacondas curled up fast asleep. We let them slumber in peace. Why kill them? Anacondas are lords of the jungle, they measure anything up to 25 feet long and weigh over two hundred pounds; but they're not poisonous. On the other hand, I constantly had to slice the heads off the tree-dwelling snakes hanging from the branches above the water. A single injection of poison from one of these is fatal.

Standing on watch in the bows, Kenou suddenly stiffened. He had spotted, a hundred yards away, on the edge of the carpet of vegetation, the rounded nostrils and humped backs of the alligators.

I decided we had better camp there for the night and not disturb them till morning.

When I awoke, Kenou was already up and about. I roused Pablo and Pedro, for I knew that at daybreak the alligators would start heading for the *cochas* and no longer present an easy target on the bank. It was therefore necessary to go into action while it was still dark.

We were about to set off when a strange figure loomed up in front of us, brandishing a bow and arrows in one hand, a sizzling torch in the other. He was stark naked and the broad grin on his painted face revealed a row of pointed teeth. To my intense surprise, this apparition started talking in fairly comprehensible Spanish. 'My name is Aray. I'm a Chama Indian. I saw you with Padre Henrique. You're going to hunt the alligators. He told me to help you; it was he who taught me your language. My tribe is at your service.'

It was in my interests to accept his offer and make a demonstration of good will, so I presented him with a brand-new *escopeta* which I had bought at Jesus Garcia's. Our alliance appeared to be cemented.

'It's a good thing you have come,' he said. 'The alligators eat our fish and sometimes even our children. But you mustn't fire on them at random, otherwise they'll scuttle off in all directions to hide and then they'll be more dangerous than ever.'

And so for several days, with remarkable skill and in complete silence, he and his fellow-tribesmen showed us how to drive the alligators off to a safe distance before killing them. At the end of the hunt he asked me back to his village for what he called 'the feast of deceived husbands'. I could hardly believe such a ceremony existed, but, as we made our way upstream in his pirogue, he gave me a rough account of it which roused my curiosity. 'Tomorrow I cut a man's head,' he concluded. 'You'll see, it's a great feast.'

As we approached his village, he imitated the distinctive long-drawn cry of the *getusa*, a nocturnal bird, to which someone replied by imitating the cry of the *pangil*, or wild turkey. Then the pirogue was literally lifted into the air by a group of Indians who loomed up on the steep, slippery bank.

A fire had been built in the middle of the clearing, and round it stood some tall earthenware jars decorated with black and red designs and containing some beverage or other to which the inhabitants helped themselves, scooping it up in their hands. Judging by their expressions and gestures, it must have been highly alcoholic.

'It's *masato*,' Aray explained. 'The women chew *yuca* until it's soft, then spit it out again. And in that jar there's *lluasca*. Very good too. Here's our *curadero* who's come to greet you.'

The *curadero*, or witch-doctor was also the chief, and the only man in the village to own an *escopeta*. I presented him with my gifts and offerings: knives, tobacco leaves, little chains and artificial jewels, at which he demonstrated the most spontaneous joy and insisted on pouring me out a calabash of *lluasca*. I found it induced a state of exceptional lucidity and alertness.

Aray was obviously proud to have me next to him during the meal. We were served grilled rat, *pirarucu* fish, hearts of palm tree, and big white worms that are eaten alive by way of dessert. The *curadero* came up and offered us yet more *lluasca*. By this time most of the villagers had collapsed and were lying on the ground, staring into space.

Next day Aray tried to explain the reasons for the ceremony: 'When a Chama Indian desires a woman who is already married, he can follow her into the forest and fling himself on her. She must defend herself, just a little, without crying, without yielding. Then presents are exchanged: a necklace for her, a bracelet for him. But she must hurry back to the village and show the necklace to her husband. You understand?'

'Yes.'

'Afterwards the man is entitled to that woman and the village knows all about it. But, mark you, the husband wreaks his vengeance on the feast day, which is today. He wears a little knife with a curved blade round his neck. That's the instrument of vengeance – vengeance for which he has been waiting a whole year!'

He left me then to witness the ceremony on my own, but without telling me he was going to be one of the principal participants. I wandered down to the river and stayed there during the preparations, for the inhabitants seemed to be getting more and more drunk. By the time I came back, the ceremony had begun. One man was already on his knees. Behind him stood another, brandishing his little knife, with a woman, evidently his wife, beside him. At a given moment he made an incision in the victim's neck. It was not very deep but the blood flowed, honour was thus satisfied.

I was about to move on, when I saw Aray, standing bolt upright, clad in a length of homespun cotton – a superb ceremonial *cusma*. There was a strange smile on his lips and suddenly he pounced upon a man by the name of Aupy. The circle closed round them. Aupy refused to kneel. In fury, uttering piercing cries, the women of the tribe forced him down. Then, eyes flashing, Aray plunged the blade of the knife into his neck. The blood spurted at once, in abundance, and he plunged the knife in again. Aupy collapsed, streaming with blood. Smiling, with an almost angelic expression, Aray thereupon helped him to his feet. He was avenged. Some old women led Aupy off to a hut to bathe his wounds. I lent a hand. The gashes were so deep that I couldn't stop the haemorrhage. He died during the night, while I sat with the witch-doctor by the big fire, drinking the sugar-cane spirit I had brought as a gift.

Next morning Aray paddled me back to the *cocha* and I bade him farewell.

I had heard about a huge quantity of mahogany trees further east, towards the Rio Chesea; but to get there entailed travelling for several days on foot and leaving behind our only possession, our only means of getting back to civilization: the pirogue which had enabled us to penetrate as far as this. I decided to camouflage it under some branches at the back of a little creek, which would serve us as a base camp. Then, with our axes slung on our shoulders, our machetes in our hands, our survival rations wrapped in rubber bags, we set off.

After eight days' march we came across the first stands of mahogany trees. They were two metres in diameter, and there were also large quantities of cedars. We made a note of the spot and pushed on. On the fifteenth day we reached a grassy plateau, a sort of pampa, in the middle of which I noticed an abandoned bamboo hut. There was no sign of life, either in the immediate vicinity or within the fairly wide radius we reconnoitred, so we decided to spend the night there. In the morning we found ourselves surrounded by some thirty Indians: silent, superb, all armed with bows and arrows. Even Kenou was astounded. 'Piros,' he whispered to me.

Our weapons lay on the ground at our feet. We made no attempt to pick them up, for fear the gesture might be misinterpreted. In fact we drew back several paces. The Piros reacted at once by withdrawing to within a radius of a hundred yards. The thought flashed through my head: 'Since they didn't kill us during the night, they're not likely to kill us now. All we can do is wait.'

We waited for hours, in complete silence. Towards noon ten other Piros arrived. The chief addressed them, then they all disappeared, leaving only six guards who drew closer, bows and arrows at the ready. I realized that any false move on our part would be fatal. My mind was still working rapidly. I thought it would be a good idea to hold my arms above my head and, while still in a sitting position, push my rifle towards them with my toe as if offering it to them as a gift. No reaction. I went through the same motion with four other rifles and then, so as to make my intentions clear, rolled over on my side as though going to sleep and told my companions to do likewise. The Piros still didn't react. Towards five in the afternoon I began to get worried. In an hour's time it would be dark. And what then?

Eventually, just before nightfall, some more of them arrived, carrying calabashes and bunches of bananas which they placed on the ground in front of us, without a word, without a smile, without a trace of expression. Not one deigned to pick up our rifles, still less fire them.

We remained in this situation for three whole days, during which we lived on water and bananas, water and bananas, water and bananas ... On the morning of the fourth day the banana-carriers didn't appear. But some new Piros turned up, with another chief who 'examined' us with a rapid glance, picked up our *escopetas*, cocked the hammers and fired them into the air. Then he beckoned us to follow him. We fell into step behind him and the other Piros brought up the rear. The chief set a brisk pace and we had difficulty in keeping up with him. I had the feeling we were going to certain death.

This impression ceased as soon as the forest reappeared and we were back again on the damp spongy soil, among the giant ferns, beneath the green roof so familiar to us. At an angle of the river, after a long day's march, the chief halted and silently waved us on. It took me some time to realize we were free, that we had been conducted beyond the borders of the territory on which we had unwittingly trespassed. Within a few minutes our naked escort had disappeared.

For all Kenou's instinct, it took us a good ten days to get back to our pirogue and the food supplies. Luckily we had not been searched, so that I still had my hermetically sealed match-box in my pocket. Hunting produced such a meagre bag that by the sixth day we were reduced to feeding on snakes and white worms. Kenou ate them raw, my *seringueiros* preferred them roasted; I tried both ways and liked neither. Luckily our pirogue proved to be intact, but it had been thoroughly inspected by the Piros in our absence. We had each lost ten kilos by the time we reached it, our feet were bleeding, and we were shivering in every limb since we all had malaria.

In my delirium I had a series of nightmares. I was back in the forest, but the vegetation was more monstrous than in reality. I struggled in the black water of the *cochas*, seized by giant arms. Vegetable tentacles wrapped themselves round my body, lifted me into the air, carried me off to the tops of the tallest trees; alligators yawned on the ground below, waiting for me to drop into their jaws.

I surfaced at the end of a week, which Kenou had put to good use by collecting all our rafts together at Pucalpa. According to him we had over four hundred skins. So I felt we could call off the hunt. Now that my fever was over, everything seemed fresh and new. Pablo and Pedro had recuperated a few days before me and they too looked rejuvenated. They had made friends with a couple of Campa Indians who offered to escort us towards the frontier of the Cachivos. The Cachivo Indians had a bad reputation, admittedly; but on the edge of their fiercely guarded territory the two Campas reported numerous mahogany trees.

'Let's go and see, it will be our last expedition,' I said.

After a few days' march the Campas told us we were approaching the Cachivo border. For these primitive people there are no maps, no treaties, no written agreements; but their instinctive precision is as extraordinary as that of birds defending their territory. After a bit I myself eventually recognized the signs: seed pods suspended in clusters from short lianas. 'We mustn't go beyond them; they're put up as a warning,' my guides explained. Remembering our mistake with the Piros, we gave them a wide berth. I plotted the position, with the intention of later drawing up a little map of this frontier region which was indeed rich in mahoganies; then, well before nightfall, we withdrew several miles in order to underline our peaceful attitude.

One morning Kenou discovered the fresh tracks of some wild beast only a few hundred yards from where we had camped. The Campas were positive and scared: 'Jaguar. Two jaguars. A female and a cub.' Now the jaguar is a dreaded killer and I felt this female

144

was a danger to us, in spite of our weapons, for if she was roaming round here it meant she was hungry.

I have always loved wild animals and decided to capture these two in order to try and tame the cub. I still remembered the primitive traps in which my Pahuins in Africa used to capture panthers, and set to work on building something similar a mile away from the camp. On my instructions, Pablo and Pedro marked out a rectangle and started cutting some wooden stakes to plant in the ground. By the end of the day we had constructed a cage equipped with a sash door designed to drop as soon as the bait was touched. I checked the lianas connected to the latch. Then we baited the trap with a big haunch of antelope.

Darkness was falling. For safety's sake I arranged for each of us to stand guard in turn. In the middle of the night we were woken by some thuds and growls; but I felt it was advisable to wait until daylight before going to investigate.

At dawn, clutching my Parabellum, and followed by my troupe with their weapons, I found the female jaguar and her cub struggling furiously inside the cage. She kept hurling herself against the wooden bars ripping them with her claws. I took careful aim and fired. She leapt backwards and collapsed, with two bullets in her skull. Surprised, the cub suddenly stopped growling and greedily lapped her blood as it dripped on to the ground. We managed to immobilize him with two big wooden forks and, while Pedro and Pablo held him down, I stepped inside the cage, tied the female's paws together with a thick liana and dragged the body out. Then the door closed once more upon the cub. I christened him Bouli-Bouli and gave him his first meal.

Following our usual procedure, we carried the dead jaguar down to the river, skinned her, cut up the rest of her body and flung the pieces into the water. Kenou pointed out how dangerous she would have been, for her milk had run dry. In this condition a female jaguar becomes terribly aggressive and is liable to attack even in day time. I felt less remorse for having killed her and devoted all my attention to the cub. After ten days or so, with great caution, I managed to put him on a home-made leash. When he was more or less trained to it we struck camp and he set off with us on the return journey to Pucalpa.

Jesus Garcia was astonished to see me appear one morning with my two *seringueiros* carrying bales of skins with which to settle his famous bill. From his expression I realized he had never expected to be paid. He was so pleased that he spontaneously offered me further credit and undertook to furnish supplies for the huge raft we were going to float down to Belem.

His 'sincerity' surprised me; yet I could see he wanted to let bygones be bygones. And I couldn't help feeling grateful, a few weeks later, for the judicious advice he gave me: 'Don't sell your skins at Iquitos, *Señor*. For such a large quantity, you'll need a special permit. Smuggle them across at night into Colombia or Brazil. I know a big merchant beyond Chimbote who'll buy your whole stock and pay you in cash.'

I felt I may as well trust him and so one morning, after spreading the rumour that we were going to prospect up north along the Maranon, we took our raft in tow and set off in the opposite direction down the Amazon.

As we approached Iquitos I stopped the motor and, adopting the smugglers' usual procedure, drifted silently in midstream. Then we had a stroke of luck: a storm broke just as the lights of the town began to appear. The thunder roared, the rain beat down, and I had no hesitation in starting the motor again. By the time the sun rose over the yellow water we were already miles away. But we still had to get past the frontier posts and Colombian customs house at Leticia. It was only when we were safely across the border that I was able to breathe more freely.

Beyond Chimbote I began to keep a sharp look-out, since the merchant's riverside house which Jesus Garcia had described could not be very far off. Presently a light flashed on the bank; I manoeuvred so as to come alongside at the given moment. I noticed a little *casa* overlooking a wooden jetty and called out. A man appeared and, without any sign of surprise at this nocturnal visit, led me up to the house. The owner stood outside, barefoot and in pyjamas. In one hand he held a hurricane-lamp, in the other a revolver. The exchange of words was brisk:

'I have some alligator skins to sell.'

'Come in, *Señor*.'

I entered and found myself in a big clean room furnished in mahogany.

'You have the skins with you, I suppose?'

'They're on my raft.'

146

'How many?'

'About four hundred.'

'My prices are fair. We'll clinch the deal when you've had some sleep. May I show you to your room?'

'I'd rather get back to the raft with my men.'

In the evening he examined the skins, sorting them carefully in various categories, congratulated me on their quality, and offered me a price that I considered more than handsome.

'You pay cash?'

'Naturally ...'

Thus the business was settled. That evening I accepted his hospitality and arranged with him for the return journey of Kenou and the two Indians. As for myself, I planned to make for Belem in the pirogue with Pedro and Pablo. But I never did, for my host offered to buy the pirogue as well, and also both motors. I saw no reason to refuse, and my two *seringueiros* and I completed our trip more comfortably by steamer.

A few weeks later I was in mid-Atlantic on my way back to Europe, rich from the proceeds of the hunting expedition and the sale of the pirogue. Every day I came and fed Bouli-Bouli, who was housed on deck in the dogs' cage. My heart went out to him, for after the freedom of the jungle I too felt caged.

21

Like my monkey on a previous visit, Bouli-Bouli proved to be a problem. How was one to live in Paris with a baby jaguar, however tame? I had chosen a hotel where the proprietor, an old Gabon hand, didn't mind my keeping my pet attached to a strong chain in the courtyard. But a few days later a worthy police inspector asked to see me.

'You're keeping a wild animal here!'

'My little jaguar?'

'Yes. He's dangerous, you must give him to the Zoo.'

'The Zoo? Not on your life!'

'I'll allow you two days to get rid of him.'

Once again I had an unexpected stroke of luck. By an odd coincidence the actor Teddy Michaud called on me that very evening: 'I hear you have a baby jaguar. I'd like to hire him.' A few weeks later Bouli-Bouli paraded proudly at an automobile *concours d'élégance* by the side of the actress Marthe Massine; and subsequently I saw him on the screen, in a totally absurd film in which he appeared in a harem with Teddy Michaud and plunged into a pool in the midst of the half-naked houris. A film star within a few months! I wished him a long career, unconfined and unleashed.

Europe, at all events, seemed very circumscribed to me. I found people had changed for the worse, and business appeared to be at a standstill. The only topic of conversation was Germany: *Mein Kampf*, Hitler, Nazi parades, the Maginot Line. French industrialists were forever sneering: 'The Germans are most inventive. They're trying to manufacture butter and edible fats from coal. They must either be raving mad or starving. Yet they want to make war!'

I went to Germany to see for myself. The country looked prosperous, business appeared to be booming, the factories were spotless, the workers well-fed and disciplined. The managers received me most amiably; they were extremely interested in my timber and were already dealing on a big scale with various French colonial firms. So, despite the rumours of war, money still talked! Yet behind all this order and efficiency there were warning signs: too many parades, too many flags, too many youths in uniform, too many photographs of Hitler. In such blind obedience and discipline I discerned the beginnings of slavery, a parody of true law and order. I left Germany with a number of contracts but determined to tread warily.

Back in France, at Nancy, I concluded my official mission and managed to interest the Ecole des Eaux et Forêts in the training of Peruvian executives. After an exchange of cables with the presidential palace at Lima, the French Government took action: two inspectors were officially appointed, one at Cayenne, the other at Toulouse, and put at the disposal of the Reccavaren brothers. I had at least succeeded in bridging the gap.

The more I saw of Europe, the more disappointed I became. There was no spirit of enterprise, no boldness. Even a businessman as reputable as Misraky (he was my last hope of financial backing) shook his head in despair: 'The rumours of war are increasingly alarming. Later perhaps ... You're in a strong position, but the general situation is too precarious ...' One morning, however, I received a letter from a Dr Kurt Weigelt of the Deutsche Bank und Discontgesellschaft – a complete stranger to me – asking me to call at the German Embassy. I arranged to meet him instead at the Hotel Astoria, so as to steer clear of the official services of Count Welczek, Hitler's ambassador to Paris.

Dr Weigelt arrived punctually at the rendezvous but asked me to come with him to a private house. He was a powerfully built man of about fifty, haughty and austere. I hesitated for a moment, then sat down beside him in a huge Mercedes. In the Boulevard de Courcelles the car drove through a porte-cochère and into an inner courtyard. Dr Weigelt invited me to step out and, using his own key, opened a tall ground-floor door giving on to some vast deserted offices. One room, right at the back, was luxuriously furnished. The German asked me to be seated and offered me a cigar, then came straight to the point: 'We'd like to buy your concession. Name your price.'

I told him my concession was not for sale. Whereupon the conversation went on in this vein:

'Think it over. Our price would be substantial.'

'I'm a forester. I like the life out there. I want this concession for myself.'

He smiled:

'Our agents weren't far wrong in the report they gave us as to your character. But couldn't we come to terms? We'd buy the business and you'd manage it.'

I then asked him why he was so keen on this particular concession. He replied that it was no secret: Germany had no colonies of her own and was interested in developing large forest zones.

'Count me out,' I said. 'I want to remain my own master.'

After selling the last of my nuggets and some diamonds which I had bought cheap at Belem, I had a nice little sum tucked away in my leather bag. I had failed to get financial backing but could now return to Peru with enough orders to start felling and to enable Peru, for the first time, to export her wealth from the Upper Amazon.

On the way, I disembarked at New York for a few days. I didn't like it. With its gimcrack skyscrapers, it seemed to be living out its final days as a civilized town. Everything was rushed, no one had time to spare, and the garish lights reminded me of a firework display.

One evening, at the Waldorf Astoria, I involuntarily overheard a conversation between three Canadians. They were talking about fishing:

'Cod's out! Shark's the thing!'

'Are you sure?'

'Sure, I'm sure! Vitamins are the great discovery of the century. A cod liver gives only 850 units of vitamins A to the gramme, and it's small. A shark has an enormous liver, yielding 30,000, 40,000, 100,000 units. So shark's the thing.'

'Maybe. But where do you fish?'

'In the Pacific, off the Galapagos.'

Then and there I changed my plans. I decided, before going on to Peru, to have a look at Ecuador. First thing in the morning, I booked my passage to Guayaquil. During the voyage I learnt that one of the islands in the Galapagos Archipelago still belonged perhaps to the King of France. I pictured myself, just for fun, locating it, confirming the ownership and planting the French flag there.

With its wooden buildings, rococo façades and wrought-iron grilles, Guayaquil was a town after my own heart: chock-a-block with tropical produce of every kind, every species of fruit, every foodstuff imaginable, which provided a blaze of colour under the sparkling sun. I rented a nice little apartment down by the harbour and started to look around for a boat.

I found what I wanted almost at once: a forty-tonner that would enable me to make a quick dash to the islands and then sail on to Callao and Lima. To make sure she was sea-worthy, I probed her timbers from deck to hold with the point of my knife, then went up to my apartment for a siesta before returning to clinch the deal.

On waking I had a shower, then came back in to the bedroom. I stopped dead and rubbed my eyes: there, on the floor, was my leather bag! ... I snatched it up: it had been slashed three times with a razor and was empty. My spare cash, a couple of nuggets I had kept for luck, two big diamonds and several sapphires, had all disappeared. The equivalent of about two hundred million old francs! I rushed round to the nearest police station. Luckily my wallet, in the hip pocket of my trousers, still contained a substantial sum; but my fortune and my Galapagos expedition had simply gone down the drain.

After being kept waiting for some time, I was received by the chief of the secret police, a lean brawny man with cold, piercing eyes. He listened to me, flanked by a couple of henchmen, and the more I talked the more ill at ease I felt in front of these three inscrutable and rather forbidding figures. My complaint was registered however, and next morning the local newspaper came out with the headlines: *A Frenchman Robbed of Jewels and Cash to the Value of 200,000 Dollars!*

Two days went by. No news. I went back to see the chief of police, and was curtly told he was away. In desperation I applied for an interview with the Governor himself; to my surprise it was granted. He was a pleasant, distinguished-looking man with thick white hair. In spite of the heat he wore a well-cut black serge suit. He spoke perfect French, but didn't appear very disturbed by the theft of my fortune. He talked about French culture, the Paris theatre:

'Sarah Bernhardt ... admirable! What an actress! I remember ... one evening ... Edmond Rostand .. '

I did my best to keep him to the point, but he kept reverting to his blasted Sarah Bernhardt, her gestures, her voice, her pearls, her bath-tub. I couldn't contain myself a moment longer and burst out: 'Yes, but what about my money?'

He looked at me as though I had been impertinent, and simply went on: 'I love France. Ah, Paris. Now there's a real capital! ...'

It was enough to make one explode. I dashed out in case I did.

The next day I found a hastily scribbled message under my door: 'Beware, Señor, our thieves are powerful.' What was I to deduce from this? I went back to the Governor, who mercifully spared me his memories of Sarah Bernhardt and came straight to the point: 'Our policemen are wizards; they've tracked down the thieves. Can you tell me the origin of your precious stones?'

I replied that I was a tourist in Ecuador, my papers were in order and I could see no reason for this sort of question. He looked embarrassed and finally confessed that the chief of the secret police himself had prompted him to ask.

I dashed round to the chief, who went on in the same vein:

'We're on the tracks of the thieves, but the sum involved is substantial. Can you participate financially in the investigation?'

I was flabbergasted, and refused categorically.

'What proof is there that these stolen jewels and money belong to you?' he continued.

'Let's not reverse the roles. I'm the plaintiff and victim. I'd rather not be treated as a suspect.'

He went no further. But that very evening another anonymous letter provided me with further information: 'Don't pursue the matter. The thief is the chief of police in person. His gang have just stolen a store of whisky belonging to the Bank of Guayaquil. You're not in a strong position.'

I didn't know where to turn for help. If even bankers came to terms with this gang, it was obviously going to be difficult for me to fight it by myself.

The chief of police brought things to a head by calling on me in person. 'I'm giving you a friendly warning,' he said. 'It's indispensable for you to prove the origin of your stolen goods. Otherwise the case will turn against you. Try and show a little understanding, Señor.'

I realized I would have to act quickly. No sooner had he left than I decided to move out of my apartment. On returning with some stevedores and a cart for my luggage, I found a third letter which was even more explicit: 'Get out of the country at once. You're in danger of your life. If you don't leave you'll be killed.'

I moved out in double-quick time and went to ground in a shabby little hotel where I chose a room looking out on to the street and with a door that could be locked and bolted. There was also a restaurant on the premises so that I didn't have to risk going out for meals. But I still had to find some means of leaving the country.

I put on my thinking cap, sent word to a friend and thus learnt that an Italian boat, the *San Henrique*, was leaving in three days' time for Callao. But the Governor now refused to grant me an exit visa. This was the limit. I dashed round to see him, brandishing my anonymous letters:

'What's wrong with your rotten town? I want to get out of here.'

He went white in the face with anger, but he obviously wanted to see the last of me.

'All right, you'll have your visa in half an hour. However, you must report to the secret police before your departure. You're sailing on ... ?'

'A Grace Line boat, in three days' time.'

I had given false information about the boat and therefore had no wish to report to the secret police. As soon as I was given my visa, I notified the captain of the *San Henrique* who arranged for two of his sailors to come and fetch my luggage from the hotel after dark. Then I left an envelope in my room addressed to the manager, containing a sum of money that would more than cover what I owed, and went down to dinner.

At ten o'clock in the evening the dining-room emptied and I sat down in the lobby to wait. Eleven o'clock struck: still no sign of the sailors. The porter was already nodding in his little lodge. A clock kept ticking away the minutes. I couldn't account for the delay and grew more and more impatient. I gazed in turn at the walls, the carpet, the ceiling. I got up and went and hung my panama hat on a peg in the dining-room. Midnight struck, and each stroke was like a knife thrust. The whole hotel was fast asleep; so was the street outside. I pictured the boat leaving without me. I waited and waited. I was about to give up when I saw two half-caste Indians on the pavement. I rushed towards them:

'You're from the *San Henrique*?'

'*Si, Señor.*'

'Come in. Quick! And don't make a sound.'

We crept past the porter. I gave them my luggage to carry and told them to wait by the stairs until I signalled that the coast was clear. Then I went to the porter's lodge:

'I think I've left my hat in the dining-room. Could you go and see, *Señor*?'

No sooner had he gone than I signalled to the two Indians who slipped out and disappeared into the dark. I thanked the porter for bringing back my hat and waited till he sat down again to resume his interrupted sleep. Then I in my turn dashed down to the harbour. The silhouette of the boat stood out against the wharf; the engine was turning over. The two Indians scuttled nimbly across the narrow plank which served as a gangway. I followed suit. I felt a reassuring slap on the back from the captain. He had heard all about my adventure and was delighted to be helping in my escape.

One morning, after a week's leisurely sailing, the *San Henrique* anchored in the port of Callao. I collected my luggage together, said good-bye to the captain and drove to Lima in a taxi. I was glad to see the Hotel Bolivar again, and above all Colonel Reccavaren. He spread his arms in a wide embrace, but his eyes and voice were rueful:

'Don Fernando, you're back, but look ...'

I read the telegrams and papers he showed me: France and England had just declared war on Germany. In one second all the orders I had collected became null and void, and my project for exporting to Europe was reduced to a Utopian dream. Yet it didn't occur to me to feel discouraged. On the contrary, I tried to revive the colonel's spirits:

'Didn't you once tell me that Peru was short of wood and you had to buy it from North America? An absurd situation. Anyway now there's a war on, the United States probably won't be able to provide you any longer. Why don't you open up your eastern province and get the wood from there?'

'Are you dreaming?' he said rather sharply.

'I could do it, with your help.'

My confidence finally convinced him:

'Go and see my brother, come back with a detailed plan.'

Meanwhile I heard some more bad news: Rosita, my lovely spy, no longer lived in Lima. She had moved to the Argentine, and her absence affected me cruelly in this town where everything reminded me of her. I decided to bury myself in my work.

Next day I went round to the Ministry to see the colonel's brother, the engineer and economics expert, who was enthusiastic about my project. His secretary, Arturo, produced some maps for us, then donned his little spectalcles and stood up like a school-master about to deliver a lecture :

'If we have to choose somewhere, the obvious area is Satipo – here, where the mule track ends. There's no road. But for years we've been trying to connect Lima to this isolated, this god-forsaken hole.'

'Why god-forsaken ?'

There was an embarrassed silence.

'I'll leave you now,' said Reccavaren. 'Arturo, don't discourage our pioneer.'

He disappeared. Arturo took me by the arm, as though to implore me.

'Don't go to Satipo. It's a dreadful place ! Hundreds of poor wretches have left their bones there. We still haven't managed to complete the road across the double cordillera, from Concepcion to Pampa Hermosa. We've had to dynamite our way through solid rock. Prisoners, priests, emigrants, Negroes, half-castes have gone out there in the hope that one day the road will reach them, and they've found themselves cut off, victims of nature and an evil shadow.'

'What evil shadow ?'

He refused to explain and merely said : 'If you go there you'll see for yourself.'

The more I looked at the map, the less crazy and impossible did the project seem. Arturo's remarks merely whetted my curiosity. When Reccavaren reappeared, I told him I wanted to reconnoitre Satipo straight away.

He smiled at my determination :

'Arturo will give you a special permit and you can have an official truck. I'll just scribble a letter of introduction for you to my *compadre*, *Señor* Urco, who lives at Pampa Hermosa. Be sure and call on him.'

I left Lima next day with a minimum of luggage and arms. The truck whisked me away from the fleshpots of the coast, the elegant villas of Miraflores. I had shaken off my depression and discontent, and had no eyes for anything but the cordillera which my *cholo* driver seemed eager to negotiate at full speed. The road zig-zagged up the imposing mountain face. We sped along the edge of multi-coloured precipices, the rock varying in tone from pink to purple, and I gazed in admiration at the royal blue and mauve of more distant heights with condors flying above them. From time to time we passed squat little women in coarse green skirts walking in groups of eight or ten – descendants of the Incas, my driver explained. These *serranas* were in fact pure Indians from the Andes, with firm, finely chiselled features, and a constitution capable of tolerating the murderous altitude.

We crossed the first rocky barrier and started heading downhill towards Concepcion, an unexpected oasis in a huge valley covered with broom and eucalyptus. Here we halted for the night. Next morning there were further crests to tackle. We climbed to over sixteen thousand feet and the dust from the unmetalled road transformed us into earthenware statues. Every so often we came across caravaners, in striped ponchos and phrygian bonnets, driving strings of heavily laden llamas.

'They're carrying coca,' my driver told me.

And indeed I was conscious of a strange pungent smell at each of these encounters. Hundreds of kilos of leaves are transported in this way, destined to provide a sort of miracle drug, a staple diet for the poor Andeans who chew it to alleviate their hunger.

Beyond the pass, the road began to dip towards Pampa Hermosa in a series of zig-zag bends overlooking dark gorges where giant cacti grew cheek by jowl with bamboo. At six thousand feet the edge of the track became a blaze of colour from the giant geraniums and wild fuschias. The whole landscape altered before our eyes; the first stunted trees heralded the nearby zone of lichen and brushwood. It was warmer down here and all the perfumes of the forest rose to meet us.

Suddenly the driver slammed on the brakes and switched off the engine.

'*El derrumbe!*'

'What is it?'

'Look!'

A few hundred yards further on, in an impressive, almost total silence, as though plants and animals alike had sensed the danger, the whole forest with its giant trees still standing upright was slowly subsiding into the valley.

I was mesmerized, unable at first to believe that an entire forest could thus be on the move. And yet the green, muddy avalanche started gathering momentum. For centuries the thin layer of topsoil had held firm; now, undermined by the rains, it was being swept

156

away by the heavy load of vegetation. The landslide accelerated to a fatal speed, and the valley and gorges reverberated with the shattering crash of the trees and the monstrous thunder of the rocks.

My driver went off to look for help, cautiously working his way round the lower edge of the avalanche of mud, rocks and trees. Presently he came back with a mule and a little black horse, accompanied by an Indian of a type new to me, a villainous-looking *serrano*. His jaws were munching coca, his purplish lips bore the mark of the drug and he peered at me with a mixture of intensity and lassitude.

My driver no doubt thought I needed reassurance:

'The road's blocked. This man will act as your guide. Don't worry, he knows the country, the forest. I'll come back and wait for you here in two weeks' time. Good luck! See you soon!'

The *serrano* loaded the mule, but insisted on carrying my leather suitcase on his own back. Leading the horse by the bridle, I followed him downhill towards the muddy morass. He kept glancing back at me. Beyond the avalanche, I mounted and drew level with him:

'What's your name?'

'*Napoleon, Señor. Para servir.*'

Napoleon at my service! I felt I was dreaming.

Thanks to him, we reached Pampa Hermosa just as darkness was falling. *Señor* Urco was waiting for us with a lantern outside his front door. He was dressed in coarse woollen clothes, with a big threadbare hat on his head and a chopper hanging at his waist. I greeted him and gave him my letter of introduction. He read it, put it away in his pocket and asked me to dismount so that he might welcome me with the traditional *abrazo*.

We talked together until late at night and, as I told him my plans, he looked sad. 'I can't stop you going to Satipo,' he said. 'But do be careful of these wretched *colonos*, those disillusioned pioneers. They're simply wallowing in their own misery.'

I asked him about the evil shadow to which everyone kept alluding in veiled terms.

'I can't tell you,' he replied. 'Go there and see. Keep your eyes open and your mouth shut. I'll let you have Napoleon, who knows the place, and I'll provide you with mounts. It's appalling to think of the colossal effort of those pioneers toiling away for years in the hope of a road that has never reached them. The result is poverty, disease, ill-feeling. I too once believed in Satipo,' he concluded, shaking his head. 'You'll see the big fly-wheel of my saw-mill outside. But I'm better off than most. At least I own my land and I grow coca.'

His wife, a superb Indian woman, asked us to come in to dinner, and afterwards I went to bed in a bare room with a wooden floor where hundreds of sacks of coca awaited the next caravan. At one moment, in the middle of the night, I woke up suddenly and drew my revolver. When I lit the lamp to see who on earth could be chattering away in such bad Spanish, I saw a parrot which appeared to be talking in its sleep.

We set off at dawn next day, Napoleon mounted on another old mule, myself still on the little black horse. The track leading down towards Satipo was not practicable for motor traffic, but it seemed quite firm and I saw it could easily be widened.

For our midday meal we halted between the 'toes' (roots) of a superb *oje*, a type of ficus yielding a milky sap which cures fever and destroys hook worm, while its bark is shredded and used for making loincloths. From a packet of leaves Napoleon produced a huge roast duck, a gift from *Señor* Urco, which we washed down with *aguardiente*.

A few hours later we reached a clearing, with some sickly plantations of maize and bananas bordered by some shabby huts. I noticed faces peering at us through the slats. 'Libertad,' Napoleon whispered.

So this place was called 'Liberty'!

Towards five in the evening he pointed to a little iron bridge a few hundred yards ahead: the entrance to Satipo. I tightened my belt, checked my Parabellum and *escopeta*, crossed the bridge and found myself in a little square with a flag-staff, some wooden shanties, groups of men in broad-brimmed hats dozing outside them, a modest general store, several hitching-posts – a cowboy village, in fact.

Before I even dismounted, three men had risen to their feet. Their features were drawn with hardship and malnutrition. They all wore choppers at their waists and stared at me warily. Napoleon arrived in time to reassure them: 'Don't be frightened, this gentleman is my boss.' I went into the store, but the men prowled round suspiciously for some time before resuming their siesta.

'Where can I get a glass of *aguardiente*?' I asked.

'Here, *Señor*. My name's Quiroz and I'm the only shopkeeper in this god-forsaken place. May I venture to ask who you are?'

There was no arrogance in his tone and I trusted him instinctively. He led me along a bamboo passage leading to a little garden fragrant with flamboyants, banana-trees and frangipani, and after he had produced the drink and a couple of packing-cases for us to sit on, I told him why I was here. He listened to me attentively, keeping his head lowered. But from time to time he peered at me intently, and his sickly face then betrayed the despair I had already seen in *Señor* Urco's expression.

When I had finished, he went out to make sure no one was listening and then started talking in his turn. Within an hour I knew more than anyone in Lima about the curse hanging over Satipo. 'We're at the end of our tether, *Señor*,' he explained. 'With you, I'm no longer frightened to speak. All the others would tell you the same, if they dared: Martig the Swiss, the Hungarian Tacatch, the Indians themselves. We could have made a success of this place. The soil was good; we had any amount of enthusiasm. We all believed in our future prosperity when we saw the first harvests, the forest reclaimed and planted with banana-trees. In spite of the rains the government sent some engineers and a doctor. *Señor* Urco set up a saw-mill at Pampa Hermosa and sold us splendid timber for our houses. The road was even opened to small trucks. And then the tyrant appeared.'

'The tyrant?' I echoed.

'Yes. I hardly dare utter his name.'

So that was it! At last I had my finger on the evil shadow behind all those cautious allusions. I urged Quiroz to spill the beans, to get it off his chest. Not without reticence he told me the identity of the 'tyrant' who had delayed the acquisition of title deeds, sabotaged the land reclamation, prevented official investigations, and gradually brought the *colonos* under his sway. Then, one day, the last agronomic engineer had been recalled to Lima. Although enquiries were made, no one was ever able to discover why work on the road had stopped in the middle of the dry season. The maize had rotted in tons, the oranges and tangerines had dried up on the trees, insects and diseases had completed the damage. Even now it was still the 'tyrant's' deadly hand that doled out the rare title deeds.

'What's he aiming at?' I asked.

'He wants to get rid of the original *colonos* and that's why he represents us to the authorities at Lima as drunkards and idlers. If you have any power, any means of protection, help us. And I only hope the others will confide in you as I have.'

I spent that night with him and next morning went off to visit his neighbours.

Martig, the Swiss, was prematurely aged; his face was ravaged, worried and careworn; but a broad grin spread over it as soon as I addressed him in French. He asked me to stay to lunch in his cosy little house and what he told me cast an even more tragic light on the situation at Satipo:

'I'm doomed, Monsieur, and I know it. I only keep alive for the sake of my wife and children. I shall pay a heavy price for this struggle, for I've worked myself to death trying to hold out against the wild animals, the armies of ants, the diseases. I'm in a fairly strong position, being an agronomic engineer and owning my own land. All the others will be driven out by Pancho de la Cruz.'

He was racked by a fit of coughing. When it was over he offered to show me round his domain. I soon realized the tremendous efforts he must have made. He even had a herd of cows: Holstein cows which he had had sent from Ronatullo and which had cost him a fortune. But his wife and children owed their health to them.

'And look over there: my pigs. They eat all the fruit since we can't sell it because there's no road. Everything grows here, but what a waste!'

I began to see what was needed in Satipo: capital funds, a land reclamation programme, and a road practicable for five-ton trucks. When I said so to Tacatch, the Hungarian, his careworn eyes started sparkling and he took my hand and cried: 'You're our last chance!'

'I'll see about the road if you help me,' I assured him.

'How can we help?'

'Tell all your colleagues that I want to buy your trees. I shall fell them professionally.'

'That gangster Don Pancho won't let you.'

'I'll deal with him.'

He looked me straight in the eye:

'God be with you, Don Fernando. I'll send my kids round all the neighbours this evening.'

'Just tell me where I can find this famous tyrant of yours.'

'Three hours' ride from here.'

I shook hands with him and said:

'I'll go and see him tomorrow morning.'

22

At first light, freshly shaved and as smartly dressed as possible, I set off for the tyrant's house. Napoleon led the way, opening up the track, thus enabling me to devote my attention to the wealth of the forest. Shortly before noon we reached a clearing, in the middle of which stood a neat white American-style ranch-house. Half a dozen cows grazed on the thick grass, and there were stables and poultry-yards behind the building. I dug my spurs into my horse and galloped up the drive, eager to come to grips with the enemy.

I was in for a surprise: on the balcony stood a handsome man dressed in a smart white suit. His lean frame, piercing eyes and fine features contributed to his natural elegance. I introduced myself:

'I'm Don Fernando. A Frenchman. Your government has authorized me to prospect in Satipo.'

'Pancho de la Cruz. An engineer. What can I do for you?'

'The minister suggested I call on you.'

'Please come in.'

I dismounted and climbed the steps. It seemed a far cry from the Maltese grocer and his scruffy little gang. The enemy had changed in nature and in scope. La Cruz led the way into a large living-room-cum-office, and I noticed the butt of his Colt protruding from its raw-hide holster. He sat down behind a huge desk, leaving me to find a chair for myself, then crossed his legs and peered at me sardonically. He was obviously waiting for me to open fire. I therefore took the initiative, remembering that this bandit with the face of a Spanish grandee was in cahoots with the authorities in Lima.

'Your superiors have decided to make use of my abilities as a forester,' I said. 'They commissioned me to reconnoitre Satipo, which has impressed me most favourably: mahogany, cedar, camphor in abundance. One ought to be able to cut down thousands of trees here and reclaim the forest for agriculture. If the *colonos* sell me their standing timber, they'll find themselves not only with the ready cash they lack but also large tracts of arable land.'

Pancho de la Cruz didn't turn a hair. I delivered a thrust which I felt was bound to unsettle him:

'Of course, work on the road will have to be resumed. Some of the *colonos* say it was stopped after your arrival here?'

He remained absolutely inscrutable. Not a flicker of an eyelid, not a twitch of impatience. Snakes are often endowed with this sort of immobility. I outlined my programme – a couple of weeks in which to prospect and submit my report to the government.

'I shall probably advise them to open up the road. Have you any objection?'

'None whatever.'

'What is your honest opinion, *Señor?*'

'Probably the opposite of your own,' he replied in a firm, ruthless tone. 'But you're a professional forester. Do as you see fit. I shall take the necessary steps. Would you like a couple of my men to act as guides?'

'No thank you, *Señor*. I've already chosen my assistants.'

I stood up. He looked me straight in the eye and it was clear to us both that we were now engaged in a fight to the death. It was therefore pointless to shake hands.

As I made my way back to Tacatch's house, I had to admit that the tyrant's cruel and at the same time captivating aristocratic face concealed an even more dangerous determination, an even more perverse intelligence than I had imagined. Napoleon had instinctively divined the hazards confronting us and we rode back together in silence. It was very hot. We came across a little stream of reddish water. As he dismounted and plunged his face into it to cool off, I heard a slight rustle on my left and was horrified to see a *surucucu*, one of the largest poisonous snakes in the world, heading straight for the water. In a flash I emptied my *escopeta* into the triangular head. Napoleon sprang to his feet, drew his chopper and sliced the writhing body in two. When we had recovered from the shock we looked at each other and laughed; both of us felt we had liquidated the tyrant!

I soon realized Tacatch had not wasted any time. The *colonos* had assembled at Quiroz's and, still better news, a Campa Indian from the Rio Pangoa was expected to arrive that very evening: 'He might be useful to you.' Apparently he came here from time to time because he trusted the inhabitants. His name was Akrim and his tribe lived on the edge of the river. His personal history partook of the miraculous. Abducted in childhood by a rival tribe, he and his brother Kinchokre had been taken into the forest for a ritual sacrifice. They were about to be burnt alive when a Spanish missionary appeared at the head of a little expedition. In a flash the Indians vanished into the jungle, abandoning their victims. The two boys had thus been saved and were subsequently taught Spanish at the mission, until they escaped one day and went home to the Rio Pangoa.

'If you can get Akrim to take you there, maybe you'll find more trees,' Tacatch added.

Akrim arrived at nightfall, with some wild honey. Sprightly, gentle, rather frail-looking, he listened to me with increasing interest and offered to guide me and Napoleon next day to the upper forest where his tribe lived. Without him it would have been impossible for us to find our way through the successive barriers of rattan hedges and short spiky palms. Any prospector would have given up at this hostile and impenetrable vegetation. But we pressed on, despite the unbearable heat to which our guide seemed impervious. After an hour we came out on to a lovely palm plantation large enough to supply an entire oil factory. 'Our store-room,' Akrim explained. 'The first of several. We still have further barriers to cross before reaching my brother Kinchokre, but you're now in our territory. No white has ever been'here before.'

He went over to a felled palm-tree in which some arrows were embedded, and from this hiding-place produced a bow, a little bag and a purple tunic. Then he slipped out of his shirt and trousers and donned his proper Indian dress before proceeding. During another halt, in another palm plantation as large and closely guarded by hedges as the first, he told us something about his Indian kinsmen and said:

'No white man will ever go beyond this point, except you. For on this spot two Indians were killed by a *caouchero* who's still alive and belongs heart and soul to Pancho de la Cruz.'

'What's his name?'

'Vilarette. He wanted to expropriate our palm plantations, to which he had been guided by an Indian woman. Two of our scouts stopped him here and ordered him back. Without a word, he shot one of them dead. Before he could fire again, the other one dashed off to warn his kinsmen. When they returned, Vilarette's woman was lying on the ground, her head split open with a blow from a machete. He hoped, on getting back to Satipo, to make the white *colonos* believe that the Campas had killed her and that a punitive expedition ought to be mounted against them. But friend Tacatch knew Vilarette, he guessed the truth, and so the trick didn't work. Ever since then we have been waiting for the hour of vengeance and, for fear of Indian reprisals, the tyrant has respected our frontiers and Vilarette has never dared violate them again.

'We must move on,' he concluded. 'It's not so far now.'

He uttered the throaty cry of the jaguar, deliberately, three times, and repeated it again and again as we advanced: 'I'm notifying my brother Kinchokre that I'm not alone. All the Campas must be warned. I'm not entitled to act without their permission. Now they know. We'll wait for them here.'

Napoleon built a fire on which to roast an *agouti*, a rodent with a thick coat and flesh like a rabbit. A smell of cinnamon rose from the flames. Without knowing it, Napoleon had come upon a fine stock of balata wood. I realized the Campas were still masters of an exceptionally rich region.

During the siesta hour I watched in admiration as Akrim put on his war-paint. From his woven bag he took out a bamboo sheath and drew some red and dark-blue lines on his face with a thin blade dipped in *rucu* paste. He now seemed ready for his meeting with his brother. 'Kinchokre is cleverer than all of us. He can read in a man's eyes,' he told me proudly.

'If I came and settled here – and I'm a rich man – would the Campas come and work with me?' I asked.

'The Campas lead a happy life in their forest, they don't need other men. Kinchokre alone may know. He says the *colonos* are liars and poor.'

'Would you agree to cutting down big trees?'

'Perhaps, if in exchange we received *escopetas* to kill the jaguars, ant-eaters and big anacondas.'

Suddenly he sprang to his feet. The stark-naked Indians were advancing towards us without my having heard a sound. Akrim parleyed with them, then they disappeared after holding out their open hands. Each of them carried a large cutlass in a sheath strung round his waist.

A few moments later Kinchokre appeared, clad in a faded blue shirt and trousers. He exchanged a few words with his brother, then came towards me. Slim, rather short, with firm features, he had 'dressed' for our meeting, not wishing to appear for the first time in front of me in Campa garb.

'I'm Kinchokre,' he said. 'They call me "Killer" because I organized the defence of the Campas.'

Whether savage or civilized, a bush-whacker or a business tycoon, this man would have been a leader anywhere. I realized at once that what he expected from me was frankness and plain-speaking. Acquainted in his youth with whites, he was able to discern their failings. Responsible for his kinsmen who were too often victims of the *colonos*, who in their turn were too poor to be able to keep their word, he had opted for the shelter of the jungle and complete isolation. I felt he was summing me up and a smile must have flitted across my face; no doubt he was aware that at this moment, confronted with the gravity of his own features, I was thinking of my encounter with the Piros. Dimly I perceived how my long months in the jungle with Kenou and my apparently useless hunting expeditions had prepared me, without my realizing it, for this moment.

I heard myself reply in a voice I hardly recognized. The words came of their own accord. It was as though I had shed my white skin. I felt I had been here for thousands of years, naked, a child, a brother to all men, as I told Kinchokre of my dream for Satipo.

After a long silence he looked me straight in the eye and told me where there were large quantities of cedars, mahoganies and *huara-caspi*. Then he added: 'If you come back and if you keep your word, I'll be notified. You will then see me appear in Satipo itself. According to the advice I am given and the discussions I have with the elders, either you won't see me again or else you will have Campa Indians to work with you. Akrim, guide this white man; take him to see the trees I mentioned and protect him. *Adios.*'

We had five days in which to explore the jungle and note the quantity and extent of the stands. This entailed marching over ten hours a day, counting the trees on the way. Akrim and Napoleon quickly understood the system: one tree, one twig. And in the evening, as we sat round the fire, I would add up the total, to the great joy of my two novice prospectors. At every halt Akrim would leave us for a moment and reappear infallibly with a couple of wild pheasants and some palm wine. He explained that throughout the region his tribe possessed secret stores and were fully conversant with the habits of the local wild life. On the last night I fell asleep happy in the knowledge that I had discovered an absolute gold mine: thirty-two thousand trees between thirty and fifty metres tall, and sometimes over six in diameter.

I could have pressed on further; but I thought of *Señor* Urco, who had lent me Napoleon, and the Fomento driver who must already have set off to meet me at our rendezvous. So I packed some fifty samples of wood into several rice bags and we started back. On the way we killed an impressive number of coral snakes, whose poison kills within a minute. But despite these hazards we reached the little square of Satipo safe and sound.

Quiroz came up and I asked him to circulate the following information for the benefit of the population: 1. I had contacted the Campa Indians and they had not been hostile. 2. The quantity of trees in their jungle was worth over three hundred thousand dollars. 3. I expected the *colonos* to sell me every stand of timber on the land they had not yet reclaimed. From Quiroz's enthusiastic embrace I knew that he would do the job properly and I was thus able to move off again at dawn. I presented Akrim with two machetes, two long knives and a length of cotton cloth; then I mounted my little black horse, as eager as Napoleon to get back to civilization and determined to take immediate action.

The mule was almost invisible under the bags of samples, as we climbed towards Pampa Hermosa. I wanted to reach *Señor* Urco's old saw-mill before nightfall. After a short siesta, therefore, I urged Napoleon on. I didn't want us to be caught unawares on the track. Natural caution or intuition? I don't know. But as we advanced, wending our way between the rocks, I felt rather uneasy.

Suddenly a shot rang out, reverberating in a series of echoes. I thought it must be some hunter or other, but a second shot struck the cast-iron cooking-pot attached to my saddle. I spurred my horse and it leapt forward. There was a third shot and I flung myself on to the ground. Thinking I had been killed, Napoleon flung up his arms and yelled:

'Mi patron es muerto! Patron! Patron!'

I lay inert deliberately. Total silence ensued. The unknown marksman must have skedaddled, confident he had scored a bull's eye.

An hour later, to my great relief, we got back to *Señor* Urco's and I gave him an account of our adventure.

'You're sure it wasn't an *escopeta*?' Urco asked.

'Look at the cooking-pot, you can see for yourself. It was a carbine.'

'Pancho de la Cruz is the only man around here who owns one. It's a Winchester. There's no doubt about it: he wants to put paid to you.'

Now I knew what to expect from the tyrant. No doubt he had sent Vilarette to ambush me. During the drive back to Lima I had no time to study the landscape, I was too busy trying to work out the next step Pancho de la Cruz was likely to take in the hope of thwarting my plans.

When I reached the Hotel Bolivar I fell into bed, but didn't have much of a sleep. Early in the morning the telephone woke me and a strange voice, in a disguised tone, issued this anonymous warning: 'Don Pancho de la Cruz will be in Lima tomorrow. He is preceded by a courier who is representing you as a bandit and trouble-maker. Apparently, you have sown terror in Satipo and stolen some mules. Take care.'

I decided to go straight round to the ministry, knowing to my cost what a powerful weapon calumny can be. From the colonel's attitude I realized at once that the rumours had already taken effect.

'Let's be frank, Monsieur.'

His voice sounded icy and I noticed he had stopped calling me 'Don Fernando'. Before I could reply, he went on:

'We build the road, we start a forestry business, we give you a development permit. Fine. But what do you contribute? A saw-mill will be needed, not to mention a fleet of trucks and financial backing. I'm afraid you haven't the necessary funds.'

'That's true, but I'll find them. If you can vouch for the road, I'll see to the rest.'

'You're up against it. The Chamber of Deputies is hostile to the principle of your concession. You'll have to prove your worth.'

'I shall.'

I started dashing round Lima in search of a rapid solution, as though the tyrant's accusations, the rumours, were a gang of killers at my heels. I had to protect myself, safeguard my project, somehow find the money, the trucks, the saw-mill ... Suddenly I had a brainwave – Victor Marie, a Belgian agronomic engineer, who had been appointed senior administrative officer. I rang him up and he came round at once: 'A saw-mill? You want a saw-mill? Go to the Calle de Francia. No, better still, I'll take you!'

As we drove there in his superb American car, he explained: 'Seven years ago a Japanese turned up. He was very rich and started a big saw-mill; but the logs came from Iquitos, were floated down the Amazon, and made their way here via Panama. Was it because of this long, roundabout journey? Bad organization? Who knows? Came a time when there were no more logs. So the Japanese had no timber for his mill. One morning his bank informed him that his account was overdrawn. He committed hara-kiri in his villa. At noon – too late! – they rang again and said it had been a mistake! ...'

We reached a vast open area surrounded by walls. A watchman let us in. I couldn't believe my eyes. As though in a fairy-tale, the machines lay slumbering in their coating of dust – strippers, vertical saws, planes. A huge slide-bridge stood out against the sky. Some rails led to a railway line. Granted, it all needed a bit of dusting and a touch of oil! But everything seemed ready to start up again at the stroke of a wand, as though by magic. The Japanese had even equipped himself with splendid Guillet saws. A French make in Lima! I felt I had taken on a new lease of life. Infected by my enthusiasm, Victor Marie hastened to explain: 'The saw-mill was put up for sale and Augusto Benavides Canseco was the only buyer. He's the cousin and brother-in-law of the President, although he belongs to the Opposition. Would you like me to approach him on your behalf? It'll be easy, he's a clever, civilized man.'

How could I not accept? Within a few days we had agreed to go into partnership: Augusto Benavides provided the saw-mill, I would contribute the funds and the timber. I still had to find the trucks and convince the banks.

Next morning the telephone rang and the strange disguised voice delivered another message: 'Don Pancho de la Cruz has not confined himself to following you to Lima. He has turned the pioneers at Satipo against you. That's where you're being attacked now.' The warning was so brief that for a moment I thought it was a practical joke.

An idea then occurred to me, so absurd that I couldn't resist it: why not dash back to Satipo, make my presence felt, show them all that I was alive and prepared for a fight to the death? But how was I to get there? By car? I couldn't afford it. Besides, since the landslide the road was out of commission beyond Pampa Hermosa.

Another brain-wave, and a few hours later I had the perfect

vehicle: a powerful Harley-Davidson and sidecar. And, in front of the outraged porter of the Hotel Bolivar, I loaded on to it a tool chest, spare cans of petrol, my mosquito net and arms, then swung into the saddle and roared off.

My appearance on the little square, heralded by the noise of my exhaust, caused a sensation. Thinking it was a plane, everyone was looking up at the sky when I arrived in a cloud of dust. Their faces went blank with surprise. Quiroz flung his arms round me. I had covered the distance in two days and demonstrated that Satipo was not cut off. I learnt that Vilarette had indeed launched a campaign to discredit me immediately after my departure. But most of the *colonos* had seen through it.

Two hours later the entire population knew about my arrival. Martig, Tacatch and the Tante brothers arrived, barefoot as usual; and that evening, in Quiroz's garden, in the heady atmosphere of the tropical night, a ceremony took place. By the dim light of a hurricane-lamp, in the deep shadows cast by the mango and banana trees, the six of us took a solemn oath that from now on we would form the initial nucleus of overt resistance to the tyrant. We swore to stand firm against the man who had caused the ruin or death of so many pioneers. We undertook to restore the confidence of the survivors. The news spread during the night, reviving the spirits of this handful of desolate *colonos*. I was able to leave again, happy to have heeded the anonymous voice.

As soon as I was back in Lima I found that my partner had likewise been busy. The board of directors had been formed and two experts had drawn up estimates for putting the saw-mill into working order; according to them, we would be able to start operating in a couple of months. 'On the other hand, there's bad news from the bank, my friend. *Señor* de la Cruz has cut the ground from under your feet. He has cast doubt on the Satipo timber. The bankers are now wary about the whole business. What can you do?'

'Fight back! Provide evidence!'

I was furious. At all costs I had to overcome the bankers' distrust, once and for all. My bags of samples ought to convince them. But, as I knew to my cost, a financier is not a technician. Again I applied for help to Victor Marie: again he provided the answer: 'Engineer Bert. Come round here at once. I'm going to take you to the Caproni factory.'

This Italian firm specialized in aircraft built of laminated wood.

So it naturally possessed a well-equipped laboratory for analysing the material used in the construction of its machines. Engineer Bert, another timber enthusiast, accepted my samples and undertook to submit them to a detailed test, accompanied by an official testimonial for each species that might be of industrial interest. I remained with him for four days, during which thirty-five of my samples were given certificates. As I left the factory I felt my two bags were worth their weight in gold. And when, a few hours later, I deposited my blocks of pink cedar, mahogany and rosewood on the desk of a Lima banker and showed him the Caproni testimonials, I was gratified to hear him apologize: 'I had my doubts. But no longer. In the circumstances I can advance you half the capital requested.'

Only half. Again my hopes were dashed. It would now be impossible for me to buy the eighteen trucks I needed; in fact I would have barely enough money to cover the cost of the logging camps, forestry equipment, labour and maintenance of the saw-mill. But I couldn't afford to hesitate. I accepted.

Don Pancho de la Cruz, however, was still on the war-path, as yet another anonymous telephone message showed: 'The tyrant knows that the bank is backing you. He's now trying to get his own men appointed to the Water and Forest department you are going to create. Act quickly.'

Within a week I had found the means of ensuring the absolute probity of the Water and Forest staff. I had contacted the air force pilot, Lieutenant Gal'Lino, and with his agreement applied for his immediate transfer to supreme command of the Peruvian Forestry Corps to which he appointed his own assistants. The tyrant thus had his guns spiked.

Like the descent from the Cordillera after a long hard climb, everything now seemed easy and help began to pour in from every direction. A certain Cuisano undertook to negotiate the exchange of some old Decauville rails in the saw-mill against a new truck (he was a genuine seer; he had dreamed about these tons of unused rails, had looked for them on waking up, and come across them lying in a corner). I found a priest, Padre Santa Maria, who agreed to join us in due course, depending on permission from his bishop. The village of Cajamarca, tucked away in the Andes, volunteered to provide two hundred and fifty labourers to build the road or fell the trees; and their leader, Jesus, presented me with a white horse which was to be delivered direct to Satipo ...

Everything now seemed ready for our departure. I loaded the truck with stores and equipment, and was making final arrangements for our move when the telephone rang. The voice was disguised, as usual, but sounded more impulsive: 'Don Fernando, I congratulate you. You've put up a good fight. Good luck in Satipo!'

Some almost imperceptible inflexion gave me the clue. Now I knew who it was. I tried to speak, but only one word came to my lips:

'Rosita!'

There was a long silence. Then I heard her real voice whispering in my ear. But it pierced me to the heart:

'Yes, it's me, I'm here, I never moved to the Argentine – that was a white lie – but I couldn't wait for ever. I'm married.'

I heard a sob at the other end of the line. Nothing else. Silence.

With my head in a whirl, I dashed out of the hotel and started up the truck. Clinging to the wheel, like a drowning man to a life-buoy, I drove away from Lima to immerse myself in action.

23

Altitude clears the head. I began to feel happy again. I knew that Gal'Lino was following, a few hours behind, with his corps of foresters. There was a storm blowing up, but I decided to drive on and try to keep ahead of the big black clouds.

Suddenly I slammed on the brakes. Not only was I blinded by the mist but I had a presentiment of danger. Simultaneously I felt my front wheels drop into the void. I got out my torch and saw that the front half of the truck was hanging over a precipice, counter-balanced only by the load in the back. I decided not to touch it by myself and lay down by the side of the road to wait for Gal'Lino.

At first light I was woken by the sound of his Ford. He too had run into the storm and mist, but had cautiously stopped. Within half an hour, thanks to the horsepower of his vehicle and the brute strength of his men, we were on our way again and presently Pampa Hermosa came into sight.

When *Señor* Urco saw our convoy arrive, he couldn't conceal his stupefaction. Tears came into his eyes: 'So Satipo is going to be saved? I want to be in on it! Don Fernando, make full use of my house; I'll look after the trucks for you until the road's built. I'll organize a mule and manpower transport system.'

Napoleon then stepped forward, snapped to attention and said in his gruff voice: 'Don Fernando, please let me stay with you.' Urco gave me the reason for this unexpected request: 'Since your departure he has been going round in a daze. Of course I'm his *dueño*, his boss, but in your service he recovered a taste for hardship and danger. So take him with you. This is my real gift to you, because it costs me more than any other.'

Napoleon broke into a little jig, flung his arms round Urco and immediately prepared for our departure. I too was eager to get to Satipo as soon as possible and start work on the camp site, huts and office. I couldn't forget that within a few weeks a horde of labourers were going to arrive and that everything had to be ready for them.

As soon as I reached the little square, our secret committee was convened and Quiroz offered to negotiate the best sites for us. 'I want to pay the *colonos* straight away for the plots we'll be occupying,' I said. 'That'll be a slap in the face for Don Pancho de la Cruz who has always delayed the official signing of the title deeds. I look upon the sellers as the real owners of the land.' The news spread instantly; money was at last arriving at Satipo! Never in the whole of my career had I been conscious of the power of collective action. The colony of pioneers spontaneously volunteered to clear the ground and then build, free of charge, the hundred and fifty huts that would be needed.

Within a few days the foundations, drains and gutters had all been dug. An Austrian carpenter by the name of Jose had appeared, and volunteered to build my private residence. Tacatch, who had appointed himself works manager, insisted on its being constructed of solid mahogany and perched on piles. Gal'Lino meanwhile saw to his own quarters while waiting for Jesus's caravan to arrive from Cajamarca. From time to time Napoleon and I went roaming along the banks of the river. I still hoped that one day Kinchokre would come and offer me the services of his Campa kinsmen, as he had promised. No doubt he was biding his time, for I felt sure that the merry cries of the *colonos* engaged on the construction of the huts had long ago announced my arrival to him.

In due course I moved into my mahogany bungalow. Late one night, while still at work on my maps and plans, I suddenly heard Napoleon spring to his feet. Only a second before he had appeared to be fast asleep on the floor. I grabbed my pistol while he kept watch at the door. A strong, steady voice addressed us: 'I'm unarmed and I want to speak to the boss.'

A man appeared, a white, but as savage in appearance as an Indian. He said that his name was Rios, that he lived far away and had come here because one of the tyrant's servants, whose life he had once saved, had warned him that our village was to be burnt down next day after dark:

'Vilarette has got the kerosene ready and he'll make out it's a revolt of the *colonos* against you.'

'How can I thank you?'

'By taking precautions. I knew you were on the level. I'm going back now; but I want that swine Pancho de la Cruz to be unmasked.'

I embraced him. He refused any other recompense and disappeared like a messenger from the Beyond. I never saw him again.

Lying on my bed, I racked my brains to find the best means of preventing this act of sabotage. I tried to envisage how an experienced crook like Vilarette would set about the job. Logic suggested he would make a detour to reach the site and I felt almost certain that to avoid being spotted he would approach along the banks of the river. Napoleon and I undertook a thorough search of the immediate vicinity of the camp and after an hour I heard a whistle: Napoleon had just discovered a heap of tinder-dry palm leaves and, a few yards further on, a camouflaged hide-out containing a couple of cans of kerosene. He grinned broadly, picked up the cans and without a word disappeared in the direction of the river.

Soon he reappeared, still with the cans, and beaming all over his face. 'Have a sniff, boss,' he said. 'It's water, but I kept back a little kerosene for the sake of the smell. The rest I emptied into our own lamps. That's why I've taken so long.'

We still had to set the trap so as to enable us to catch the culprit red-handed. That evening I convened the secret committee in my bungalow and, after closing the shutters and leaving two hurricane-lamps burning to give the impression that we were still at work inside, we crept out through the empty stables at the back and made our way down to the river.

It was a long wait and I was beginning to fear no one would ever turn up, when a rustle announced someone approaching along the bank, and presently a tall silhouette appeared. All of us immediately recognized Vilarette. He advanced calmly, confidently, certain of being unobserved. First he dragged a sheaf of palm-leaves up to the nearest hut, then came back for the cans, dragged more sheaves up to several other huts and sprinkled the kerosene around. His technique was perfect, his gestures slow and precise. I heard the scratch of a match. The flame illuminated his face. At that moment I leapt out of my hiding-place. Before he had time to turn round, my rubber cosh came down on his skull and he collapsed in a heap.

When he recovered consciousness we carted him back to my bungalow and deposited him on the floor. For several hours he refused to talk, in spite of my threats of a long prison sentence. Then Napoleon made a suggestion: 'Boss, he'll talk if you place him under your protection. We must safeguard him against his master. He's

afraid of being killed if he talks.' Vilarette darted a glance of gratitude at Napoleon and then declared he was indeed ready to tell us
the truth.

I took down his statement, which amounted to a condemnation
of Don Pancho de la Cruz. Arson, murder – a full list of his crimes
was drawn up, followed by the signatures of the plaintiff and wit-
nesses. Armed with this confession, I leapt into the saddle to put
an end to the tyrant. 'You're responsible for the prisoner!' I shouted
to the others as I rode off. Despite my protests, Napoleon had
mounted his old mule and was already galloping after me.

The ranch-house in the clearing looked deserted. I called out in
a loud voice: 'Don Pancho!' He came out on to the balcony,
looking less pleased with himself than at our first meeting. I hustled
him into his study. 'Don Pancho, choose quickly. I'm giving you
a chance, your only chance after what happened tonight. No one
knows about it yet. Here's a copy of Vilarette's statement. Either
you leave Satipo straight away, and for ever, or this evening you'll
be arrested by my pioneers and taken under escort to Lima. There'll
be years of prison ahead of you. Don't argue. Answer yes or no.'

'I'll leave straight away,' he replied coldly, 'if you give me your
word you'll stifle the affair completely.'

'I give you my word, on condition you never lay hands on
Vilarette. Don't forget, I have a copy of his statement.'

That was all. Back in my hut, I released the bewildered Vilarette.
'Get the hell out of here! And no more monkey business. Is that
understood?' He tottered down the wooden stairs and each member
of the committee promised, in the interests of Satipo, not to say
a word about this business. That evening, when Gal'Lino triumphantly
informed me of the abrupt departure of Don Pancho de la Cruz,
I had to feign surprise.

Shortly afterwards a messenger arrived from Cajamarca, announcing the arrival of Jesus's caravan within the next twenty-four hours.
Everything was ready for them. My pride and emotion may be
imagined when, towards noon next day, old Jesus at the head of his
twenty pack-mules and oxen appeared on the square, followed by
some two hundred and fifty *serranos* laden with huge bundles and
cages containing cocks and hens. Shod in goat-skin, glistening with
sweat, they advanced, a silent horde that tomorrow was going to
tackle the forest and start work on the felling sites. There was
another piece of good news: two hundred and fifty more *serranos*

had likewise left their plateau to follow an engineer who was coming to build the road. Thus I learnt that my partner Benavides had kept his word: the twenty miles separating us from the world were henceforth to be reduced day by day.

After two days devoted to settling in and celebrating the newcomers' arrival, I formed the various gangs, issued the respective tools and gave the final orders. Then the felling got under way, in spite of violent storms. The rhythmic strokes of the machetes responded to the rain, the crash of trees to the thunder. I felt I had taken on a new lease of life; so did the *colonos*. The 'green darkness' was thrust further and further back by the strokes of the huge felling axes. Sometimes as many as fifty giants toppled almost simultaneously. I began to estimate the thousands of tons that must be lying there already.

A few days later, much to my surprise, a Campa Indian appeared outside my bungalow with a score of fellow-savages:

'I'm Ernesto. I've come to work.'

'Are you on good terms with Kinchokre of the Rio Pangoa?'

'No. Our clans don't fight any longer, but Kinchokre's a chief and a witch-doctor, he's very powerful. He despises me.'

'Then if you want to work I'll allot you a site of your own.'

'Will I have a lovely knife, like Jesus?'

'Yes, if you agree to fell the trees.'

'We'll fell any amount; more than your *serranos*.'

The felling continued despite landslides, snakebites, epidemics. Gal'Lino and I transformed ourselves into doctors, doling out medicine, dressing wounds, improvising a primitive hospital. I was constantly haunted by the thought that I still had to find eighteen trucks. Nevertheless, I started building a stock of top-grade logs to feed the sawmill when the time came. A hundred men felled a hundred trees a day, and it was true that Ernesto's Indians outclassed the others. Meanwhile the remaining two hundred were perfecting themselves in the construction of forest tracks and 'biscuit bridges' made of branches and dried mud, while another little gang was employed on counting and marking the logs.

One morning Kinchokre at last arrived and said by way of explanation: 'I wanted to see how you treated the men who work for you. Now I've seen. Come with me to the Rio Pangoa. It'll take two days.'

'I'll come.'

176

'It's an honour I'm doing you. No white or stranger to the clan has ever been inside our village.'

'I know. We'll leave tomorrow, before sunrise.'

After a month of responsibility and toil it was an immense joy to plunge into the forest again. I didn't feel I was deserting Satipo; on the contrary I was opening it up to the secret tribal world. The track wound between two dales, then crept into the orchid-scented undergrowth. A sudden hot-house atmosphere proclaimed the density of a vegetation which in order to keep alive assumed every colour, every ruse, every charm. Much to my admiration, Kinchokre seemed to glide along, to flutter, light and silent as a leaf. I followed, spellbound by the beauty of our surroundings.

Suddenly, straight in front of me, I noticed a solitary mottled mahogany tree over six feet in diameter. Kinchokre saw the gleam in my eyes: 'If you like it I'll give it to you. We'll fell it and roll it to your place.' I accepted and thanked him: it was a princely gift. Further on he stopped dead and drew his bow. His arrow flashed, he plunged after it into the undergrowth and came back a moment later with a wild pheasant, a superb *paujil*. I felt rather ridiculous with my rifle; I hadn't even seen the bird. Even so I earned a compliment: 'You march well, for a white.' Thereupon he forced the pace and I had the greatest difficulty in keeping up.

After several hours the track suddenly stopped, obstructed by a hedge of dry branches. 'Follow me,' said Kinchokre. 'But don't ever show anyone this passage.' He went forward, ducked down and started crawling, which was fairly easy for him because of his short stature. I had to struggle along behind him, constantly protecting my eyes from the artificial entanglement of dry and rotting wood. For over an hour we crawled along like this, until at last Kinchokre straightened up again, as fresh as though he had woken from a siesta. The smell of smoke and the sound of water heralded human habitation nearby.

We made our way down to the river, and from there I gazed in admiration at the Campa settlement on the opposite bank. The huts, simple leafy shelters without walls, formed a perfect rectangle. Nightfall imbued every outline, every figure with an aspect of mystery and tranquillity which was further accentuated by the fires. Kinchokre uttered his shrill cry. Instantly over a hundred naked men armed with poles leapt on to a balsa raft to fetch us from the bank. Darkness endowed our arrival with an atmosphere of solemnity.

Kinchokre sat me down by a fire and his fellow-tribesmen gathered round to listen to him. Towards the end of his speech he took a five-*sol* silver coin from his little bag and showed it to them. They seemed as happy as children. 'I've just told them how they are going to work for you,' he explained. 'Fifty of them with their families will settle in your camp under my command. They'll fell the trees you want. You'll pay them in coins like this one. They are pleased.'

Within forty-eight hours he had settled in with his contingent. Every day he gave me fresh evidence of his intelligence and knowledge: 'Against mosquitoes, look, burn pieces of termitary ... Here, these *jambu-assu* flowers: chew them and you won't have toothache.' From him I also learnt about the strange power of *niopo* and I understood how many of the Indians had been able to protect themselves at certain moments against all invaders: 'You grate some *parica* seeds. When dried, they turn to powder. That's *niopo*. You blow it into the air or else scatter it on the ground: your enemy goes mad, stamps, shouts, kills himself.'

'And what about *jambu-y*?' I asked.

'That's the same as *parury*. It's for putting lead in your pencil.' He smiled and added: 'A man like you ought to have a mate.'

'We'll see about that later,' I replied. 'First of all I have to go to Lima and find some trucks. Would you like to come with me?'

It was a flying visit. I took Kinchokre to his first cinema show. The adventure film did not strike him as at all extraordinary: 'It's the same with us, at Rio Pangoa. The brave man keeps his lands. He kills his rivals. Why didn't you kill Don Pancho de la Cruz?' But he was very impressed by the saw-mill.

Meanwhile I suffered two setbacks. The banks refused me further credit, and none of the truck manufacturers would do business without a substantial deposit. Luckily I heard of a European who had invested all his capital in a depot for the transport of wool and other goods between the southern cordilleras and Lima. The enterprise had failed and he was heavily in debt. On the spur of the moment I called at his office and offered him a contract. I undertook to buy all his trucks at a high price but only by instalment, depending on the volume of each load of timber that eventually reached the saw-mill.

'What security can you give me?' he asked.

'My stock, which is fully itemized. The completion of the road, which the arrival of the trucks will accelerate. The saw-mill, which I invite you to visit.'

After verifying the size of the development, calculating the liquidation of his debts, and seeing the saw-mill at work, he signed. I now had a fleet of trucks, and I hadn't doled out a penny.

Next morning I called at the bank to draw the Campas' pay and asked for it to be made up exclusively in five-*sol* silver coins. The clerks looked dismayed. I explained why it was absolutely necessary for me to have such a considerable sum in such a small denomination and Kinchokre backed me up. The manager tore his hair but promised to have it ready within twenty-four hours. Next day we loaded the cases on to my truck. The clerks gaped in surprise at this treasure being driven off to the jungle.

A week later the first eighteen trucks arrived, not empty but with tons of stores, medical supplies, tools and equipment. The *alcade* of Concepcion and *Señor* Urco himself, as well as some of the *serranos*, had insisted on using the vehicles to provide us with fruit, cola, maize, rice and alcohol. The enthusiasm was incredible. I declared the next day a holiday for everyone and there was a general gasp of delight when Gal'Lino opened the cases full of silver coins. The pay-out started straight away. It continued all next morning and it must have been about midday when the square, which was teeming with boisterous labourers, suddenly fell silent. I peered over my account books and Gal'Lino sprang to his feet. Then I heard Napoleon murmur: 'Old Vilarette.'

The wretched *caouchero*, prematurely aged, was indeed advancing towards the table. I saw before me a man with drooping shoulders, a man who was diminished and had come to beg my pardon. I stepped forward and to everyone's amazement, stretched out my hand. He seized it. With this gesture a period of hatred came to an end. Gal'Lino likewise shook hands with the old rascal and the sound of voices, the bursts of laughter started up again all the more loudly.

Suddenly a clap of thunder echoed over the little square. Yet there wasn't a cloud in the sky. I turned to Kinchokre, who was a witch-doctor after all, in the hope of an explanation. There was a faint smile on his lips. Guttural cries could now be heard in the forest near the Indian camp. Suddenly several trees came toppling down.

179

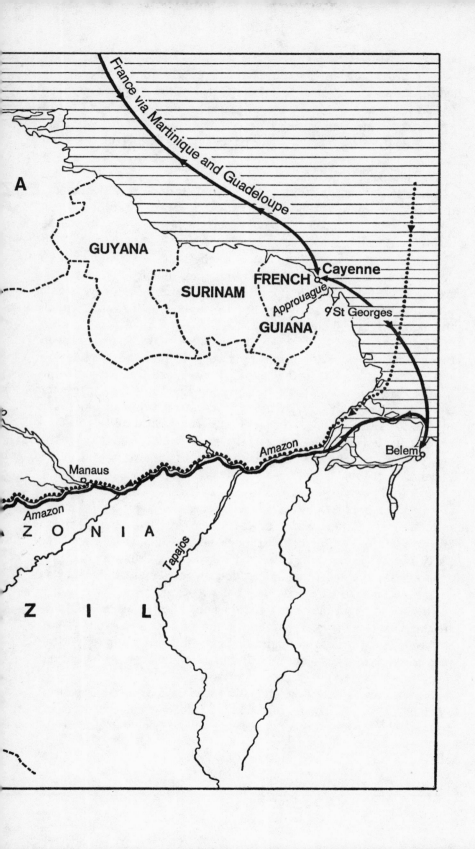

We dashed across in that direction, apprehensive, prepared for a catastrophe. The crowd followed, curious, intrigued. Only the Indian wives and children were all roaring with laughter. And then I saw, naked and yelling with delight, Kinchokre's tribe arriving, rolling in front of them a huge mahogany trunk weighing several tons.

'My promise,' Kinchokre merely said.

Like a huge snake wending its way through the forest, the rolling-track ended up just behind the Indian camp. That evening five huge mottled mahogany logs were outside my hut, waiting to be transported to Lima.

Next day Jesus came and told me that the *serranos* had been devoting all their spare time to adapting their huts for their families. At this evidence of faith in the future of the enterprise, I gave orders for ten of the trucks to drive off at once to the Upper Andes to fetch the men's wives and children.

No sooner were all these families installed than the first caravan of eighteen trucks set off for the passes, laden with trees. With Kinchokre and myself in the leading vehicle, and Gal'Lino bringing up the rear, we were at last transporting the first Peruvian timber from the Upper Amazon to the wagons waiting on the other side of the Cordillera. In Lima I organized a demonstration in the saw-mill. Delighted with the process, the bank manager bought up the entire load of mahogany to decorate a villa he was having built. Benavides, always the perfect gentleman, insisted on my keeping these initial twelve thousand *sols* for myself.

I used the money to buy a Buick roadster and give a big reception in honour of the Reccavaren brothers. The President asked them to congratulate me on his behalf though he was unable to attend the party himself. 'He's not sure that Pancho de la Cruz mightn't still try to turn the Opposition against you or even send trouble-makers to Satipo. So take care!' the colonel whispered.

This warning put me on my guard again. Infected by the euphoria of the last few days, I had lost sight of the menace that still hovered. I slept badly that night, trying to think of a way of putting paid to the tyrant once and for all. But by the morning I had found a solution.

Why shouldn't Satipo be officially recognized as a municipality? With Urco as the *alcade*, and Quiroz, Tacatch and others as his assistants? This scheme would provide several benefits: title deeds, police, a town council. I decided to tackle the authorities at once. I went round to the ministry and this time, against all my expectations, even the politicians proved efficient. The papers still had to be drawn up, and the motion passed, but I was given an absolute assurance.

As we set off on the return journey, Kinchokre was fidgeting with impatience and wouldn't believe we were going back until we began to negotiate the first zig-zags of the Cordillera. At Pampa Hermosa I abducted *Señor* Urco from his base camp, then drove on to Satipo where Gal'Lino had been holding the fort. Since my departure the trucks had continued to ply to and fro: five convoys, not a single accident, not a single setback. My white horse had arrived at last. I decreed the following day a holiday.

Next morning, Kinchokre came to my hut and tactfully reminded me: 'We have been to Lima together.'

'Yes, I know.'

'You said that after you had been to Lima you would get yourself a mate. I'll show you a woman of my tribe.'

Well might I seek a way out, every day he became more pressing. Shortly afterwards he drew my attention to a very young girl, little more than a child: 'Let her roam round your house and venture inside. Don't talk to her. I want her to get used to you. She's a real woman. Her name is Pangoate.'

Next day I noticed her, clad in a loincloth, hanging about at the back door. She continued to loiter like this, until a couple of weeks later Kinchokre arrived with her parents who flung her into my arms, roaring with laughter. This simple ceremony, Pangoate's reserve and her grave face may have made me more embarrassed than I need have been. At all events I felt shy of showing her into my bedroom. Whereupon, sensing my modesty, she went in of her own accord and with the utmost tact made it clear that she wished our marriage to be consummated, totally.

Thus for several months we loved each other, without exchanging a word. Then one day a miracle occurred: she addressed me in Spanish! After the first few phrases her speech became less clear, but she was able to explain that Kinchokre had secretly given her lessons to enable her to converse with me. I held her hands, then clasped her in my arms. Every day she made progress in the language, but nothing ever took the place of our long silences or the profound peace born of a mere touch of the hand.

'Horse', my beautiful white horse, would often poke his head out of the stable and whinny at her by way of greeting. He had acclimatized himself admirably and developed an 'ambling' pace, which enabled me to train him to long expeditions in the forest without any risk of laming. I had had some rough grass sown so that he could graze and, sometimes, to amuse Pangoate and the other Campas, I would make him 'salute'. When 'Horse', under a slight touch of the heel, lifted his hoof and waved his tail, even the *serranos* were brought to a standstill.

Despite the rains, the humidity, the outbreaks of jungle fever, the trucks went on plying to and fro. Urco, whom I earmarked as *alcade*, came and settled at Satipo as soon as the official papers arrived from Lima. Every day I was forced to reconnoitre further stands to prevent our stock from dwindling. The war raging elsewhere, which I was scarcely able to follow, had the effect of compelling Peru, like so many other countries, to live on its own resources. We all had an additional reason to keep our factory on the coast supplied.

One evening, after a year or so of this arduous life, Pangoate arrived looking radiant and seized my hands more firmly and gravely than usual. 'Father, I'm expecting a child by you,' she proudly announced. 'I speak Spanish too badly, but Kinchokre will come tomorrow. Listen to what he says. We are all agreed he should tell you.'

Kinchokre did indeed come next morning and spoke to me at great length. It was the first time his tribe had agreed to a non-Campa marrying one of their women, he said. He had himself suggested this union because he had observed me for a long time and saw that I didn't resemble any of the whites of Satipo, still less any others he had met.

'But you are a white,' he went on, 'and we know you will not stay here forever. We won't let you take your children away to the whites, who are barbaric, sickly or stupid. When you leave, I myself will look after the child and he will remain a Campa.'

I looked him straight in the eye. It pained me to realize that he was already thinking of the day when I would no doubt have to move on from here. I couldn't reply without being evasive, captious or untruthful. I therefore fell in with the decisions of the tribe.

Shortly after she was delivered Pangoate got up to show me the infant. She clung to me for a moment, then asked if all three of us could set off on my big horse and ride into the jungle together. So I mounted her and the child behind me and for several hours, as we made our way slowly through the forest, I felt her warmth against me and her hand in mine. Back in the bungalow, she held the child out to me again and I clasped it to my breast while she stepped back to contemplate us both with a joy that I have never since beheld on the face of any woman. Taking the child back in her arms, she said: 'We shan't go for any more rides together. It was for the sake of your child. When you've gone and he grows up, I'll be able to tell him that you took us on your big white horse and we were very happy.'

At the end of three unforgettable years we had two children. By then, despite several outbreaks of jungle fever, probably due to foul water which we had to cover with a film of kerosene, business was thriving to the great satisfaction of my partner in Lima. But suddenly – was it overwork or a relapse? – I was laid low by a bad attack of malaria. The doctor at Satipo was adamant. Only proper treatment, on the Pacific coast and for several months, could save me. Kinchokre, who spent all day at my bedside, was well aware that I didn't want to go away. But he gently insisted: 'The real father of your children, Fernand, are the men of the tribe and, behind them, the ancestors. We gave you a wife; she bore you children. They must not leave our forest. They are *our* children. You are sick, you must be tended, and therefore you must depart. Those are my orders as the chief. You must obey our law. Depart without fear.'

Through my fever I heard him repeat the words: 'You must depart. You are sick. Depart without fear.' He told me again that the Campas would never work for anyone else and that after my departure they would return to where I had first found them, on the banks of the Rio Pangoa: 'We shall withdraw further into the forest to escape from the whites. For one day they will come to kill us.' Then once more he assured me: 'I shall look after your wife and children. Go in peace. We shall never meet again perhaps, but we shall always think of you.'

The evening before my departure, I got up and spent a last few minutes by the fire in the Indian camp. I wanted to clasp Pangoate and my two children in my arms and show that I refused to be sad as white men are. The Indians looked grave and, to mark the event, had adorned their faces with thin black lines relieved by little dots. I peered at them intently so as to engrave their image on my memory. When the fire ceased to blaze, everyone retired to his hut, for the death of the flames is the signal to disperse. Pangoate didn't come back with me that night. I abided by the rule.

Next morning, after loading up the Buick, one of the foresters came to fetch me. Beside the car, immobile, wide-eyed, stood Pangoate with my two children. I kissed them one after another, as though I was coming back that very evening. I was bowed down with fatigue, fever, sorrow, but at that moment I wanted to be worthy of my Indian wife. Through a haze I saw the pioneers wave farewell. Quiroz, Tacatch and Napoleon ran alongside for several yards to hold my hand or stroke my arm. It was a wrench to leave this little square I had crossed so many times, to quit this site where I was leaving my heart, my very life behind me.

An hour further on, as we were leaving the banks of the river to start the ascent towards the passes, Kinchokre appeared on the edge of the road. In silence he approached the car. I can still see his lean face, his calm and at the same time piercing gaze, his features tense with emotion. He stroked my shoulder, then continued on his secret way through the forest. I realized this gesture was intended to convey that I had been a distinguished guest, an esteemed kinsman, but that the tribe was going to close in on itself, on my wife and children, forever. And indeed I never saw any of them again.

THE PACIFIC AND
THE SHARKS

1942-1945

24

The climate of the Pacific, the peace and quiet that surrounded me, the vigilance of my friends had a beneficial effect. After many weeks of constant medical attention I grew stronger and had every reason to look forward to a complete recovery provided I took things easy and abandoned all forestry work. I was no longer delirious; the fever, the virus seemed to be under control. Soon I was allowed out of bed and gradually recovered the use of my legs.

One morning out of the blue, I received an invitation to call at the American Embassy. There I was introduced to the head of O.E.W., the department dealing with economic warfare, who asked me point blank to locate the largest possible quantity of balsa wood. (I realized much later, at the time of the landing, how important this material was in the manufacture of gliders, since it was very light in weight and could be easily compressed.)

Within one month, despite the shrill cries of the doctors, I had ordered the production of Satipo to be intensified and flown to Ecuador to reconnoitre the rivers and especially the Rio Vinces. Within three months I had submitted my report and pin-pointed two sites which, when developed, would provide precious material for D-Day and the war in the Pacific. By way of thanks, O.E.W. offered to install me at Guayaquil to keep an eye on the coast where smuggling was on the increase. I decided not to commit myself until I was on the spot.

O.E.W. in Ecuador operated far more like a military department, as I saw for myself as soon as I reached Guayaquil. I was therefore all the more reluctant to commit myself. I wanted to remain independent, an adventurer at my risk and peril, refusing to conform, refusing to join the herd, continuing to give my desires and instincts full rein. And one of my desires at the moment was to buy a boat.

I therefore spent my time wandering around the harbour, casting an eye over fishing vessels and the men who manned them. One evening, I heard about an old half-caste sea-captain who earned a good living from transporting tin cans. This sounded intriguing, so I decided to go up the coast to Manta, where his boat was anchored, and find out what these cans contained. By next morning, after standing a round of *aguardiente* to the crew, I had actually got hold of one. I prised it open with my knife. It contained liquid rubber.

I went back to Guayaquil, dashed round to the O.E.W. office with my booty and told them I was looking for a boat. The Americans, good sports as usual, had nothing to say against this, but asked me to contact their consulate next day. Meanwhile they were very interested in my discovery. It appeared that I had just put my finger on a nice little rubber-smuggling racket! These cans apparently reached the Pacific from the Amazonian forest and were then shipped through the Straits of Magellan to be picked up by the Germans in the Argentine. Henceforth the Americans would be able to intercept them before they reached their destination.

At the consulate next morning I was handed a document. '*S.O.S. to the fishermen of the Pacific Ocean*,' I read. It appeared that an appeal had just been launched in London: England, the United States, all the Allies were dangerously short of vitamins. Under-nourished children, wounded airmen, convalescents were in danger of their lives unless professional fishermen volunteered to help the researchers and scientists by methodical shark fishing.

'So far the appeal has evoked no response,' the consul said. 'Would you like to attempt the experiment?'

Straight away I recalled the conversation in the Waldorf Astoria, and one name in particular: the Galapagos. They lay directly opposite, 620 miles out to sea. The Pacific coast was teeming with shark.

'Yes,' I replied, 'on condition I'm given the necessary information.'

'Here are some figures: shark liver oil yields a minimum of 3,500 I.U.V.A. (international units of Vitamin A) as against cod liver oil's 850. Certain species have livers amounting to 100,000 I.U.V.A. Would you like to make some tests? If so, we'll notify our services and provide you with documentation and measuring apparatus.'

At eight in the evening the old Mauresque clock overlooking the docks of Guayaquil struck its derisory notes. The streets, the houses, the passers-by had no more significance for me. I had made up my mind and was heading towards my new destiny: the old coaling jetty where a few days before I had spotted a boat for sale, the *Pelicano 32*.

By the light of a torch I jabbed my knife again and again into the inside of the old hull. With her black dust, her empty hold, her rustic timbers, the *Pelicano 32* was not very elegant but she was sound. The owner, disgusted with the sharp practices of the tunny fishermen, couldn't wait to get her off his hands. Thus I became master of an ocean-going vessel, for which I now had to find a crew.

At dawn next day, wearing a *Monte-Christi*, which in Europe is erroneously called a 'Panama', I entered the shop of the 'Dangerous Brothers', Los Peligros, at Santa Rosa. One of them, a low-browed, lantern-jawed *cholo*, sat drinking at the bar. The other, in faded linen trousers, was busy stacking sacks of maize and red beans.

'Victoriano's house?' I asked.

'Why?' they retorted, distrustfully.

'I'm looking for a pilot to go shark-fishing.'

They pointed to a cliff at the end of the village and, after buying a bottle of *aguardiente*, I headed in that direction.

Victoriano wore a plain cotton shirt and threadbare shorts reeking of fish and smoke. He spoke Spanish interspersed with *cholo* words, but I saw straight away that he knew the coast and the deep sea like the back of his hand: 'I've been a fisherman all my life. So why not shark?'

He introduced his son, a thickset stocky Indian, whose eyes gleamed at the thought of sailing in a boat with an auxiliary engine.

'You'll see to the sails, Pablo,' his father told him. 'For shark one has to manoeuvre, it's not like tunny. We must take on "Double-Chest" and old Suarez as well,' he added. 'They're experts with sails and harpoons.'

He gave a shout and mysteriously the men appeared at once. I poured out the *aguardiente*. By the end of the evening I had engaged four seamen, located an isolated house on a cliff and, late at night, steeped in alcohol, my crew and I caught a truck back to Guayaquil.

I still had to make the boat seaworthy, repair the sails, look for an engine and a mechanic, put the papers into proper form, prepare the fishing tackle. Because of the war, material and equipment were unobtainable; we had to improvise. Victoriano manufactured some tow out of pulverized coconut fibre. The others caulked the seams of the hull by mixing this with chalk and linseed oil. I found an old Cadillac engine in a warehouse, which a half-caste by the name of Pepe undertook to put in working order and adapt for the sea. Infected by the sense of adventure, he also agreed to being taken on as mechanic.

In a short time the thirty-foot vessel, fitted with a jib, staysail and mainsail, began to look rather different. I had the deck cabin removed, since we needed all the available space for cutting up the catch. I bought some iron bars and had them converted into big thirty-metre hooks. I studied the documents the consul had given me: instructions for preserving in salt, hints on the manufacture of double-saucepans and a makeshift laboratory. It all seemed quite clear.

In the harbour the yachtsmen and sailors round us smiled ironically: so many fishing concerns had come to grief! A Norwegian company had met with failure; did we, with our makeshift barrels, patched sails, and lines salvaged from the steel cables of an old oil well, think we could succeed? Yet gradually respect succeeded irony and less than a month later I loaded up with a thousand litres of petrol, two drums of sweet water, food supplies and wood for the kitchen stove. We were ready.

As I gave orders to cast loose, I thought of the shark infesting the high seas – blue, white, hammer-head. Which variety were we going to find? I checked the chains and swivel fastenings, the harpoons and curved knives for cutting up the catch. I tried out the two spotlights on deck, trained them on the bank. They functioned properly. Thanks to them we would be able to work at night without any risk.

Victoriano's son made some coffee. At the end of ten hours we rounded Death Island. The black backs of the dolphins heralded the open sea. We waited for them to come closer in the hope of harpooning one and using it as bait – the cruel law of the ocean. While 'Double-Chest' lowered sail, Victoriano took up his position by the cable, his son got ready to launch the harpoon, and old Suarez stood on watch.

'Dolphins ahead!'

The long steel weapon flashed, the cable unwound – much too fast. I rushed over to help block it before it reached its last fathoms. Our bodies were arched, our muscles flexed. The sea boiled and turned red. 'Double-Chest' got ready to launch another harpoon as a coup-de-grace. The victim was hooked and hoisted out of the water. It flopped on to the deck, spattering us with blood. Then it gave a death-rattle – two deep, drawn-out notes, as though it was trying to speak. Victoriano seemed deeply affected by this and for a moment I thought he might be superstitious. I peered at him intently but he mastered his feelings and merely wiped his face with the back of his hand. 'It died like a Christian,' he muttered.

We cut the carcase up into three-kilo hunks with which we baited the hooks. I switched on the engine to make for deeper water. Our two bottom lines, gigantic trawls, were weighted with stones since anchors weren't to be found at Guayaquil. Balsa trunks took the place of floats. I rather regretted not being able to try out more than ten hooks at a time, but I hoped to improve upon this later. The main thing at the moment was to learn how to catch a shark.

'Cast anchor!'

Well might Suarez cavil at the spot I had chosen, I felt it was pointless to go further out to sea for this initial attempt. With precision, almost ceremoniously, we dropped the first stone. The line with its baited hooks uncoiled in a depth of fifteen fathoms. In an hour the lines were laid. We sailed on and stopped again a mile away to bask in the sun and wait.

At the end of two hours my *cholos* couldn't contain themselves any longer; they felt it was time; they wanted to see. So we started up the engine and headed back towards the floats. Without a word old Suarez cleared the decks. And suddenly the others started yelling with excitement. Above our lines a shoal of dog-fish was thrashing about in the sea, their fins flashing in the waves: 'They're fighting! They must be attacking the ones that have been hooked. Shall we have a go with the harpoons, Skipper?'

'Let's try.'

Pablo and Suarez snatched up the weapons. I stood by the tiller: 'Easy ahead, Pepe!'

I nosed the prow gently towards the brownish patch which seemed to be the centre of the carnage. My two harpooners stood motionless as statues. Then two arms were raised, and two harpoons flashed through the air. I saw Pablo's line slip through his hands. 'Block the winch,' I shouted to Victoriano, who promptly did so.

Gradually we wound in the lines and at last I saw the two hooked sharks struggling wildly. We hauled them alongside. Pablo's was enormous; it leapt into the air, falling back into the water with a resounding thwack, and would have been dangerous had he not stabbed it several times with another harpoon. The line dragged its head above the surface and a spasm forced its jaws open, revealing twelve rows of triangular teeth. Straight away I gaffed it.

'Lash it, quick!'

It was nineteen feet long – a tiger shark, apparently, which we made fast against the hull. Pablo put one leg over the side, flexed his buttocks and adroitly lashed the tail. Then we rushed over to the second beast, which seemed less lively. It allowed itself to be hauled up, while Pablo straddled the rail and plunged his long knife into its gills.

We were utterly exhausted and our hands were bleeding by the time we got both carcasses aboard, and over the deck there already hovered that typical, pungent odour which no shark fisherman can ever forget: reminiscent of cod liver oil but a hundred times stronger and more clinging.

Before lifting the lines I thought we had better cut up the catch so as to get into practice and make more room on deck. I claimed the privilege of operating on the first victim. The instructions I had been given by the American services indicated the order in which the operation should be performed. With my long cutlass I sliced off the dorsal fin and pectoral flappers, slit the belly open and removed the entrails. The huge tobacco-coloured liver then lay revealed in the gaping wound.

'We'll salt it soon,' I said.

We flung the remains overboard and washed down the deck before lifting our lines. I was eager to see how our makeshift tackle had behaved and how many fish were hooked. The reflection was blinding as Pablo grabbed hold of the balsa float and we started heaving on the steel cables. Presently we caught sight of the first shark caught on our lines. It emerged from the sea like a monster of the Apocalypse: jaws agape, flesh in tatters, with only one eye which gazed at us blankly. It was dead, having been torn to shreds and devoured. There followed a string of three smaller dog-fish then two empty hooks, one of which had been twisted into a corkscrew by a jaw that had prevailed over the tempered steel.

All that remained was to make for some island, anchor there for the night, and then test the livers for their vitamin content. Meanwhile Pablo and Suarez disembowelled the second shark, 'Double-

Chest' again washed down the deck, and I cut the liver up into thick slices, sprinkled them with salt and lowered them through the hatchway to Pepe in the hold. Our first barrel of shark oil was safely stowed away in the belly of the *Pelicano 32* by the time we reached the little bay in Death Island.

As we were about to land, I suddenly felt a strange urge and went below to the *bodega*, where I had stowed away half a dozen kilos of shark meat. Yes, I wanted to eat shark that evening, to vaccinate myself, to commune with the enemy! Victoriano, who was going to do the cooking, looked scared when I told him. But in the end, to exorcize his fear, he agreed: 'Yes, you're right, Skipper, but we shan't tell the others until they've eaten it.'

Later, in the moonlight, my famished crew having devoured the contents of the pan, I gave each of them a swig of *aguardiente* to celebrate our first salted barrel and then said: 'By the way, Victoriano, what was it you gave us to eat?' When he told them there was a short silence, then their faces glowed with pride, as though from now on they shared the strength of the enemy.

Next morning Victoriano and I stripped naked on the beach and went for a swim. I was floating on my back, basking in the rays of the rising sun, when I heard him give a shout and saw him dash out of the water towards his clothes: 'Skipper, the crabs are eating our togs!' He shook his rags and dozens of red crabs tumbled out of them. I rushed up and found my own clothes shredded by an absolute army feeding on them. I contemplated the disaster: from now on I was condemned to wearing these Robinson Crusoe tatters, since I had to keep my other shirt and trousers for my next visit to the consul.

Meanwhile Pepe had brought ashore the little Lamotte laboratory the Americans had given me and I set to work on my analyses. I selected a piece of each of the livers, poured out some tetrochloromethane and plunged the first sample into a measuring tube. Only 10,000 units! Well below standard. Some of the others reached 12,000 units, but not one of them the 25,000 I had expected. I wasn't disappointed, only worried. Would we find any shark up to standard? We might have to sail up and down this coast for days, sounding the bottom, selecting the species. I decided to inform the crew. They looked grave but far from discouraged. Old Suarez made a remark which went straight to my heart: 'Never mind, Skipper! give us time.'

'Let's get going, then!' I said.

'Double-Chest' was already loading the pirogue when Victoriano suddenly drew my attention to two figures coming towards us along the beach. I cocked my Parabellum – no point in being caught napping by smugglers who would do anything to seize a sailing-ship – while Suarez and Pablo picked up their cutlasses. From this distance it was hard to see if the two men were armed or not. I shouted: 'What do you want? Stay where you are.'

'*Somos abandonados!*'

Marooned! Marooned on this island? I turned to Victoriano, who took over from me: 'Drop your knives and come closer to talk.'

The two men obeyed: 'We're hungry. We're not thieves, we're fishermen.'

Victoriano gave them some shark to eat and started questioning them. Their story sounded true. They had been working for a Peruvian smuggler, but for two months had received no pay. When they asked for their money, they had been sent ashore and ordered to cut wood for the galley. The launch in which they landed had failed to come back and pick them up. They now begged us to take them on. They looked tough and muscular. I glanced across at Victoriano and saw that he shared my opinion: eight of us aboard wouldn't be too many.

Only a day later the two newcomers saved Pablo's life. At nightfall, in a heavy swell, he fell overboard trying to grab the last balsa float. Hanging over the rail, attached to a cable, Chankai and Cabeza – these were their names – managed to grab hold of his arm in a fearful trough before his head was smashed against the hull.

We had just waged our second battle; the deck was littered with sharks which we had surprised in deadly combat with some 'emperors', those live torpedoes known sometimes as sword-fish. In the morning my analyses showed a remarkably constant yield of 12,000 units, so we had improved somewhat on the previous catch.

I felt we ought to get back at once and deliver the first two barrels of samples. I wanted to check the results of my tests. At sunrise, when all I could see of the ocean was its deep blue colour, Victoriano gave a cry:

'*Una mancha!*'

'A patch? Where?'

I couldn't see anything, but he drew his knife and pointed: 'Look over there.'

195

It was a shoal of tunny or bonitos. I felt we may as well take a few samples of their livers as well, so I headed for the patch, while Victoriano muttered: 'Later on, up north, we ought to hunt the shark that eat the tunny.'

'Why?'

'Maybe their livers are better.'

This struck me as sound advice. Meanwhile we proceeded to harpoon a couple of dozen tunny and bonitos. Their raw flesh, mashed up with lemon, would give us outstandingly sharp sight, according to Suarez. 'It's called *seviche*,' he said. I made a mental note of this and started cutting up the catch. The proceeds from the sale of these fish were destined for the crew, but I kept the livers and packed them carefully away in some small tins, for I knew from my instructions that they contained Vitamin D2.

Just as we had had to wait after setting our first lines, so now we had to wait again to know the outcome of our effort. It seemed a very far cry from the forest, from Satipo. A barrier bigger than the Cordillera separated me from my kinsmen of the Rio Pangoa. But I had now found a new family in these Indians of the ocean.

25

Even after having a bath and changing into clean clothes, I still stank of oil when I called on the consul. 'I'm sorry, sir,' I apologized, 'it's the sharks ...'

As luck would have it, he was an old sailor: 'Don't worry about that, Skipper. If I had my way I'd be on a boat myself. Well, how did it go?'

Sheepishly I described my initial catches and told him the result of the analyses.

'Don't be discouraged. The Washington Laboratory in Seattle is still interested. Look.'

And he showed me the following telegram: '*Willing to buy several hundred kilos of livers. Provisional price one dollar per kilo, cash down, additional payment depending on analysis of samples. Please notify captain's moorings.*'

Just then the telephone rang to announce the arrival of my barrels and boxes of samples.

'How much do they weigh?' the consul asked.

'Four hundred kilos.'

Then and there he made me out a cheque for four hundred dollars.

That evening, after a fairly lengthy binge, my crew and I ended up in a smart night-club. There was a heavily decorated general there who was carousing with some friends and several girls. I sat down alone at a table, while my men remained at the bar.

'There's a terrible smell of fish,' the general presently said in a loud voice.

I sprang to my feet and replied in the same tone:

'Yes, it's me. I fight shark. What about you? How did you win all those medals? Playing ping-pong?'

He was taken aback for a moment, then burst into a loud guffaw and ordered us a last round of drinks. From then on I was known to everyone at Guayaquil as 'Captain Shark'.

This name seemed all the more appropriate when, a few weeks

later, I accidentally fell overboard off La Plata Island and had to stab a shark to save my life. This was merely a natural reaction, something I did on the spur of the moment. But from then on, in the eyes of my crew, I was invulnerable. Meanwhile the Indians along the coast talked about our expeditions and the adventurous life we led, and volunteers began to pour in from all directions. It reached such a point that I even envisaged enlarging our flotilla, especially when I put into Manta harbour and found the following telegram waiting for me:

'Send unlimited quantities shark livers from 12,000 to 25,000 I.U.V.A. identical to your samples. We pay 50 cents per pound F.O.B. Guayaquil. Guayaquil and Manta banks notified. Washington Laboratory, Seattle.'

Next day a second message was brought out to me on my fishing grounds. It had been forwarded from Guayaquil:

'Captain Fernand Fournier-Aubry, Pelicano 32, Ecuador. Willing buy all quantities tunny and bonito containing Vitamin D2. Preparation identical to your samples. Price fifty cents per pound salted F.O.B. W.L. Seattle.'

The man who brought this message had a lean, weather-beaten face. A huge scar bisected his head from brow to lip, and one eye was absent from its socket. The other peered at me intently: 'My name is El Tuerto. The harbour-master is my compadre. I'd like to work with you.'

He offered me the use of an old warehouse and undertook to ship our future catches to Guayaquil. Since our hold was already crammed full of salted livers, I welcomed his offer. Meanwhile he started buying up empty lard and manteca drums from all the merchants, who were only too pleased to sell us salt in vast quantities. I sealed my pact with him and was thus able, with the help of my crew, to persuade all the little fishing villages to join in the enterprise. I would leave them drums and salt, organize practical demonstrations of the method of treating the tunny and bonito livers, and El Tuerto would call to pick up the goods. And the further we progressed the greater was the urge I felt to enlarge my fleet.

One evening, as we were coming back with sixty shark livers on board, I felt I couldn't wait any longer. I made some mental calculations and decided to buy three new boats, increase my business with the fishermen, confirm El Tuerto in his functions, open a bank account for him in Manta, and above all find a suitable base with storerooms for fuel, food supplies and stocks of salt.

I felt like singing as we sailed into Manta harbour. I already foresaw that henceforth I would be spending all my time between this delightful little colonial town and the creeks of Machalilla, Salinas or Esmeraldas in the north. Having unloaded the barrels, we got down to some serious drinking and presently tongues began to wag. Thus I heard that evening about La Cruzita.

Once upon a time, so the story went, a smuggler landed on an island opposite La Plata, inhabited by impoverished fisherfolk. He arrived with two *balandras* loaded with building material, wooden beams and sacks of lime; and his ten *cholos* started reconnoitring the south of the island in search of a spot suitable for a house. Meanwhile, ambling along the coast, he came across a little cross of white stone half buried in the sand. He cleared the sand away and discovered what appeared to be a tomb. Next to it was a little chest made of *guayacan*, that very hard wood found in Ecuador, and from it, much to his surprise, he drew a big tortoiseshell comb and a yellowing sheet of paper which said: '*On this spot I killed and buried the woman I loved. Whosoever you be, respect her tomb and her cross.*'

'Double-Chest' and Cabeza went on to explain that the smuggler, far from respecting the tomb, had had a huge house built on top of it and had subsequently come to a sticky end. But the house, La Cruzita, was still standing. Their two voices proclaimed in unison: 'There are cisterns and cellars there, Skipper!'

'And a good mooring.'

'And we could even install a light-house.'

I promised to sail across the next day, after seeing about the boats, and we all fell asleep amid the sacks in the storeroom.

The boat business was quickly settled; there were only three available. I told El Tuerto to supervise the fitting-out and paid an initial deposit. Then, after saying good-bye to the harbour-master, I set sail for La Cruzita.

From afar it looked splendid. A sandy beach pink with shells stretched across a sheltered bay. Wild pigeon took wing at the approach of our *bongo*. Above the dunes stood a massive, impressive building. Goats grazed on the shrubs round it. I wanted to wait until we were all ashore before visiting the premises. But no sooner had Chankai and Cabeza landed than they started climbing towards the house, so I followed them and headed for the big wooden door.

'Look out, Skipper! Come back, it's dangerous!' Chankai warned me, then he crept forward whistling and shouting: 'Yoo-hoo! Tomala!'

'Steer clear, you buggers!' came a voice from inside.

'It's our captain,' Chankai went on shouting. 'Open up! He's come to buy La Cruzita ...'

A stocking cap appeared at a window, and beneath it a contorted face.

'Bugger off, you yellow bastards, or I'll stick you in the gizzards!'

'Yellow bastard yourself! He's come to buy the place, I tell you.'

'Have you a letter from the *dueña*? She doesn't allow anyone inside.'

The cap disappeared from the window, but footsteps resounded on the stairs and presently the door opened an inch or two. I caught sight of a bandy-legged little mannikin who glared at me suspiciously – Tomala, the janitor.

'If I let you in, will you give me a letter for the *dueña*?'

'Certainly.'

We all stepped forward, but he drew a cutlass about as big as himself. 'No, only you,' he said to me. 'Not these two buggers.'

'Well, lead the way.'

I followed him into the muggy atmosphere of a big bare hall, where bats hung in clusters from the ceiling. On the staircase I suddenly began to itch all over. He smiled: 'It's the fleas. They're hungry. The *dueña* won't give us enough diesel oil to sprinkle on the water.' My inspection of the premises was perfunctory, for I kept having to stop and scratch.

'Primavera! Come and fetch the captain's clothes!' Tomala shouted to his wife. Then he trotted across to a cupboard and came back with some branches: 'Take off your togs, I'll rub you down with these *cochayuyu* leaves and the fleas will jump off.'

While he applied the leaves to my skin, I said: 'You seem to be a good fellow. If you like I'll engage you as major-domo.'

'At what salary?'

'Whatever you please if you're good. A kick in the arse if you're not.'

He gazed at me with a pensive smile, while his wife took away my clothes. 'Shake the fleas into the fire and look snappy!' he shouted after her. 'The captain's stark naked!'

Chankai and Cabeza in their turn were eventually allowed to

visit the premises and I heard them counting out loud: six big store-rooms, one office, several other rooms. Then they went to investigate the condition of the cisterns. My clothes were brought back and, while I dressed, Tomala disappeared for a moment, then reappeared with a greasy piece of pasteboard bearing the owner's name and address: 'La Elefanta – Villamine'. I thanked him and bade him farewell, but he followed us down to the edge of the water, shouting: 'Look out for the Elephant. The last person who tried to buy this place was stabbed to death!'

We headed straight back to Guayaquil and as soon as we arrived I jumped ashore and into a taxi. The old Negro driver peered at me disapprovingly in the rear-view mirror when I gave him the address: 'That's the brothel quarter, boss!' Scarcely had we entered the narrow, noisome streets than we were assailed by clusters of children who clung to the sides of the car. We drew up outside a heavily studded door, while the brats milled around and pissed on the front tyres. 'It's here,' said the driver, and roared off without even waiting for his fare.

Confronted on my own with this gang of juvenile delinquents, I could think of only one way out. I delved into my pockets and scattered a handful of change in the street. The brats went chasing after the rolling coins and left me free to push open the front door. It gave on to a patio with another door at the far end. This slowly swung open as I approached, and I saw a huge black shape peering at me from the shadows beyond. Then I discerned a bed, some ox skins, some lemons, a demi-john, a chamber-pot, a machete: the interior of a fearful den, reeking of musk, alcohol, nutmeg and cigar smoke. A hand grabbed hold of me and dragged me inside.

No light penetrated the patio; the room was illuminated by a flickering hurricane-lamp. Its inmate, who was now sinking back on to the bed, was presumably the Elephant. She must have weighed over twenty stone. She puffed at a long cigar and peered at me intently. Even though I had known the famous Negress of Cayenne, the convicts' banker, I was overawed by the size of this mastodon. A strange paralysis seized me as she started to speak. Her voice seemed to emanate from the depths of her belly, enveloping and subjugating me. Its tone was so infatuating that I could barely grasp the significance of the words: 'All whites are stinkers. I only like Negroes and Indians.' She exhaled a cloud of smoke. I noticed her arms: columns of muscle. Her hands tugged at my sleeve, claiming my attention, and I found myself listening to her life story.

Her ancestors had been tortured and sold into slavery. At the age of five she had seen her mother die at work. Somehow she had made her way to La Cruzita and hidden in a hole in the rocks, where she was eventually found by an Indian seaman: 'He grew rich, because he was engaged in smuggling. Sit down and have a drink, Skipper.'

She filled a hollow coconut with white rum and handed it to me, then poured another for herself. I sat down.

'When the Indian died he left me La Cruzita.'

I watched her as she drank. She seemed to smile into her glass. Her teeth were magnificent, unusually large and regular. 'What's your real name?' I asked.

Her face changed, assuming a pensive expression: 'Margarita. Come closer, Skipper. Men are frightened by my size, I know, but I'm an affectionate soul.'

I recoiled. So this monstrous pachyderm was going to be sentimental! I felt I had fallen into a trap. Her hands groped for my shoulders. I had to head her off at all costs, distract her somehow, so I put all my cards on the table and said: 'I came to see you about renting La Cruzita.'

'I know.'

How? I concealed my surprise and told her about my shark fishing. She pretended to be interested, but could not prevent herself from snuggling against me. Then her deep voice whispered in my ear: 'I'll rent you La Cruzita for ten years, Captain Shark, payment in advance.'

Preparing myself for an exorbitant sum, I asked her the price. She merely bubbled over with laughter. 'How much, Margarita?' I persisted.

'One dollar a year. Ten dollars altogether.'

Again she laughed, mischievously, incomprehensibly. Again I feared a trap or some misunderstanding:

'You know how much the dollar is worth?'

'Yes, Skipper. Shall we sign the lease?'

I produced the ten dollars, a ridiculous little banknote for such a splendid fortress as La Cruzita. But she accepted it without a murmur, then called: 'Tomala!'

To my stupefaction, the little dwarf shuffled in, carrying a portable writing-desk. 'He arrived just before you did, Skipper,' Margarita explained. 'That's how I know all about you. You're a French-man and you respect the Indians. Otherwise I wouldn't do business with you.'

In a clumsy hand she drafted the lease and I countersigned it. Tomala gave me a conspiratorial wink before disappearing again. Then she poured out more white rum: 'Right, Skipper, let's drink to it.'

We did so, again and again and again. By the time I had drained my twelfth glass, I was beginning to feel rather the worse for wear. But she apparently hadn't turned a hair. Suddenly I felt a heavy mass of flesh bear down on me, herculean arms held me fast, and I was tumbled backwards on to the bed. I had the impression of drowning under a landing-craft crammed to the gunwales with white rum. Unable to struggle, I let myself sink to the bottom.

In the morning, woken by a loud snore, I surfaced slowly and realized my companion must have passed out a few minutes after I did. I disengaged myself gently. The lamp was low, the wick was smoking. With a final glance at the slumbering body, I snatched up my cap and made for the door.

As I came out on to the patio, Tomala sprang to his feet from behind the pillar where he had been standing guard. 'Skipper,' he said, 'I'm going to tell everyone. I'm proud to be your servant. The servant of the man who lasted a whole night in the Elephant's bed!' Why disillusion him? The legend would go down well with the *cholos*.

It was already light as I crept out of the house. In spite of the stench of refuse, I inhaled deeply. Two figures sprang out from a porch: Chankai and Cabeza. They jumped for joy at finding me safe and sound. Stout fellows! They had kept watch all night, fearing the worst, ready to answer my cry for help.

This was a turning point in our fishing business. In Europe the landing was about to take place and I was asked to increase my deliveries. I prepared to enlarge my establishment and availed myself of these few days at Guayaquil to overhaul the *Pelicano* and scrape the barnacles off her keel. During this enforced pause, a distinguished-looking old man, a former sailor, a real *caballero*, offered me free of charge the use of some large warehouses where my barrels could be stored pending their departure for the United States. Through his good offices I was also able to recruit a reliable agent who became the official despatcher for all my deliveries to Seattle.

In a few months, with the help of my coastal network and on the proceeds of fishing and occasional whisky smuggling, I managed to equip a flotilla of ten sailing-boats. We plied between the Galapagos and the coast, known to all, greeted and welcomed everywhere, engaging in every method of fishing – harpoon, line, net, even dynamite – in order to increase our output. Shark no longer had any mysteries for us. The hazards diminished to the point where familiarity with them bred contempt. Injuries occurred, but La Cruzita served us as an asylum and hospital.

One evening, in La Plata Island, we heard that an aircraft had been seen coming down in the sea. We immediately headed in that direction. It was pitch dark and the sea was infested with tiger shark, some of them thirty foot long. We patrolled all night in vain. But in the morning, as we were coming into Puerto Cariyo, some Indian rowing-boats signalled to us: they had just picked up a survivor. In the village I found an American airman who was clearly in a state of shock. I took him on board and we headed back to Manta. On the way he gradually recovered his wits and told us what had happened. His plane had been forced down and began to sink as soon as it touched the water. He and the two other members of the crew had donned their inflatable life-jackets and started to swim, but in the dark they had become separated. My Indians realized at once that his companions must have been devoured by the sharks. I asked him what he had done all night to be able to survive. 'I prayed,' he replied.

Cojimie, in the north of Ecuador, affords perfect shelter on condition you know how to manoeuvre between the sandbanks and find the channel. I thought of settling there for some time to explore the high seas which were infested with shark.

The Indians of the *pueblo* announced our arrival. As we lay at anchor off shore, a man paddled out in a pirogue. He introduced himself as one of the rare shark fishermen in the area and asked me to follow him. We moored opposite a lovely house, surrounded by coconut palms and scarlet hibiscus, which we had noticed from the bay. 'My name is Marco Tupac Ramirez. Please make yourself at home.'

The hospitality of his family went straight to my heart. His mother, Doña Josefina, had the distinction of an Andalusian lady and his father, Don Luis, was endowed with all the best characteristics of the coastal Indians. Ayde, his sister, was very beautiful and resembled them both. She must have been about twenty. As we shook hands she trembled slightly, so that her brother teased her. 'Caramba, Ayde looks rather disturbed!' In a swirl of skirts and scent she rushed out of the room.

We talked things over and I suggested staying here several weeks to clear the bay and shallows of the dangerous sharks, if Marco would like to come to sea with us. Then I took my leave. As I went out, I noticed a statue of the Virgin Mary with a little oil lamp burning in front of it. For a long time that evening I dreamt of Ayde's lovely face.

Next day Marco came aboard and we resumed the chase. From then on, every evening, we would come back to find Ayde waiting for us, outlined against the setting sun. Often, after dinner, she and I would sit together on the beach or on the verandah, imbued with tender and romantic feelings. One evening, which happened to be her birthday, I described some of my adventures in the Amazon. Two old Indians were singing softly in the background. The house was fragrant with the scent of the oranges, mangoes and bananas in the fruit basket. She was sitting opposite me and looked increasingly disturbed. Marco suddenly spoke up and put me in a very embarrassing situation: 'Ayde, your face betrays a great deal of affection for our new friend. What do you say, Skipper?'

I was in duty bound to reply frankly to such a frank remark. So I told him that in spite of being constantly on the move I had often dreamt of settling down with a woman like Ayde.

'And what about you?' he asked her.

Without any false modesty, after a brief moment of revolt at having her secret feelings forcibly revealed, she confessed that she felt a profound tenderness for me.

That night we again went down to the beach together, and on her forehead and lips I planted a first kiss. We stayed there, on the sand, until dawn. Then she left me and went back to the house. I heard her singing as she drew away. But I was sad: I had known for several days that despite all our efforts the fishing was poor. Though my holds were full, the vitamin content of the livers was as low as ever and I therefore had no excuse to prolong my stay. My heart ached at the thought of leaving.

When Marco arrived in his pirogue, I knew that this would be our last day at Cojimie. He too felt that after this expedition he wouldn't see the *Pelicano* again. We laid our lines together for the last time. That evening we found Ayde waiting for us as usual, in a flowered red dress and with her black hair falling down on her bare shoulders.

I told her I was leaving. She listened in silence, gazing at me with her great big eyes, then took the red hibiscus she was wearing in her raven locks and handed it to me. I planted a kiss on each of her moist eyelids and went aboard the *Pelicano*.

Back at La Cruzita, I received another telegram: *'Please expedite deliveries. Allied military hospitals counting on vitamins A and D2.'*

I set to work again with a vengeance, fishing with nets off the estuaries and even, despite the danger, using dynamite. But I came to realize that the effort was insufficient. So I flew down to Costa Rica and bought a refrigerator ship which would enable us to visit all the *pueblos* which were not accessible by road. And so, one day, the *Cecilia* appeared off La Cruzita – a magnificent vessel with an insulated hold, cooling system and 120-horsepower engine. I was now in a frenzy of impatience to scour the seas and raise a whole armada.

For the last year I had had sixteen sailing-boats at work. I had caught more than eight thousand sharks. Several tons of livers, hundreds of barrels had passed through Tomala's hands. And yet I had the feeling that the end was near. Why? Impossible to explain. It wasn't lassitude. On the contrary, the Indians all the way along the coast were helping us; never had my agents been so punctual with their deliveries; never had my crews been so productive. And, though the war was over, the demand for livers was as great as ever. So what was the reason?

It wasn't long before I knew – synthetic vitamins. As soon as I heard about this new discovery my foreboding turned to alarm, and my alarm was confirmed shortly afterwards when Seattle abruptly cancelled all further orders.

It was difficult to believe at first. The vessels lying at anchor off La Cruzita seemed to mock me. Every morning I contemplated the *Cecilia*, knowing that no one on this coast could afford to buy her. The *Pelicano* 32, the *Letty*, the *Tiburon*, the *Santa Cruz* and all the others lay idle. These vessels were utterly unsuitable for the little *cholos* who were too poor to run them. I was going to have to sell them off for a few hundred dollars.

All sorts of crazy ideas flashed through my head; I thought of going on a bender all the way along the coast or trying to arrange a sale at Guayaquil ... I wrote to a few friends and a little miracle occurred; three young Americans, former naval engineers, offered to buy the *Cecilia* and all the shark-fishing tackle. They arrived a month later to clinch the deal. I was heavy-hearted as I accepted their wad of four thousand dollars and saw my lovely ship disappear for ever.

I let my loyal fishermen have the other vessels for a song, and was preparing to close down La Cruzita, when one day I saw a man come climbing up the dunes. 'It's Picoudo the smuggler!' Chankai shouted. I knew him; he was the enemy and rival of Guyacan, a crook who two years earlier had played a dirty trick on me.

He had asked me to allow a specialist on board to conduct experiments on a shark in order to verify some secret preserving product. These experiments were to be carried out while we sailed to Callao, where, for security reasons, the shark would be transhipped to a yacht waiting off shore. I was only too willing to oblige – for a certain fee. Unfortunately the transhipment took place in a heavy swell, during which the shark crashed against the mainmast. Where-upon its belly split open and spewed out hundreds of wrist-watches! I went straight down to my cabin, wrapped my fee money up in a bag and tossed it on to the deck of the yacht. Then I pitched the shark overboard, still spewing its contraband contents. Guyacan never forgave me ...

It was an old story now, but I was reminded of it at once by Picoudo's unexpected arrival. The old rogue gave me a comic salute, and then made a suggestion which at once restored my spirits. Would I like to get my own back on Guyacan? If so, all I had to do was to go to Panama and load up with twenty tons of lard that would serve to undercut his business in Ecuador. 'It's quite simple,' Picoudo explained. 'I buy over there cheap. You drop the barrels off La Plata. I pick them up at night and sell them here at a lower price than Guyacan. He'll be ruined. I also have two thousand bottles of whisky waiting for you at Panama, and a boat. On your share of the pro-ceeds from one trip alone you'll be able to pay half her cost; she's for sale at fifteen thousand dollars.'

Why not have a bit of a laugh? Three days later I set sail for

Panama in a Mexican three-master, and a week after that, at dead of night, I found myself again off the coast of Ecuador in a vessel flying the Panama flag and manned by an exceptionally tough crew. My hold was full of hermetically sealed drums of lard and bottles of whisky. I had bought the superb 80 ft two-master, because it had a name I liked, *Aventura*.

A torch flashed a signal, to which I replied, and the faint throb of a motor heralded Picoudo's approach. He climbed aboard with sixteen other pirates and inspected the cargo. The drums were pitched overboard and towed to the coast where several lorries stood waiting. I gave Picoudo a farewell embrace. The *Aventura*'s engine roared again. I swung the wheel and she came about. I headed due north for Panama. The operation was over.

26

It's a great thrill to be in command of an 80 ft boat. Even moored in Panama harbour, a thirty-ton two-master fires the imagination. Anchored among the fishing-coasters, I dozed on deck, revelling in a well-earned rest while I waited for the forwarding agent of the Washington Laboratories of Seattle.

I soon heard the sound of an engine and saw him approaching in a launch. I wondered what new business he would suggest. At all events I refused to earn a living from smuggling, which had never been more than an occasional amusement for me. But all he had to announce was the imminent winding up of the Laboratories and that synthetic vitamins had prevailed. 'Do you know I still have your last seven tons of shark liver on my hands?' he added.

On the spur of the moment I replied:

'I suggest a straightforward deal. Sell me those vitamins at half price. I'll take them back to Europe, where they may still be useful.'

He looked astonished, but I told him my conditions: I would buy the livers at half price, provided he saw to the shipping-bills and also bought the *Aventura* from me. The simplicity of the deal attracted him and the thought of owning a two-master was an additional temptation. Next day he came aboard with his answer and the fifteen thousand dollars on which we had agreed.

A few days later I was on board a freighter bound for Portugal and Marseille, with my barrels in the hold exuding the stench that was so familiar to me. I smiled at the thought of the pungent smell of shark following me all the way back to Europe.

I was proud to be coming home with a lot of vitamins which were badly needed. My amiable American had given me the address of an importer in Lisbon who, at the sight of the cargo, declared himself willing to take four tons then and there and pay for them by cheque on a French or Italian bank. But the Portuguese Customs refused to let me unload them unless I could produce an import licence. And

I couldn't. I had the loading-bills from Panama all right, but I wasn't a merchant, hence the snag.

This put me on my mettle: 'Well, if I can't unload the livers here, am I entitled to pitch them overboard off shore?'

Was it my seaman's cap that impressed the customs officer? At all events he took his colleague by the sleeve and led him out into the corridor. When he came back, there was a broad grin on his face: 'You needn't pitch your barrels overboard. You can unload them here if you like. We know you're not a smuggler.'

In Marseille I had no such difficulties. A big firm bought the rest of my cargo from me, and all that remained of my five years' activity in the Pacific was a sack of shark fins which I stored with Carthis's concierge in Paris until I could sell them to a Chinese restaurant. Meanwhile I moved as usual into the good old Hotel Terminus Saint-Lazare, where I hoped to stay for several weeks.

Before leaving for Lima in 1938 I had left a nice little sum at the bank: two million francs. I now decided to blow the lot before setting off again. But I was in for a shock: what had been a small fortune before the war was now barely sufficient to buy a five-ton truck! So I would have to get down to work at once. What I wanted was to start a lobster fishing industry off the Galapagos or Mexico, and I was looking into the possibilities when a telephone call came through from a big foreign investment company: 'We're starting investigations north of Magellan. We need a prospector.'

The over-friendly voice put me on my guard. But it was a tempting offer: I didn't know the South Pacific and its isolated islands. I listened with growing interest as the voice went on: 'The climate is dreadful: storms the whole time. But you're the first person we thought of. What do you say?'

I asked for further information and two days in which to think it over. But it appeared that the mission was urgent: the Guaytecas Archipelago and all the neighbouring islands belonged to Chile; the subsoil and forest had to be prospected, and their resources determined, within seven or eight months at the latest. I was required to reply at once. Since the conditions the company offered were extremely generous I accepted, and a few days later I flew out to Santiago.

Since I had only seven or eight months in which to submit my report I felt the best thing I could do was make an aerial reconnaissance of the region. So, after moving into an hotel, I went

France by plane

S. Miguel de Tucuman

C H I L E

Coquimbo

Valparaiso

Mendoza

Santiago

ARGENTINA

Valdivia

Puerto Montt

Pto Quellon

Iles Guaitecas

TIERRA
DEL FUEGO

straight to the civil aerodrome to enquire after air taxis. A plane had just landed as I arrived, and out of it stepped a passenger wearing a bowler hat and carrying an umbrella. He was obviously one of those gentlemen who no matter what the climate would rather be seen dead in a ditch than improperly dressed. The pilot, a sporting young Chilean, quickly fell in with my plan. Spreading out the maps, we plotted our itinerary together. And a few days later we took off and headed due south towards Tierra del Fuego.

Flying at an altitude of only five hundred feet, I was able to study the indented coastline and islands in detail. Though this area was said to be uninhabited, some isolated wooden huts and even a few small villages betrayed the heroic presence of human beings. But what a distressing landscape! Here, even after Magellan had sailed through, the Alcalouf Indians, like the wreckers of Finistère, used to light fires to lure the rare ships on to the rocks and then loot them. Since then whale fishers coming from Norway had in due course founded families and settled along the coast. I felt it required immense courage for their half-caste descendants to continue to live here, in the mist and permanent icy drizzle which seeps into one's very bones. 'Summer? It lasts a couple of weeks!' the pilot told me.

The big kidney-shaped island of Chiloe attracted me more than the others. With its snow-covered volcano, lake and burnt-out cypress forest, it struck me as being the most accessible for future development. I therefore asked the pilot to land me here and, after circling round to find a suitable spot, he eventually deposited me on a stretch of open ground. I arranged with him to come and fetch me in seven months' time, then we said good-bye and he took off.

So there I was left, alone with my meagre luggage in the middle of a bare field. The thermometer stood at 42°F and the humidity was fearful. Suddenly, as though from nowhere, a little girl appeared, barefoot in a homespun woollen dress. She smiled and presented me with a bunch of flowers she had just picked, then seized my hand and guided me to a little adobe hut. A man came out to meet us, a stocky, thickset figure, obviously a mixture of Nordic and Alcalouf, with a weather-beaten, care-worn face. He was kindness itself and offered to show me the way to the little port of Quellon, but insisted first of all on giving me a cup of hot coffee. Like all the other *sufridos*, or local inhabitants, he did a little farming, wove his own wool and went fishing for crustaceans and molluscs in his wooden rowing-boat. He had never known any other life.

At Quellon the formalities were soon completed. The amiable policeman and harbour-master didn't have a visitor to deal with more than three or four times a year. My passport was passed from hand to hand like a new toy. I explained the purpose of my mission and told them I wanted to buy an undecked, ocean-going sailing vessel and to recruit four *sufridos* to man her. Meanwhile I moved into the primitive little hotel.

The toughness of the local population surprised me. The women were as hardened as the men. They rode their little ponies bareback, and barefoot unloaded huge sacks of crustaceans and molluscs from their boats. Everyone seemed to be bursting with health – just as well, since there was no doctor on the island.

After a few days the harbour-master called on me: 'I've found a boat for you. And here are your *sufridos* – the Colivaros.' He introduced four extremely resolute-looking characters, the eldest of whom was over fifty, the others being between eighteen and twenty-five. And by dinner time I was the owner of a big boat with four rows of oars and a stubby mast to enable the sails to be taken down in a flash. It was splendid to feel one was on the threshold of a real battle with the elements.

That evening a robust young man came up to my table and introduced himself. He looked just like a sailor but, to my great surprise, was wearing a brand-new cassock. 'I've put it on in your honour,' he told me, and went on to explain that he really was a priest, the son of Polish emigrants, and that he plied between the islands in an old boat bringing absolution and the sacraments to his scattered parishioners.

'The men you've engaged are not recommendable,' he said. 'None of them is legally married and they're inclined to be light-fingered.'

I replied that it was the outlaws, pariahs, rejects of this world who had always served me most loyally and I therefore had no use for choirboys. He looked at me in amazement for a moment, then his expression changed as we summed each other up. I realized he had warned me out of pure kindness of heart, but he was obviously no judge of men.

Next morning we set off on the long haul to the Guaytecas. The harbour-master came down to bid us farewell and, as a parting present, gave me a case of tinned condensed milk. The north-easterly wind blew all day, deadly, nerve-racking, as we headed for the

Island of San Pedro where we hoped to camp for the night by a spring of sweet water known to my men.

Not far from the spring was an adobe hut which must have been built by some intrepid predecessor hunting otter, seal or nutria. There were dry logs inside, so we were able to have a fire and cook some rice before dossing down on the bare floor. My *sufridos* had proved themselves excellent seamen and cheerful companions. I had every reason to be pleased with them.

But in the morning I realized I still had a lot to learn. As we were setting off, I saw that the case of tinned milk was no longer in the boat. Was the young priest right, then? Were these men really thieves? I looked each of them straight in the eye and asked: 'Where's the milk?'

They withstood my gaze, but none of them replied. I went back into the hut and found the case hidden under the straw we had used for bedding. 'What's the meaning of this?' I asked. Again none of them batted an eyelid. I glared at old Colivaro, thinking that he, being the eldest, probably had some influence over the others. He stepped forward, inscrutable, noble, without taking his eyes off me for a moment. 'I did it,' he confessed.

'What for?'

'For whoever might need it.'

Chiouaye, younger and more talkative, then explained that this was the custom here. When you're rich – that's to say when you have enough food for the next day – you leave something behind for the poor or needy. 'A drowning man, even if he's your enemy, must be rescued,' he added.

This was a real lesson to me. I thanked them all and put the milk in the straw. Then we set sail for the south of the island, opposite San Pedro, where I noticed the cypress forest came right down to the water's edge.

In the evening, after reconnoitring the coastline, we landed in a tiny estuary affording perfect shelter for the boat. Old Colivaro drew my attention to a clearing with a wisp of smoke rising from it: 'There's a woman who lives here.' And indeed, as we drew nearer, I caught sight of a tall, queenly figure with a little girl standing beside her. 'Her husband was shipwrecked,' Chiouaye explained, 'and she has stayed here ever since.'

No one had been here for over a year, so she welcomed us all the more warmly into her simple hut with its wattle partitions and rush matting. Impossible to refuse her offer of a separate room in which to sleep, so happy did she seem at the prospect of receiving us. Chiouaye poked the fire and started cooking. The others went off to fish and unload the rice, flour, salt and coffee.

During dinner, which included some huge sea-urchins, old Colivaro described how this young woman, who was no more than thirty, had absolutely refused to come back to Chiloe after her husband was drowned. She had buried him here, and here she intended to stay until her daughter was old enough to marry. 'My husband is always near me,' she herself added. 'What more do I want?'

After several weeks of prospecting we had to tear ourselves away from this blissful little island; and it needed all my powers of persuasion for our heroic hostess to accept some coffee, salt and a few fishing hooks. As we sailed out of the little bay I vowed that if I ever came back here I would bring a trunkful of clothes for her and her little girl.

Our next port of call was a cove from which I would be able to reach the lake I had spotted from the air. It was dominated by a wooden hut surrounded by vegetable plots. 'We'll have to stop here for the night,' old Colivaro announced, and I let myself be guided by him.

We were received by a large family whose patriarch sacrificed a grilled sheep in our honour. After dinner we sat round the big log fire and one of them started telling a local legend. Others followed suit and thus it was I learnt about the sea fairies and the ghosts of the mist. Then Chiouaye asked me in my turn to tell a story and I found myself describing Europe, the rush hours, the traffic jams, the pension system, the social security service, the everyday activity of the average Parisian ... A pensive silence ensued, then a female voice remarked:

'What a wretched life it must be!'

The young girl who had spoken wore a long homespun dress with an old-fashioned pleated bodice. Her name was Carmen. She had strong hands and wrists, regular Nordic features. Our eyes met and suddenly I realized she was the woman for whom I had been searching all my life. From various allusions I knew she was unmarried; husbands were not so easy to find in these god-forsaken spots. So perhaps I stood a chance ...

Next day I started reconnoitring the lake. Unexpectedly, it

offered exceptional resources. At Santiago I had been struck by the number of electricity failures: twice a week on an average the town was without current due to lack of generating power. On seeing this mass of water, miraculously situated at an altitude of over six hundred feet in a country with a constant rainfall, I felt it might constitute an important supply of energy. For ten days, in the icy drizzle, on board a makeshift raft and with improvised equipment (some big reels of white cotton, because they were visible at a distance) I sounded the bottom at regular intervals and took various measurements. Then I drafted a detailed report and went into Quellon to cable it to my company before proceeding further north.

The vision of Carmen continued to haunt me. I imagined her every morning heading out to sea alone in her boat and returning in the evening loaded to the gunwales with *mariscos* and giant clams. I had not given her a hint as to my feelings, but I vowed to come back as soon as I had finished my prospecting and ask her to marry me.

Meanwhile I sailed up north with my four *sufridos* to reconnoitre the burnt-out forest. A huge stand of cypresses had once caught fire on the island, but the trunks were still valuable provided they could be shipped. I sounded the bottom off shore and found the depth sufficient for cargo-boats of a thousand tons. I also went otter-hunting, observed the playful antics of the penguins (which I had to forbid my men to kill), explored the holes and caves of the coast and collected samples of the stones.

One evening old Colivaro told me a strange story about a *cueva* – a cleft in the rocks a few hours away which contained hidden treasure. Next day, in spite of heavy seas, we headed for that point on the coast. Sure enough, I discerned a curious cavity some thirty feet above sea level. It looked to me like a wreckers' lair and I felt it deserved closer inspection. We landed with picks and shovels and started digging. Suddenly Chiouaye gave a yell: his shovel had come into contact with a piece of wood. No doubt about it, it was the lid of a chest. We got down on our knees and scraped the earth away with our hands, until the whole chest was revealed. It contained a second chest about sixteen inches long. I opened it carefully. Inside I found a wooden statue of Saint John, another of Saint Francis of Assisi and, right at the bottom, a terracotta head of Christ. Doubtless some Jesuists had sought asylum in

216

this grotto on their flight westwards, or perhaps they were themselves victims of wreckers on the look-out for refugees sailing up from the Guaytecas. At all events we carried off our 'treasure' as a souvenir, making haste since we still had to build a hut in the interior before darkness fell.

There was no trace of game in this desolate spot. All we had to eat for several days was 'billiard ball' – flour boiled into a paste, the staple diet of the *sufridos* when on the move. Not once did the sun appear; we lived in a permanent drizzle. Never mind, I found several samples of gold or platinum and reconnoitred two big forests and another lake before I decided to go back to Quellon.

Instinct must have dictated my decision; for on my return I was informed that a delegation from my company was expected in Quellon in the next few days. They duly arrived and I elaborated on my proposals for reclaiming the plateau to create pastureland, building an electricity works to supply Santiago, etc. But there was one secret I kept to myself: how to manufacture soup from seaweed. I had studied the *sufridos*' method. First they constructed a channel about two metres long and covered it with stones heated to splitting point. Then, withdrawing the embers, they stuffed it while still burning-hot with blue seaweed which was thus baked to the consistency of a brick. Cut into slabs, it served as the basis for a soup with a delicious taste of iodine. (A few months later I flung one such slab on to the desk of Professor Bellon at the Oceanographic Museum of Monaco: 'Here, analyse this. Do you know what it is? I eat it.' Years afterwards I heard that this gesture of mine had resulted in the creation of a factory for seaweed extraction in the south of Chile.)

The evening my delegation was due to leave, I gave them a farewell dinner to which I invited the intrepid Polish priest. He turned up in his new cassock, which he only donned for special occasions. At the end of the meal I stood up, delved into my pockets and flung down on the table all the banknotes and coins I could find. 'Gentlemen,' I said, 'make a contribution. Here's a poor sailor priest who's going to kill himself at the rate he's going. He carries God around with him in a leaking boat. His parishioners are destitute. Fork up!' The tycoons emptied their pockets, so as not to appear more stingy than a mere prospector like myself, and the priest was thus enabled to buy himself a new boat.

My mission was coming to an end. I collected my notes together.

The image of Carmen kept rising before my eyes, as though beckoning me to come to her. Then I had a stroke of bad luck. As I was returning in the evening from my last expedition, a huge breaker overturned the boat. I felt a heavy mass crash down on my arm and leg. Somehow my men dragged me ashore and got me back to Quellon where my broken limbs were put in splints. Unable to move, I now had to wait several weeks longer before being able to join the only woman I felt was capable of sharing my primitive and hazardous life. I was furious, but what could I do?

As soon as I was able to limp along with the help of a stick, I went down to the harbour in search of a vessel more comfortable than my own boat to take me to the cove where Carmen and her parents lived. The harbour-master hung his head, then looked up and gazed at me steadily, without saying a word. The silence dragged on. In the end, awkwardly (and I shall never forget his voice) he said: 'I didn't want to tell you, but the other day ...'

'When?'

'The day of your accident. That same evening Carmen and her entire family disappeared in a storm. Mother, daughter, granddaughter. They were bringing back some boats loaded to the gunwales. A wave capsized them. Here's the *carabineros*' statement...'

I read and reread the short report of the tragedy. Carmen dead, drowned! There was nothing left for me on this misty island. Nothing but despair. Behind the dry official words on the sheet of paper in my hand, behind the little black hieroglyphics on which my eyes remained riveted, I beheld the heroic woman to whom I now wished I had confessed my love. I remembered her sitting by the fire, serene and radiant in her long woollen dress. I remembered her standing proud and upright in her boat. Yes, through my tears, I saw her still alive. For in my memory she could never die.

FORBIDDEN ASIA

1955-1956

AND RETURN TO AMAZONIA

1956-1971

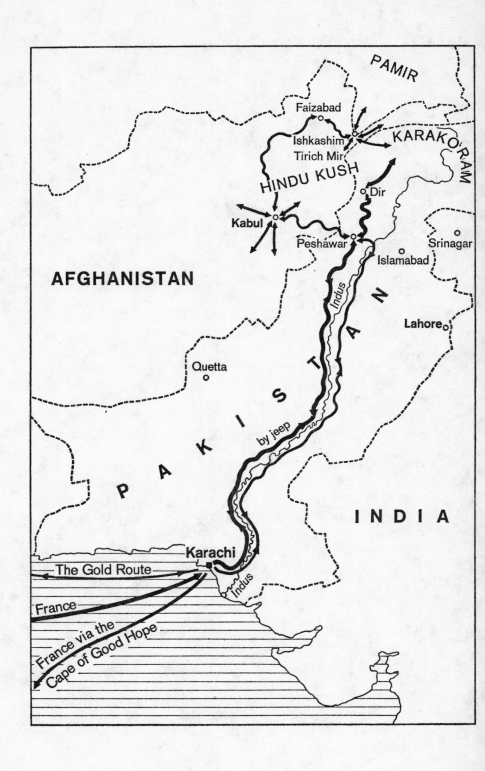

27

Once again I found myself back at the only permanent address I had in the world: the Hotel Terminus Saint-Lazare. In the golden light of autumn, Paris glowed. Despite the faint early-morning mists the weather seemed mild to me: for nearly a year not a ray of sunshine had caressed my face. I sat on the terrace of the hotel, watching the hordes of anxious, gloomy, sulky faces go by. Gaiety and joy seemed alien to these ants filing in and out of the Metro. Their shabby clothes, their down-at-heel shoes, everything about them betrayed resignation. It was a depressing sight. Suddenly I gave a start and sprang to my feet: that man over there, in rags, shuffling along – I knew him! There was no mistaking him, I recognized the trepanning scar on his temple and his aquiline nose. I rushed over and seized him by the arm: 'Guy!' He looked at me, muttered, pretended not to know me – from a sense of shame, I realized at once. But I had a firm grip on him and was determined not to let him go: 'Don't be silly, Guy!'

'Leave me alone, I'm ill,' he eventually said.

Only five years earlier this man had owned thoroughbred horses, a yacht and a Cadillac. Now he had come to this! I wanted to know what had happened. I seized him by his grubby coat and urged him into the hotel, while he protested:

'Thanks, Fernand, but it won't make any difference. I'm ruined.'

A profound lassitude reduced his voice to a whisper. In the end he consented to come up to my room, but he eluded all my questions, saying over and over again: 'I've been walking for three days in the hope of catching pneumonia and dying.' I made him lie down on the bed and drink a glass of champagne before going to sleep. I wanted him to realize he still had a friend. Meanwhile, knowing his independent character, I felt certain I wouldn't see him again if I left him alone. So I settled into an armchair until he at last dozed off.

Midday, five o'clock, ten o'clock in the evening: he went on sleeping. I ordered a splendid supper and ran the bath, then woke him, made him spruce up and lent him one of my suits to wear: 'Come on, Guy, never say die! Oysters and caviar for us to-night!'

Freshly shaved, bathed and rested, he forced a smile to his lips and tried to pull himself together. The champagne and food loosened his tongue and at last I discovered the reason for his decline. For several years he had been dealing with some Kirghiz friends in Uzbekistan. Their business wasn't contraband, for up there, in Central Asia, the cultivation and sale of opium was still allowed; but all transactions were by word of mouth. He had been making a handsome profit until a few months ago, when heart trouble had laid him low and prevented him from going back to collect what he was owed. 'Since then I've spent thousands of dollars on doctors and hospitals. I haven't a penny left. But I won't accept charity,' he added pig-headedly.

'Granted, but you wouldn't refuse me a partnership, would you?'

He looked at me intently to see if I really meant what I said. I did mean it. Had I not been racking my brains ever since my return to find something that would help me forget the tragic image of Carmen, that would send me to some other point of the globe as far as possible from South America? Guy realized I was sincere and stretched out his hand:

'A partnership? Agreed, Fernand. Now listen.'

And he started telling me about Central Asia, the harsh laws of the steppes, the political and religious customs of the Kirghis and Kiptchaks, the greatest horsemen in the world, the nomadic life of all those old Turco-Mongol, Chinese and Indian races. 'They're the last free men on earth,' he went on. 'Neither Soviet Russia nor China nor Afghanistan nor Iran nor Pakistan have ever been able to subjugate them.'

Gradually, as he warmed to his subject, all his confidence seemed to return. His pride and self-respect suddenly gained the upper hand. He brought the conversation to an end: 'It's late, dear Fernand. Ask them to give me the best suite in the hotel. The sum can be deducted from our assets out there. See you tomorrow.'

Next morning I was woken by his deep, sonorous voice: 'It's one o'clock. You've had enough sleep. Come and have lunch in my suite. We'll spend the day working.' An unrecognizable figure greeted me. Carefully groomed, wearing a sumptuous silk dressing-gown, he explained with lordly casualness: 'I asked them to put everything on your bill, of course.'

'That's the style,' I said, delighted to see he had now recovered his spirits completely.

Our work for the day consisted of his talking and my listening, but occasionally I would interrupt to ask a question:

'What about the climate?'

'In winter, between minus thirty and minus forty. In summer, a blinding glare. Very little water, very little food, all travel on horseback or by camel – really tough. But lovely.'

The place names he mentioned were music to my ears: 'The poppy fields are south of the Amu Daria. But my friends operate between Iskachim and the Pamirs. This area is the nucleus connecting the highlands of the Hindu Kush and Karakoram with those of the Tien Shan and Kunlun. Look ...' And he drew me a rough sketch of the age-old trade routes lying across the modern frontiers of Russia, China and Afghanistan. It was impossible not to be carried away by his description of the landscape up there. I pictured myself making my way through fields of millet and buckwheat, past silkworm cultures nestling in a paradise of trees and flowers, and finally into the savage gorges, the secret entrance to China, the forbidden zones: 'Up there you get shot at from every direction, for good reason or for none at all. So think again before committing yourself.'

But my mind was already made up, and I told him so.

'Very well, then. We can now get down to brass tacks. My last transaction involved an investment of a million dollars. So there's five hundred thousand in it for you, if you manage to collect my due. You'll be contacted by a Chinaman as soon as you reach the secret pass east of Iskachim. But first of all you must go to Karachi and take a suite in the Imperial Hotel. Here your contact will be an old Moslem called Babaa who'll identify you by a little black ribbon I'll give you to wear in your button-hole. But you'll also have a letter of introduction, with your photograph attached ...'

At this point he paused and looked rather embarrassed, but not for long:

'All our agents have a scar incised on their left cheek. You'll have to have it done by a specialist. Any objection?'

'None.'

Next day he himself traced the mark on my cheek and gave me

the name and address of the specialist. When the scar was healed I flew out to Karachi.

No sooner was I installed in the Imperial Hotel than I received a visit from a man who claimed to be one of old Babaa's lieutenants and asked me to come with him to his master's house. This turned out to be a pretty villa with a garden full of flowers. A major-domo sat me down under a shady bower; tea, cakes and drinks were then served. Birds sang in the lemon-trees; cooks and serving-boys went about their business. Presently an elderly man appeared on the shadow-dappled pathway – a tall white figure in scarlet slippers, the great lord Babaa himself. He looked at my scar and handed me a posy of jasmine, then introduced his interpreter, Rani, a lively, quick-witted young man who spoke six languages including Chinese.

Through him I learnt that old Babaa was the chief of forty thousand Moslems who were devoted to him body and soul and smuggled gold on his behalf from the Persian Gulf to the northern confines of Pakistan. 'My master is as sound as any of your banks in Europe,' he added proudly. Then he started talking about the forbidden countries up north and told me that emissaries had already been sent to the famous Bandi-Nabab, who held the northern frontiers of Pakistan. 'Meanwhile you and I will go on a voyage together, just to show you that my master has complete confidence in you.'

Thus, one evening, he called for me in a jeep and we drove along the coast to a point beyond Somniani Bay, where a launch was waiting to take us out to a big sailing-ship. I could scarcely believe my eyes when I saw this marvellous vessel; her sails, poop, deck, tackle were reminiscent of the days of Sindbad the Sailor. So was the cargo – gold from Kuwait and Basrah bound for a secret cove in the Gulf of Oman.

On the second night out, in a flat calm, I witnessed the entire operation. The other passengers who served as a justification for this voyage had been invited by the captain to a special feast in the saloon and were thus kept unaware of what was happening on deck. Meanwhile three members of the crew lowered the little cases overboard. I watched the buoys to which they were attached bobbing in the sea. 'What if one of them drifts away?' I asked.

'Impossible. The reception party can't be far off. They know the exact spot.'

Spellbound, I went down to my cabin and fell asleep. When I woke, we were lying at anchor off Karachi.

A few days later Rani again called for me in the jeep, but this time we were bound for Kafiristan, haunt of the famous Bandi-Nabab who by now had been notified of my mission. The Hindu Kush formed a barrier in front of us. To the east the mountains of the Karakoram raised their snow-capped battlements. The forests of Kafiristan appeared. The road grew narrower. It began to snow.

Suddenly, to my amazement, a human figure appeared by the side of the road – stark naked and walking on all fours. We stopped dead and I peered at this wild creature with long hair falling over his eyes. He peered back. I handed him a packet of biscuits and he started to nibble them. 'He's in search of God,' Rani whispered, and went on to explain that up here some men lived like this in the hope of attaining to a higher state of consciousness. What a far cry from our monotonous Western world! The road soon petered out into a track and wound its way through gorges hemmed in by forests. A few yards ahead a spotted puma sprang across our path. Rani cocked his carbine and told me to keep my revolver handy, for we were approaching some cliffs where a group of professional hunters had been killed a few months earlier. 'Further on we'll be given a couple of bodyguards,' he added, 'but we must get to Swat first.'

Two hours later a little adobe mosque loomed up in front of us. Rani briefed me: 'We must go inside. It's a holy place, so we must leave our weapons by the jeep and take off our boots.'

We entered the modest little building. What peace! Nothing but bare walls and an earth floor. Here, yes, I could well believe in God's presence. In spite of myself I prayed, or rather made my mind a blank.

On coming out again we were greeted by two villainous-looking characters in ragged turbans. 'Our bodyguards,' Rani explained. 'Their master is the Nabab himself; his palace is tucked away in that pine forest to the west. But we'll stay where we're told.'

This proved to be an adobe building which looked extremely primitive from outside. Inside, however, we found thick carpets, two big sofas covered in moufflon skins, and a splendid fire in a curious stone hearth. It was more than comfortable, but we were kept under close and constant surveillance by our two ugly customers.

We were never received by their master. For three days we drank his black tea, listened to his musicians, inhaled his sticks of incense, that's all. On the fourth day we were told that the Chinaman I

225

wanted to see was away. 'He'll be notified of your arrival in due course. But in the meantime you must go back to Karachi and wait for further orders.'

I was bitterly disappointed, but there was nothing either of us could do. On our way back, out of habit, I made a note of thirty huge walnut trees and cautiously pierced the biggest with my old spike-stick which I had had the foresight to bring with me. I thought that if I didn't succeed in contacting my Chinaman I might perhaps be able to wreak my revenge on these splendid trees.

28

At Karachi I waited for further orders. The letters from the Sultan of Kafiristan seemed to reassure old Babaa as to the happy outcome of my mission, but he advised me to make detailed preparations for my big expedition to Afghanistan. With the help of Rani I had my money transferred to a bank in Kabul, notified a factory in France capable of receiving my walnut trees, and found an agent in Peshawar willing to see to the felling and transport of the timber to Karachi.

A week later I was ready to set off again. On the eve of my departure Babaa came and had a long conversation with me in the presence of Rani. I realized from the tone of his voice that he felt protective towards me and wanted to help me for the sake of my friend Guy: 'I now know that Guy's debt is concerned with gold not *afim*' (this was the word he used for opium). 'Everything ought to be easier for you. Farewell, I shall be following you from afar.'

Next day he saw us off, after presenting us with some sumptuous clothes: silk tunics with stripes of gold thread, light trousers which we would have to replace later by *goupichas*, the warmer Mongol garb.

We drove up through the Khyber Pass, which had not yet become the tourist resort that it is today, and eventually reached Kabul where we spent several pleasant weeks. The French Ambassador, Monsieur Brière, and a number of Afghan notables for whom I had letters of introduction went out of their way to be as helpful as possible. Rani and I had agreed that as soon as I had found a vehicle and a new assistant he would drive back to Karachi.

Everything worked out perfectly. One of my new Afghan friends sold me a jeep and provided me with a guide by the name of Aziz who came from Faizabad, up north. He spoke several languages, including two northern dialects, and had been a student in Switzerland. To put him through his paces, I decided to drive north at once on the pretext of prospecting for walnut trees – but in reality to reconnoitre the frontiers of the secret territory where I had to go later.

Rani and I thus parted company. On our last evening together there was a native feast with music during which, for the first time, I swallowed some pellets of opium with my tea. I felt light-headed and relaxed, but was not tempted to repeat the experiment. I noticed moreover that several of the musicians indulged in the drug, but in very small doses. Doubtless on account of the tranquil euphoria it induced, Rani's last words kept ringing in my ears for several days afterwards. An odd sensation: even after I had left Kabul and was driving along the forbidden road up north, the tone of his voice, the precision of his speech came back to me. I heard him saying: 'Try out your new guide, then come back to Kabul and wait for word from us. Never travel alone!'

Aziz and I drove for two weeks, further and further north, higher and higher into the mountains. We passed an occasional caravan of nomads heading towards the Pamirs. The glare was blinding. From time to time, so as not to rouse suspicion, we stopped to take samples of the walnut trees which were often to be found close to small villages. But there was a problem: how were we to transport such huge trunks without a superhuman effort?

Eventually we came upon a small stone planted by the side of the road. It marked the track to Iskachim. But we drove straight on, towards Faizabad, wending our way through vast fields of poppies. As we rounded a bend, a splendid young horseman came into sight. I drew up by a little water-fall. The air was crystal clear. The horseman dismounted and came towards us, a dagger at his waist, a carbine slung on his shoulder. His big black eyes were daubed with red paste against the glare; on his wrist he wore a broad silk bracelet. He signalled us to draw closer to the side of the track.

Then, for the first time, I witnessed the fantastic sight of a caravan on the move. Hundreds of camels ambled past in a slow, flowing motion, laden with huge brown bundles. On top of these bundles were perched children, and women without veils, their almond-shaped eyes rimmed with kohl. The camels were followed by horses, then more women and children walking barefoot, who stopped to drink at the waterfall before moving on again. They seemed to have been marching at this pace for thousands of years, tirelessly. Not a glance was cast in our direction. Not a word was uttered. The last horse went past, the dust began to settle.

228

Shortly afterwards we reached Faizabad where Aziz told me his friend Afizullah was expecting us: 'He was notified by telephone from Taligan. You'll see.' This turned out to be true. Our host had in fact been awaiting our arrival for several days. His turbanned servants bustled about: perfumed water was produced for our ablutions, carpets were spread, tables laden with sweetmeats were brought in, tea was served.

Afizullah spoke French fairly well and, whenever I could, I brought the conversation round to the famous secret route. I learnt that the Chinaman who was to contact me was not Chinese at all; he was a Mongol, a chieftain of one of those independent tribes still holding the mountain ranges where their flocks had grazed for centuries. 'Some caravanners whom I trust completely tell me he's a giant of a man. No one, so far, has been able to follow him on his constant peregrinations. They say he's also the master-mind behind the opium and gold smuggling.' Everything Guy had told me was thus confirmed.

There was no message for me when I got back to Kabul, but I heard that hundreds of Kirghis had come down from the north to participate in a *buzkachi* which was due to be held in a few days' time. And indeed I saw that preparations for it were already under way: a grandstand for the guests had been erected, also a tower reserved for reporters and photographers.

A *buzkachi* has something in common with polo, but is infinitely more dangerous. The horsemen, sometimes at the risk of their lives, vie with one another to grab hold of the carcase of a calf that has been killed the day before and soaked in water so as to make it as slippery as possible. The winner is the first to score a 'goal' by depositing the carcase in a pit specially prepared for this purpose.

On the appointed day His Majesty the King, the French Ambassador and all the local dignitaries turned up in force. In the horsemen's enclosure the men from the north were preparing for the fray. I prowled round, hoping that among them I might find someone who would lead me one day to the Mongol. Then, camera in hand, I waited in front of the grandstand. The first cavalcade, an outburst of colour and noise, came charging towards me. I began to film the scene, standing some distance away. Then, on the spur of the moment, I took a deep breath, dashed forward and kneeled down to get a closer shot. I saw the horses galloping straight at me, heard the thunder of their hooves as they flashed past and over my head.

229

Several people came rushing to my rescue. There was no need; I had curled up into a ball and was unharmed. I picked up my hat, rose to my feet, dusted myself down and bowed to His Majesty.

At the time I didn't realize the consequences of my behaviour. I had acted unthinkingly, carried away by the excitement. But a little later, while having tea in the grandstand, I heard that the horsemen were already talking about my miraculous escape. At all events it resulted in my being invited a few days afterwards to the Loy-Gergah, the Grand Council of the People, where I had the privilege of attending a meeting of all the *maliks* and tribal chiefs under the presidency of the King. I didn't understand a word of the various languages spoken – His Majesty himself used several interpreters – so I had no idea what questions were discussed. But the guardians of the Russian, Persian, Pakistani, Chinese and Indian frontiers were present.

One evening, at last, Rani burst into my room. He had driven up from Karachi with my future guide, chosen for me by old Babaa and the Sultan of Swat. His name was Tachki and he came from Kafiristan. He was armed and it was up to me to see that he remained so throughout our journey, for which he had been fully briefed. But he spoke no French, so the only means I had of conversing with him was by sign language.

Next day, we started off for the far north. The glare was even worse than on my first trip as we headed in the direction of the Hindu Kush, driving higher and higher every day, sleeping in abandoned huts, filling up with water from wayside springs. Suddenly, on the fourth day, we heard a shot and a bullet pierced the bonnet of the jeep. Tachki promptly fired back, signalling me to keep going. Three men with some shaggy dogs came leaping down the slope. I tucked my head into my shoulders and accelerated, while Tachki went on firing from the back. Luckily the track was fairly good; in a few minutes we were out of range.

Soon after dawn next day we reached the stone marking the track to Iskachim. This time we turned down it and, to my relief, Tachki gave me to understand that from now on we were safe. After a few hours he motioned me to stop. It was only then I noticed the drywall of a house among the rocks. He smiled, pressed the horn, and out of this completely isolated building poured a dozen friendly figures who welcomed us effusively. My only regret was not being able to understand a word they said, but I was infected by their high spirits. They made us park the jeep under a rocky overhang where it was more or less invisible.

Then an old man stepped forward, a perfect replica of Babaa. His clear blue eyes, immaculate turban and snowy beard commanded immediate respect and admiration. With great difficulty and a wealth of gestures, Tachki gave me to understand that we were going to leave the jeep here and continue on foot. Black China tea and Turkish delight were served. A giant of a man with a broad grin on his face suddenly arrived and handed me a message. It was written in French: 'This is to introduce Cheul. Follow him. He will lead you to the caravan that awaits you.' I looked at the messenger and gave him a fraternal embrace.

Next day we set off on foot, through a fissured lunar landscape. Without the reassuring presence of Cheul and Tachki, I should have been scared. But I had complete confidence in them. Suddenly, from behind a rocky barrier, some khaki helmets appeared. For a moment I thought it might be a Chinese or Russian ambush. But the faces beneath them were smiling, chuckling, talking. Cheul whistled and advanced up the steep path towards the rocky platform. I followed and to my surprise discovered a number of military tents pitched there. I was shown into one of the biggest, furnished with a thick carpet, a table laden with sweetmeats, chiselled trays and a small brass brasero.

We resumed our march next morning, after our packs had been loaded on to two shaggy camels. I began to suffer from the cold, especially at night, but didn't dare to ask for warmer clothing. In the afternoon, moreover, the sun was burning hot. We had to press on, follow these strange soldiers who seemed to be very lightly armed, but who could tell? Their horses and camels carried heavy loads and plodded along tirelessly.

In the evening another plateau appeared, and again I was surprised to see dozens of tents pitched there. Men and women bustled about, horses grazed, fires flickered and smoked. Could this be the caravan to which the message referred? An old man stepped forward and joined both hands in front of him by way of greeting. Cheul and Tachki showed me into one of the tents, fetched the luggage and, without a word, dressed me up as a nomad. The old man returned, looked me up and down, and appeared to be satisfied with what he saw. Then he went off again.

A musician came in and settled down to play, while Cheul and

Tachki brought in the tea. Reclining on a rug, with my head resting on a silk cushion, I listened to a long lament on the fiddle to which some little drums outside responded. What a far cry it was from the Hotel Terminus Saint-Lazare and the morning rush hour in Paris! Presently the musician departed. I was lying alone in the tent when two figures appeared: the old man who had welcomed me and, a few paces behind him, a woman enveloped in silken veils. I stood up, breathless at the sight of such a beauty.

'Azayade,' said the old man, then promptly disappeared.

I had to think quickly. Maybe this was a trap. A Moslem woman introduced into my quarters would be sufficient justification for murdering me. Seeing my dismay, Azayade smiled, as though reading my thoughts. Then, to my immense surprise, she addressed me in perfect French: 'Don't be afraid. I'm not a Moslem. I'm free from all attachments and it's your friend Babaa who arranged for me to travel with this caravan.'

She drew closer, bashfully, and I asked her to sit down. In her melodious voice she went on: 'My father studied in New Delhi where some French missionaries taught me your language. You were alone, I agreed to act as your interpreter. I'm sorry, but in your presence I feel shy.'

I could no longer think clearly. I wanted to put an end to this awkwardness, for I was deeply conscious of my visitor's charm. Spontaneously I seized her hands and kissed them, and went on holding them as we sat together in the magical light cast by the little oil lamp. Tears of joy came to her eyes as she told me the truth; it was not through Babaa that she had joined me; she had volunteered to do so after seeing me in Karachi, and Rani had made the necessary arrangements with the Sultan of Swat. I felt I was dreaming as we lay side by side, her head resting on my heart, her hand clasped in mine, and presently we fell asleep.

We woke in the morning, still holding hands. She went out and came back carrying a brass tray laden with honey cakes and boiling-hot tea. In the daylight I was all the more able to admire her regal bearing, her divine gestures, her radiant features. My body was suddenly aware of hers, and my longing for her lasted throughout the day.

That evening I bestowed on her all the love I had harboured, feasting my eyes on her lovely face, revelling in the sound of her glorious voice. I felt as though my life had had no other purpose than to lead me to this woman and, from the gleam that came into her eyes, I knew that she reciprocated my feelings.

She told me we were leaving next day and would be on the march for several weeks. Then she opened a lacquer casket and emptied its contents of gold ornaments and precious stones on to the rug: 'They're for you. You must buy yourself a horse, and a dromedary for me.' And, since I hesitated, she went on: 'You'll reimburse old Babaa.'

Next day I felt as proud as any of the local horsemen when I saw the superb camel which she mounted in her fine astrakhan cloak, while I sprang into the saddle of a lovely white stallion with my beloved's silk scarf attached to its forehead. It was as though I was living in a fairy-tale and had been transformed into a prince. Time had ceased to exist, I no longer had any notion of it. I was bereft of my past; I belonged to the Mongol, to the Sultan of Swat, to this caravan, symbol of freedom on the move between five frontiers. Tears came into my eyes as I contemplated the beauty of this nomadic community, this tenuous procession of which I was part. At night we were frozen despite our warm clothing; during the day we stifled under the burning sun. Every now and then Azayade conversed with the old leader, then told me what he had said: 'Danger lurks all round. Cheul and Tachki are riding ahead. The meeting of the two caravans is due to take place in a natural basin.'

When we reached this spot there were several dark tents already pitched there. A horseman came hurtling in our direction. Cheul galloped off to meet him. Two other horsemen rode up to us and scrutinized us in a lofty, disdainful manner. Azayade realized that if we made one false move we would be hacked to death; she told me so. To these outriders we were mere foreigners, though Cheul seemed to be well received and indeed almost venerated by them. Where did they come from, with their black silk turbans and old-gold tunics, their crimson, purple or green velvet waistcoats, their thick camel-hair trousers? 'They belong to the most exclusive clans in Kafiristan,' Cheul said, and asked me on their behalf never to reveal the exact position of this basin or anything else I might see from now on.

Azayade, who had been listening to them talking, told me that Cheul was known in these parts as one of the most trustworthy and famous lieutenants of the sultans. He was descended from a long line of nomads renowned for their intelligence and memory, and had already, at the age of thirty, acquired a reputation as a relentless dispenser of justice. For the last two years, especially, he had been entrusted with the task of keeping the passes clear of cut-throats and assassins.

As I rode past the dark tents the men outside them still appeared to scrutinize me in a hostile manner. Was Cheul aware of this? Doubtless, for he suddenly borrowed my white horse and showed off its paces, then dismounted, came up to me and, in front of Azayade, flung his arms round me and kissed me on the mouth. This was the fraternal kiss of the great nomads, the communion of breath. Henceforth all the horsemen knew I was an ally of Cheul the Terrible and, as such, a lord to be respected.

We spent several days in this enchanted basin, with strict orders not to venture outside it. One morning, however, as though to confirm his trust in me, Cheul guided me to the furthest edge. The sun was already burning hot, and the atmosphere unusually clear. Suddenly another landscape came into view; we were overlooking a defile and, from our observation post, I could see the famous gold and opium route winding into the distance towards Mongolia. A long procession of men, superbly clad and unarmed, advanced below us; behind them came their donkeys laden with firewood, their dromedaries with opium. Immense fortunes were transported in this way, protected by redoubtable outriders. These handsome nomads and their womenfolk clanking with gold went plodding along interminably, mounted on their animals in the midst of their motley baggage. Cheul seized my hand, as though to partake of my emotion, then led the way back to Azayade.

A few days later he rode off with two other horsemen, Gorgue and Roba, and Tachki told us they had gone to contact the Mongol, pave the way for me and fix the day and place for our meeting. Almost a week went by. Then the trio returned, exhausted, famished and travel-stained. Cheul's features were tense, he looked grim and pensive. He spoke briefly to Azayade. In a sad, trembling voice she told me what he had said, 'The Mongol has disappeared. Even his own warriors don't know what has become of him.'

A long silence ensued. What were we to do? Cheul decided we ought to make our way back to the jeep, but by another route. Did he foresee further hazards? Why had the Mongol vanished into thin air? Some specific danger must have prevented him from coming to Iskachim ...

234

And so the caravan set off again, with its donkeys, dogs and camels. Every day I learnt something new about the life of the Kirghis and other nomads. To them, their horses are guides whose language they understand. A whinny, a sign of restlessness, warns them of danger in advance. So the horses are well-tended, no matter what the sacrifice. The camels and donkeys and dogs can go without, but the horses must be watered and fed.

This expedition was a gruelling experience. Our route back was rougher than the way we had come, and I began to fear for Azayade's health. She wore thicker make-up to conceal her pallor, but the increasing faintness of her voice betrayed fatigue. Cheul, to whom I confessed my anxiety, admitted that he too thought she was making a courageous but superhuman effort. The abrupt changes in temperature particularly affected her. I rode beside her all day, encouraging her – 'Once we get to the jeep we'll stay in a pretty village where you can get some rest and recover your strength' – and when we halted for the night the musician came and played her a lullaby which sent her to sleep in my arms.

After two weeks we began to descend into the lowlands. With a silk scarf I made her a sort of mask to protect her lungs from the dust, but her condition continued to deteriorate. She breathed with difficulty and appeared to have a fever. And then, one evening, she gently confessed: 'The doctor in Karachi forbade me this journey. But I don't regret having disobeyed him in order to share my life with you.'

Next morning Cheul looked more cheerful. The village where we had left the jeep was only two or three days' march away, and we would find a *molla* there, a doctor. I told Azayade. I described the cosy little house on the Kabul road, the milk, the fruit that would save her, the long rest we would have before setting off again together. That evening she looked lovelier than ever and appeared to have recovered completely. I felt enormously relieved and, as she fell asleep beside me, her hands sought mine. A great windless silence enveloped us. It was warm and cosy in the sweet-smelling tent. Her hands felt cooler, her breathing sounded less laboured. I too fell asleep . . .

When I woke, her hands felt cooler than ever. I sat up to light the little brasero. The beam illuminated her lovely face. She was smiling in her sleep. I leant over and gently kissed her eyes. Her face was icy. She was dead.

I didn't weep, I didn't shed a tear. I listened to the sound of the caravan preparing for a new day. I heard Cheul's voice outside; he didn't yet know. I beckoned to him, silently. He came in and stood stock still. Never had I seen such tenderness and compassion on a man's face. But he mastered his grief sufficiently to be able to give the necessary orders for our departure.

Azayade's camel knelt as usual outside the tent. I picked up her lifeless body wrapped in its great silken shawls and settled it on her nomad throne. Then, as though she was still alive, I rode beside her. The sun shone without any warmth. My tears welled up at last.

At dusk a little oasis appeared. We halted by the trees in silence. My tears blinded me as I steeled myself to close my beloved's eyes. Then I picked her up in my arms and carried her to the foot of a big palm tree where Cheul had ordered a grave to be dug. Some men brought out the two mats that had been our bed for weeks, and lined the narrow trench with them. I laid my beloved down and watched her gradually disappear beneath the sandy soil. With her departed my heart, my soul, my mind. My body alone lived on, void, bereft.

Nothing mattered to me any more, neither days without appetite, nor nights without sleep. Somehow I dragged my carcase as far as the jeep. Tachki saw to everything, the petrol, food and luggage. When Cheul came to say good-bye before starting back for the Pamirs in his wild quest for the Mongol, I couldn't utter a word. I clasped him to my breast and gave him to understand that Azayade's camel and my white horse were to be his. He disappeared into the distance with his black-turbanned horsemen, while Tachki and I drove off in the opposite direction.

We were back in the land of the blind and I wept like a child.

29

I drifted through Kabul like a ghost and lingered among the Pathans, hoping to be struck down by a rebel's bullet or assassin's knife. Grim and dour, Tachki pretended to believe in my absurd quest for walnut trees. I watched the overworked camels drag the trunks up to the goods trucks that would transport them to Peshawar. But all this activity left me indifferent. I was like a somnambulist.

Some time later I found myself in Srinagar, in Kashmir, a guest of the Maharajah. A flag was hoisted in my honour; my car bore a pennant; some walnut trees were felled and despatched to Karachi. But nothing could rouse me from my torpor.

Then one evening one of the last of the Mongol lords was announced. He had been fleeing for his life and had only one servant left in his retinue. He told me about the death agony of his people who had preferred death to betraying the freedom in which they had lived for thousands of years. According to him, my 'Chinaman' had been murdered, or else, if by some miracle he had managed to escape, he must have gone to ground somewhere and was living like a hermit.

My faithful Tachki tried in vain to interest me in a fresh quest for walnut trees in the vicinity of Dehra Dun: a German and his secretary had apparently robbed me of tons of timber in a railway station. What did it matter? A Greek offered to look into the matter. Why not let him? All I wanted was to drive back to the oasis where Azayade lay. So one morning we set off again.

But we didn't get far. In the villages along our route rioting had broken out. I donned native dress to make myself less conspicuous. At Muree we discovered the reason for the disturbances: the Suez Canal was blocked. There was danger of world war; anti-French, even anti-European feeling was rife, and I found myself confined to the town. My pilgrimage to Azayade was no longer possible; I was under suspicion and my nationality, though unspecified, endangered the lives of my hosts who were related to Tachki.

We therefore decided to make a dash for it under cover of darkness.

For a moment, carbine in hand, I came to life again. Lights extinguished, we drove at full speed through the town in spite of the trees, pot-holes and rocks. On the outskirts a machine-gun opened fire and a bullet struck the bonnet. Tachki fired back while I accelerated. We were through.

At Karachi I found the press was extremely hostile to France. In the north a fellow-countryman of mine had been shot up and stoned. I felt it was time to leave. I knew I would never be happy again. Thanks to the Greek, my walnut trees had arrived from Dehra Dun and Peshawar — a welcome windfall.

While I waited for a passage, old Babaa lavished hospitality on me. One evening he also gave shelter to a destitute Hindu fakir from the confines of Nepal whom I found in the process of feeding a python sixteen feet long. I watched in fascination as he stroked the reptile's head and whispered something to me. Rani translated what he said: 'Show it love and it will do no harm.'

I felt touched by this advice and decided to follow it. Why not? I tried to feel nothing but love for this long sinuous body, and in due course the fakir said: 'You are truly good and calm. A snake is never mistaken.' I, who had beheaded so many snakes in my time, fell into the habit of stroking one or another of his six pythons. When he told me he was travelling right across India to join his little family in Ceylon, I offered to buy all his snakes from him at a decent price, so that he at least might one day be able to reach those he loved.

As for myself, I eventually embarked on an Italian ship which had to sail all the way round Africa to reach Genoa and France, and as the long voyage dragged on I realized there was no time to waste. Clearly, across the ocean, came the vision of the task that lay before me. Gradually the plan took shape, inspired perhaps by the memory of Azayade and the happiness I had known through her. I thought of Cheul and his horsemen, free men struggling in order to live as they had lived for thousands of years. But across the Atlantic, lost in the jungle, there were others equally free and also struggling. Though Kinchokre, my Indian brother, and my children were no longer to be found, there were still many lives to be saved. I had no right to feel apathetic or sorry for myself. I shook off my lethargy and pitched it overboard.

The radio spoke of teenage gangs, the war in Algeria, death, violence, murder. No, there was certainly no time to waste. I acted quickly. At Genoa I sold my snakes to a circus performer at so much per foot, drove up to La Rochelle in my jeep, cashed in on my walnut trees which were on their way to Le Havre, and set sail for Cuba. Within a few hours of landing there I had left again: Fidel Castro would take too many years to think about the forests.

Two weeks later, leaving the Mexico lobsters to the coastal fishermen, I was on my way to Chile, bound for Arica, a free port where I knew I would be welcomed and helped by a former agent of the F.B.I. Thanks to him, contrary to all the rules, and under the dismayed eyes of the station master, my jeep and two outboard motors were soon loaded on to a flat-car. There was plenty of room and I was able to settle down comfortably, sitting at the wheel or getting out to eat and drink as the fancy took me, while the train chugged along to La Paz.

When I got there I discovered an American company had just obtained over a million hectares in concession, soil *and subsoil* being included in the agreement which was to be signed at any moment. It was hardly my business, but I felt the Bolivian authorities ought to know the conditions in which I had worked in Peru where I had never exploited the subsoil of a forestry development. I therefore told them.

A furious political battle ensued. Convinced by my arguments and indisputable figures, the President of the Senate declared himself against the concession, while the President of the Republic continued to lend the Americans his support. What a shambles! I was attacked in the Government press. The Opposition replied. Tit for tat. I was used to being regarded as a crook or a spy, but the local left-wing papers took a serious view of the matter and flew to my defence. So why not join the fray? I pitched in with telegrams from France, letters and various other documents. Even the most conservative financial groups vouched for my integrity. Well might I regard this squabble as a ridiculous scene from an old melodrama, the actors themselves refused to leave the stage.

I remember with affection the naïve passion of one little editor in particular. With black oversleeves and the manner of an outraged moralist, he simply wouldn't leave well alone but attacked courageously, publishing certificates testifying to my honourable intentions and calling his rivals to account. Everyone was in a dither, counter-attacking and conspiring. My own position was all

the stronger in that I didn't give a damn. I didn't belong to any parish or clan. I was an onlooker. Some students held a demonstration against the American company, and various trade unions expressed their objection to the concession. Well might I try and calm down my little fire-eater of an editor, he drooled with pleasure and resumed the attack with further accusations: the American company director didn't pay his hotel bills; the deal was not so above-board as it appeared, and so on and so forth ... Such was the hue and cry that the President of the Republic was compelled to renounce the idea, and also to expel some rascals who were somewhat too compromised.

Whereupon, without my asking, the President of the Senate came to me and offered me a concession on the same lines as Satipo. Was I going to start all over again? Was it worth the struggle? Europe alone could provide me with the answer. What financiers, French or otherwise, could be induced to take an interest? We'd see. I sent off a number of cables and, just for fun, spread the rumour that I was going north to study the resources of Eastern Bolivia on the spot.

In actual fact I headed towards the jungle, the frontier of Brazil: I was determined to find out about my kinsmen who must have moved towards the Rio Picha or Madre de Dios, and nothing would stop me. I chartered a freight-carrying aircraft in which to transport my jeep and motors, my luggage and my hopes. My spirits soared as I flew over the unforgettably blue expanse of Lake Titicaca and looked down upon the frontier of Peru and the quivering carpet of the familiar forests.

But each time we landed the news became more and more alarming. The massacre of the Indians, the carnage for the sake of a few tons of rubber and ore, had condemned the strongest tribes to a deadly exodus. Armed bands were on the warpath, killing and slaughtering, under the cynical and hypocritical command of petty merchants or half-castes who were sitting pretty. Gold, uranium, oil! My kinsmen, whose only crime was having been born on unexplored territory, had died in hundreds. Ambushes, disease, gas, machine-gunning, all was grist to the exterminators' mill.

One evening some foresters who had come down from the Cordilleras of Carrabaya told me the sad end of the Campa tribes. Kinchokre, my wife, my children had remained free right up to the end. I landed next morning on the edge of the Rio Guaporo, determined to plunge into the mahogany jungle and die there myself or else discover the reason. Yes, discover the reason for this slaughter, this hatred, this gory shambles.

My plane which opened its big bay to spew out my jeep caused a sensation on the little airstrip. My papers, drawn up at La Paz, were very impressive; the mayor and police welcomed me as an influential foreigner. But I already knew I was not going to develop my concession. A cable from France had notified me of the outlook of the financiers in Europe. 'Congratulations,' was more or less what they said, 'but don't count on us, the political situation is far too dicey.' The same old tune as usual. Glory be to God! The financiers fiddle-faddled but didn't finance; money depended on ideas but no longer contributed to new ones. What a stinking world it was! Never mind, I would think of something else to do!

Miraculously I heard almost at once about a man who lived on the other side of the river – a genuine peasant, a lumber-jack turned priest, then bishop, who travelled among the *seringueiros*, suc-couring and tending. A Frenchman? Yes. A priest? Maybe. A bishop? We'd soon see.

The river formed a natural frontier between Bolivia and Brazil. I got my jeep and outboard motors across without any difficulty on a raft I had had specially built. Presently the bishop appeared and stretched out his hand. He peered at me, summed me up, and we had a meagre meal together. I felt I was in paradise. Then we went off to visit a poor *seringueiro* and the following conversation took place:

'You've had fifteen children?'

'Yes.'

'How many are dead?'

'Ten.'

'Did you weep for them?'

'No. Such is our life!'

We came back and I dossed down for the night on a pallet stuffed with maize leaves. But I couldn't sleep. I was haunted by the spectre of hunger. Yet all that was needed to combat it here was for a handful of prospectors to travel from rio to rio, reconnoitre the wealth of this unexplored region and, this time, *preserve it*. What was the point of exploiting huge concessions which would only unleash the implacable forces of blind commerce and industry? The wealth that lay dormant under the blue and green shadows of these forests ought to be nurtured and cherished.

Back in Europe labourers and company directors lived in their respective ant-heaps, the cages of their big cities, the barred kennels of their streets. Even the Rue de la Paix was nothing but a long kennel; and the luxury hotels, mere camping-sites. But didn't the spirit of adventure imply making a fresh start, beginning all over again, quitting the treadmill of outworn customs and habits, viewing real life with a sharper, more technical eye?

A strange exaltation seized me in the silence of the night. Perhaps it was the unconscious influence of my saintly host that compelled me to work out my plan. At all events I made up my mind that in the morning I would start looking for the doctors, priests, *seringueiros*, butterfly-collectors, jaguar-hunters and anyone else who was willing to join the human brotherhood I had in mind.

30

In the morning my bishop's smiling face warmed me like a glowing sun. Thanks to him, during the following days, the prefect most illegally cleared my jeep through the customs and I bought a big pirogue on which to install my motors. I was now ready to embark on my quest. But before I could take the first step I found myself in hospital at Guajara-Mirim with a broken leg – my right leg, same as before, and again as a result of a clumsy manoeuvre in my overloaded pirogue.

Jacquare, a *seringueiro* alligator-hunter, came to see me there. His marksman's eye, his ravaged face, his sense of danger designated him as someone who would help me in the future. He already seemed aware of the necessity of my plan, for he said: 'Fernando, civilization is arriving here. Bulldozers are raising deadly clouds. The place is being undermined. Let's get out of it. Let's go you know where. Far from these madmen.' He understood, he realized that the unexplored territory would be threatened next; we would have to rush to its defence before it was too late.

To keep up my spirits, I indulged in flights of fancy. I decided that if my leg had to be amputated I would have a false one made in aluminium, hollow and with a little locker for whisky. Fortunately it didn't come to this. My leg mended and, indifferent to the pip-squeaks, dimwits and faint-hearts, I resumed the quest which was to culminate eventually in my 'vitamin ship'. My plan was to provide not charity, but food; to open up a vast natural larder, starting with the twelve thousand miles of coast and tens of thousands of miles of river where the undernourished were still dying. My first step was to take out a fishing licence. Then I looked for and found several river-dwellers who would be prepared to distribute the food. My dream was taking shape: with a good boat I would be in a position to feed a thousand children a day. But I still had to find the money for it.

Once again I sailed downstream, through Manaus and its indus-

trial installations, to embark for France at Belem do Para. A boat!
The price of a wretched boat! Once again I thought I would be able
to convince some bold financiers, men with a sense of adventure
and imagination. Once again I was disappointed. Why should people
protect the jungle, when they desecrated their own beaches and
beauty spots? Well might I tell them: 'There's a forest lying
dormant over there. I've seen it. I can see it now. I can touch it, feel
it. Wake up! In the end the Americans will get it.' A waste of
breath. Music for deaf-mutes. In vain I appealed. I wanted to protect
the jungle and prevent the half-caste population from falling victim
to industrial carnage. I was offering Europe the chance to share in
this adventure. To no avail. All I encountered was silence, evasive-
ness, excuses.

To cut a long story short, I failed to raise the money and returned
empty-handed, but with the encouragement of new friends who
were determined to help me. How many times had I crossed the
Atlantic – but never with such peace of mind as now, never with
such joy at the prospect of working for others. Thus I found myself
back in Belem do Para. A long time had elapsed since my first arrival
here, but this harbour still remained a starting point for me. A
ship equipped with staterooms, built in Holland, had replaced the
old tubs that used to sail up the Amazon. No matter, I was ready
for the voyage. I felt on top of the world, and was inhaling the
familiar smells, when a fanfare suddenly broke out. A V.I.P. coming
aboard, presumably. But no, it was a group of tourists and this
ceremony was included in the price of their tickets.

Since I hadn't found the money for a two-master, deep-sea fishing
was out of the question. With the help of my little group I therefore
concentrated on the rivers. We pooled our resources and soon there
were a hundred and ten of us, strung out over a distance of four
thousand miles. Meanwhile tongues began to wag and I heard
people say: 'Fernando's back. He, too, is going to combat hunger.'
But I noticed they sometimes looked at me with a sarcastic or
rueful expression. I questioned a half-caste fisherman about this and
he told me I wasn't the only one who wanted to help the local
Indians and *seringueiros*. But he was reluctant to say any more.
Intrigued, I made further enquiries elsewhere. Yes, a few hundred
miles to the south there was a group of priests who had established a sort of distribution centre for food imported from all over
the world.

I decided to look into this. What was the point of two organizations working separately if it was possible to join forces and pool resources? A few weeks later, therefore, I made my way upstream to this mission and was straight away stupefied. Before me stood a handsome residence, rather like a Swiss chalet, with a blue-tiled swimming-pool. In front of it were parked several big American cars, one of which served as an ambulance.

I was shown in. A smell of beeswax reminded me of my youth and the church at Chatou. Far be it from me to object to cleanliness, but I was warned all the same. In the office I introduced myself and unfolded my ideas. The priest who received me was the leading character in this set-up, the purport of which I was to grasp within the next few weeks. He asked me to stay to lunch.

Though I have always led a frugal, not to say primitive life, I don't mind a good tuck-in on occasion. But I wasn't prepared for the choice, quality and vast quantity of the mission food and drink. 'So this is the way these priests combat hunger,' I said to myself. 'Well, eat your fill, Fernando. In this trying climate one must keep body and soul together!' Yet I knew that only a few miles away there were women and children who wouldn't have minded a handful of sugar and flour.

I took my leave, promising to come back. In the grounds some trucks were unloading tons of foodstuffs. Hundreds of sacks and bags were being carried into the storeroom – a solid building with a big padlock on the door.

Within a month I had completed my investigation and was able to confirm my opinion of this mission. It was flagrant, shameless, a parody of a charitable organization. It was obvious that those priests had never known hunger themselves; obvious that, with my catch and their stores, they hoped to become an instrument of power or commerce. Those tons of choice food, gifts arriving duty-free from all over the world (for charity is exempt from customs charges) were feeding a betrayal. A minute proportion was distributed for the sake of appearances. The rest went to waste or was sold – or, worse still, bartered against manual labour or alligator skins. It was all very well to deliver a little sales-talk about the destitution and persecution of the Indians. It was only too easy, in a huge country like Brazil, to create the myth of a wretched situation that was insoluble and to speculate on tuberculosis and rickets. As I was to see for myself, the situation was wretched, yes – but insoluble, no. Only, like the jungle, it created its own new parasites, because the vast distances precluded all control.

One mustn't sit in judgement, one must take action. Love of mankind will always prevail. Our lives are but seeds floating on the waters. In this book I have delivered myself of my adventures and passions, my shortcomings and failings, so that in time to come my life, my *real life*, might nourish, revive, soothe, shock, reveal, revolt, inspire, and give rise to other adventures, over and over again, interminably.

Us bush-whackers often indulge in a practice which I learnt from the Indians and *seringueiros*: when we find some good seeds in the forest we pack them carefully in a light husk or piece of bark fastened with lianas, then scatter them on the water which carries them towards the sea, in the hope that somewhere on the way a splendid tree will one day take root and grow, and the world continue in freedom. So with our lives, so with this book.

Tomorrow I shall be far away, engaged in the sacred mission I have vowed to carry out. My boat is waiting for me. I am setting off again, to immerse myself in this new quest, knowing full well that the day will come which for me will be the end of time.

On that day I shall rejoin you, Pangoate my Indian wife, and you, my children, and you, sublime Azayade. I shall lay me down to rest under another palm tree. For death will not overtake me in hospital or in my caravan, or even on my boat.

No. I want to die in a hammock, like the Campas. But I shall not really die. My friends the *seringueiros* don't view death as we do. They think they have always been alive and never die. I, too, now know one never dies. Death doesn't exist. It's just a name, another piece of nonsense. One changes, that's all. That's what I believe now. I shall close my eyes, fanned by the wind, listening to the music of the jungle. My friend the bishop or whoever else has succeeded him will light me a cigarette. My ears will be filled with the sound of singing and I shall take my leave. So simple. Every Indian dies like this, in his hammock. He rocks gently from side to side. When the rocking stops it means he has departed for another, better life.

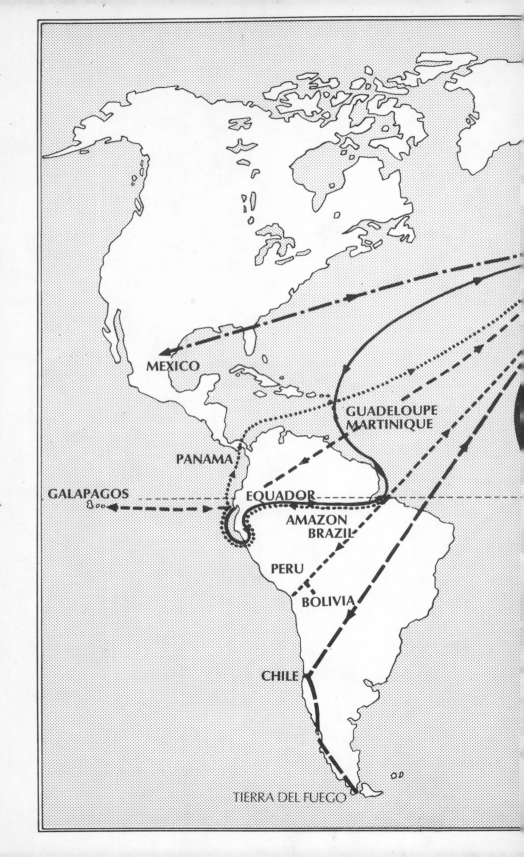

MEXICO

GUADELOUPE
MARTINIQUE

PANAMA

GALAPAGOS

EQUADOR

AMAZON
BRAZIL

PERU

BOLIVIA

CHILE

TIERRA DEL FUEGO